"Good organized advice for the woman who suspects or knows that her life is out of control."
—*Publishers Weekly*

"A lifesaver." —*San Diego Union*

"*The Superwoman Syndrome* is written in clear, non-academic language and neatly organized into bite-sized chapters. It's practical and warmly empathetic. The first part of *The Superwoman Syndrome* will help you understand yourself and your relationships, especially those with men. But it's the last three chapters that fulfill the promise made on the book's cover, showing you how to decide what's important in your life and do it well."
—*The Executive Female*

"Shaevitz's easy, straightforward sensible writing style and practical tips make the book a 'must' for all women struggling to balance home, career, family and friends with their own personal needs."
—**Dr. March Fong Eu,**
California Secretary of State

"What a wonderful book and what a great service you have performed for all of us. My husband is reading it at the moment and I am sure it will put things in perspective for him. Your style is easy, frank, and realistic."
—**Phyllis Kaminsky, Director,**
United Nations Information Centre
Washington, D.C.

more . . .

"There are plenty of books that tell women how to have successful careers in organizations. This one goes one step beyond. It speaks to balance in life—success in the personal as well as professional arena and the *difficult but possible* management act required to handle both. And the nice part is—the author actually becomes your ally and friend as she leads you through it."

—**Dr. Beverly Kaye,**
author of *Up Is Not The Only Way*

"As I read I kept thinking what a pity I didn't have a helpful guide such as this is 40 years ago. Shaevitz lays out all the facts I had to learn by trial and error. But even after 42 years married to the same man the chapter HOW MEN REALLY FEEL opened a whole new way of thinking for me. Super!"

—**Dorothy Brush,**
Community Relations Consultant
YWCA, A United Way Agency
Lansing, Michigan

"A wonderful addition to my library."

—**Senator Pete Wilson,**
California

"*The Superwoman Syndrome* is a source of useful practical information and comfort for the woman who is overwhelmed by trying to do it all."

—**Stephanie Winston, author of**
***Getting Organized* and**
The Organized Executive

more . . .

Other books by
Marjorie Hansen Shaevitz

Making It Together as a Two-Career Couple
(with Morton H. Shaevitz, Ph.D.)

So You Want to Go Back to School:
Facing the Realities of Reentry
(with Elinor Lenz)

The Superwoman Syndrome

MARJORIE HANSEN SHAEVITZ

With Men's Responses by
MORTON H. SHAEVITZ, Ph.D.

WARNER BOOKS

A Warner Communications Company

To protect the privacy of the people with whom I have worked, no case study or anecdote in this book refers to any specific individual. While illustrative material is presented, names and occupations as well as identifying details have been added, deleted, or rearranged. The personal stories represent material collected by the author in her experience as a marriage and family therapist, consultant, colleague, and friend.

Grateful acknowledgment is made for material by Virginia Satir on pages 86–91 and is reprinted by permission of the author and publisher, *Peoplemaking*, 1972 and *Conjoint Family Therapy*, 1967, Science & Behavior Books, Inc., Palo Alto, California, U.S.A.

Warner Books, Inc.
666 Fifth Avenue
New York, N.Y. 10103

A Warner Communications Company

Printed in the United States of America
This book was originally published in hardcover by Warner Books.
First Printed in Paperback: November, 1985

10 9 8 7 6 5 4 3 2 1

To my dear parents:
Evelyn and Robert Vedsted Hansen,
For applauding my efforts, enjoying my triumphs,
and accepting my imperfections.

Acknowledgments

My love and deepest appreciation to:

My husband, Mort—for encouraging me to be and do much more than I think I can, for his contributions to *The Superwoman Syndrome*, and for the pearls in New York.

My children—for putting up with part-time mothering while I was writing the book, for their ready supply of affection, and for bringing so much joy to my life.

My warmest thanks to:

Florence Friedman—for the agonies she experienced in choosing and learning how to use the computer, for time and effort beyond request, and for being my office cheering section, support system, and sounding board.

Cecilia Mary Theresa Hartmann—for six years of exquisite child care, and for staying "a little bit longer."

Carol Obermeier—for her deft editing hand, her warm smile, and for making my life a whole lot easier.

Emily Majer, Judy Bardwick and Winifred Cox—for their time and help with the manuscript.

Natasha Josefowitz—for her most appropriate poetry.

Fredda Isaacson, my editor—for taking such good care of my thoughts and words, for "being tough" when it counted the most, and for getting the jacket cover color changed to mauve.

Larry Kirshbaum, president of Warner Books—for his incredible energy and enthusiasm, for recognizing the importance of Superwomen issues in men's lives, and for his creativity.

My literary agent, Margaret McBride—for introducing me to Fredda Isaacson and Larry Kirshbaum.

Steven and Susan Polis Schutz—for their friendship, encouragement, and willingness to share knowledge about the publishing world.

Ellen Golden—for her ideas, long-distance phone calls, and generous offer of contacts, help, and time.

Spencer Johnson—for sharing his genius about books and marketing.

My dear friends—for putting our friendships on hold while I finished the book.

My Stanford connections: Ann DeBusk, Jing Lyman, and Myra Strober—for sharing ideas, providing information, and keeping me close to the university.

Erica Shaevitz, Mallery Roberts, and Maria Flores—for helping me keep my office and household together.

Donald Stevenson, M.D., and Douglas Bell, M.D., of Scripps Clinic Medical Group, Inc.—for kind and considerate health care for me and my children.

Barbara Christman and Lee Phillips at Warwicks—for keeping me informed, supplied, and referenced properly.

The many friends and patients who contributed to this book.

Contents

Preface

Why write a book about Superwomen? Isn't that a bit clichéd these days? Aren't you getting tired of newspaper and magazine articles about rich, go-getting, multitalented, successful dynamos who buy their way out of problems and responsibilities? Please . . . save me from reading about yet another gorgeous attorney who is a partner in a Wall Street firm and who, in her spare time, makes gourmet sushi for her friends, races Porsches, and runs marathons! While many of us may envy the trappings of the attorney's success, we are quick to sense the disparity between her everyday realities and ours. Some of us resent the overwhelming expectations she sets for us.

I have noticed that in the past year or so the Superwoman has also been portrayed in less heady terms. Sure, she is still well dressed and throws lovely dinner parties, but she is more likely to resemble a friend or neighbor than some far-off urban ideal. This new Superwoman is usually described as a loving wife and mother, devoted friend, caring daughter, good housekeeper, and competent worker. She is the extraordinary, ordinary woman.

This new Superwoman is ordinary in that she is neither rich nor famous. She is extraordinary in that she tries to be everything to everyone—juggling family life, social life, and commitments outside the home (i.e., career, education, or volunteer work). The new Superwoman "has it all" by "doing it all" with superlative standards and ends up feeling overwhelmed, over-extended, overworked, and underappreciated. In many ways, today's Superwoman is Everywoman.

If you are one of today's Superwomen, The Superwoman Syndrome *has been written especially for you.*

This book describes the contemporary forces pushing women to be all things to all people. It provides penetrating new insights into the differences between men and women and how this knowledge can be used to solve some of the relationship dilemmas we face. It gives practical, easy-to-apply methods for gaining control of your life, with an emphasis on your having more free time, greater personal satisfaction, a healthier lifestyle, and better relationships with those who count. Whether your current dilemmas revolve around relationship, career, children, friends, self-esteem—there is an element of Superwoman in each of us.

Individual people are usually the catalysts for positive change in our lives. Sometimes a book that comes along at a time when we are particularly receptive opens up possibilities for change and new directions. My hope is that this is the right time and the right book for you.

Introduction
Who Am I to Be Telling You What to Do?

Before I buy a book, I usually want to know who the author is, what his or her credentials are, and why I should read the book. If you are a busy woman, as I am, you probably have some of the same questions about me. Who am I and why should I be writing about the Superwoman Syndrome?

Well, my friend (and I hope we do become friends as you read this book), let me introduce myself.

I grew up on a farm in California's San Joaquin Valley during the fifties. The San Joaquin Valley, located inland between San Francisco and Los Angeles, is a rich agricultural region much like the Midwest. Especially during the fifties, people in that area tended to be rural, conservative, and very traditional. I want you to know this so that you will understand that I had the same traditional, typical, prefeminist upbringing as you probably experienced.

A TYPICAL CHILDHOOD

Eldest of three daughters, I was raised by my Danish-American parents to be "nice," achievement oriented, hardworking, and, above all, "ladylike." It was assumed by my father from the time I was born I would go to college and join a sorority. The implied goal in all this was to find my future husband, who would—with luck—be a wealthy rancher's son, smart, athletic, and of Scandinavian heritage.

Characteristic of many middle-class families of the time, my father was the acknowledged head of the household: he made the important decisions about money and the family ranch. My mother was the family parent: she took care of my sisters and me and was in charge of all the household detail.

Especially in the pretelevision days, our family spent a lot of time together, although we didn't talk very much. When we did talk, it was about the weather, community gossip, and events at our schools. We did not talk about *feelings*.

THE WAY WE COMMUNICATED

Rarely were we direct with one another about requests, anger, or personal needs. "Mind reading" was the name of our communication game. For example, if I wanted to go to a movie, I'd hint around it for a few days and hope that my father or mother would "pick up on it." If one of my parents asked me to do an errand I didn't want to do, I would never say no or challenge the request. In true passive-aggressive style, I would do it and sulk. Or I would do it poorly. Or I would suddenly get ill and avoid doing it. Or I would drive them crazy procrastinating about it. I have found these communication patterns to be fairly typical.

As I mentioned, I am the eldest of three daughters. Many social-science researchers have found that firstborn children of either sex tend to be "good kids," responsible, and achievement oriented. Believe me, I didn't let the researchers down. I was a straight-A student from the first grade through the end of high school, with the exception of algebra. Can you believe it! I had math anxiety, too. (I wish I weren't quite so stereotypical.)

Praise from my parents came with achievements at school. Like many girls, I found that being smart in elementary school was acceptable behavior. However, by the time I reached high school, being brainy was a real disadvantage. While I was very active and a good student in high school, I was not popular with the boys "who counted." It was the latter that mattered most to me.

My achievement-oriented style, coupled with a "good girl" desire to please, led to a 4.0 grade-point average in my college classes and being chosen Outstanding Freshman Woman. Again, the college men who counted weren't impressed. I spent a lot of time during those early college years trying to figure out what would impress them.

WHEN THE CHANGES BEGAN

In my senior year, while my friends were getting pinned and engaged, I was defensively beginning to think about graduate school. After all, what was a girl to do after college if she hadn't caught a man? It was then that I first began to deal publicly with "women's issues." Betty Friedan had just written *The Feminine Mystique*, and I found myself leading a group discussion called "Women's Role in Contemporary Society." Here is how our student newspaper reported that discussion:

> Majorie Hansen, President of Tokelon, described how her group debated the advisability of young women to continue their education on a postgraduate level if they had high hopes of reaching the altar. She suggested that perhaps higher education was a seed of marital trouble. In summarizing the sentiments of the group, she said, "We can't afford to become so intelligent that we lose our femininity. Then as wives we would become more of a challenge to our husbands than a confidante and helpmate."

It is amazing to me that today, twenty years later, some women still think this is true.

The mid-sixties were very exciting times for me. That was when I entered the Counseling Psychology Program at Stanford University and eventually joined the Dean of Students staff.

THE SEVENTIES

In the early seventies, I moved from Palo Alto to La Jolla, where I became director of the Adult Counseling Services at the University of California at San Diego. While there, I developed a reentry program for adults (mostly women) who wanted to go back to school. I continued my work with women's issues by providing these women with information and assistance in moving from the home world back into college or work.

It was at the University of California at San Diego that I met my husband, Morton Shaevitz. He was a clinical psychologist, serving as dean of the university's Counseling and Psychological Services. Although he was (and is) very smart, he did not meet any of my parents' other prerequisites of wealth, a Scandinavian heritage, athletic prowess, and a ranch background. He was a college administrator with little money. His cultural heritage was Russian-Jewish, he managed to jog thirty-five miles a week, and he had grown up in Brooklyn. Nevertheless, at the age of twenty-nine, I finally married, and I was sure I heard the entire San Joaquin Valley heave a great sigh of relief.

With a colleague from the University of California at Los Angeles, I wrote a book for adults who wanted to go back to school, appropriately called *So You Want to Go Back to School: Facing the Realities of Reentry.* A couple of years later my husband and I coauthored *Making It Together as a Two-Career Couple.* In 1978, I left UCSD to join my husband in private psychological-services practice. In addition, we founded an organization called the Institute for Family and Work Relationships, through which we research, write, and consult.

THE BEGINNING OF A SUPERWOMAN

When I married Mort, I not only became a wife, I inherited two stepchildren from his previous marriage.

In the mid-seventies, Mort and I had two children of our

own. About that same time, we also bought a home. By 1976, I was a wife, a stepmother, a mother of two babies, the person in charge of a home, a writer, a psychotherapist, a speaker, and a consultant. Those were the roles of a Superwoman; but, believe me, I wasn't feeling super.

When our son was born in 1974, I ostensibly cut back my work at the university from full- to part-time. I say "ostensibly" because I actually continued in the same role, with all its responsibilities, but I was in the office less. When I was at home with my baby I felt guilty about what I wasn't doing at the office; at the office I felt guilty about being away from my son. To be truthful, "guilty" is not exactly what I felt—it was more like intense pain.

During this time we had minimal household help because "I was working only part-time." I felt that hiring a housekeeper was not justified, and that my husband should take a much greater role in keeping things together. Mort kept urging me to hire outside help, but I thought this was just an excuse for his unwillingness to help. I spent a lot of time smoldering internally over his apparent recalcitrance. I took it one step further by judging that if he really loved me, he would see how hard I was working, how tired I was, and would come to my rescue with cheerful resourcefulness. Need I tell you this never happened?

I worked at work, I worked at home, never stopping to think about what I was doing. Priorities changed with each crisis that inevitably developed; time was eaten away by whatever task was before me at the moment. To stave off enormous guilt, I rarely said no to anybody or anything. I did it *all*, trying all along to meet my parents' (and by now my own) internalized "good girl" standards.

The bad news is that for *years* I felt out of control, overwhelmed, angry, tired, sick, and completely overworked. For years I was trying to be Superwoman. I didn't take time to think about how to get out of the mess; taking time was a luxury that seemed unavailable to me. Does this sound familiar?

The good news is that eventually, out of desperation, I did take time to look at my situation and do something about it.

I made time to read a lot of new literature about changing sex roles and the psychologies of women and men. I looked at the sociology of housework and at the latest information on management techniques in the business world. I also talked with hundreds of women at various seminars and workshops and found that they were experiencing many of the same frustrations. As with previous personal issues, I found it helpful to use a diagnostic formula that asks: *What* is the problem I'm experiencing? *Why* is it happening to me now? And, most important, *What* can I do about it?

As you may have guessed, the literature did not have any answers to my questions. Clearly, I had no role models to follow who were successful at meeting all these new and multiple demands. My mother couldn't help me; in fact, like many other women her age, she probably thought I was crazy to be trying. I realized that I would have to figure out the answers to those questions or wait for someone else to do it. Since I didn't think I could survive the wait, I've spent the past few years answering them. In this book I define the problem, explain some of the reasons why it is occurring, and offer suggestions on what to do about it.

There is no need to rush through this book (as most Superwomen would be inclined to do). I suggest reading whichever chapter appeals to you most, thinking it over, attempting the suggested changes, and then moving on. Trying to do it all at once will only worsen the quandary you may be in. Make it easy on yourself this time.

1

Are You a Superwoman?

SUPERWOMAN

She is a perfect mother
the model wife
the best housekeeper
the greatest cook
the most available daughter
the most effective worker
the most helpful friend.
She is wonderful at
juggling home and career
with a constant smile
and an even disposition.
She is everything
to everyone.
But who is *she*?

Natasha Josefowitz

THE WOMAN IN this poem is what this book is all about. It is about those of us who try to be everything to everyone.

I first saw the term *Superwoman* used in its present context in 1977 when columnist Ellen Goodman said that her generation had replaced Super*mom* with Super*woman*. In an article I will never forget, she wrote:

> Supermom stayed home and when the kiddies came back from school she baked them cookies in the shape of pumpkins with raisin eyes and carrot noses. But now we have before us the ideal of Superwoman who prepares a well-balanced nutritious breakfast for her children, and her children eat it. She goes off to work where she makes $30,000 a year as an executive of a law firm. She comes home and reads to the children, then serves dinner by candlelight to her husband.[1]

More recently, the manufacturers of Enjoli perfume, Charles of the Ritz, capitalized on the Superwoman concept by portraying in their television commercials a glamorous working woman wearing Enjoli perfume, slipping in and out of mother/cook/worker/wife-lover roles as easily as she slips in and out of her gown.

Ms. Goodman's description reflects a late-seventies tongue-in-cheek impression of a Superwoman. The Enjoli commercial depiction never even uses the word *Superwoman*, but the message is clear. Be the *ideal* and do it glamorously, effortlessly, happily, and perfectly. There is another implicit message: if you are not the *ideal*, you are a failure.

I am concerned about those of us who are trying to be perfect workers, perfect wives, perfect mothers, and perfect housekeepers all at the same time. I am concerned about those who go beyond the bounds of what is realistic and appropriate to reach for ideals that are impossible and debilitating.

THERE'S NOTHING INHERENTLY WRONG WITH "WANTING IT ALL"

There is nothing inherently *wrong* or *bad* about any woman wanting to have a career, to be a wife and a mother, and to have a home. On the contrary, there are hundreds of *rights* and *goods* about each of these roles individually and combined. Some women are successfully pulling it off, but for every woman who has combined these roles in a realistic and satisfying manner, there must be a hundred who have not.

ARE YOU A SUPERWOMAN?

There are some external and internal factors that are characteristic of Superwomen. The external factors include such things as how many children you have, when you were born, and what your job is like. Internal factors involve such things as how much guilt you feel, how important it is to you to be "nice," your niceness orientation, and how difficult it is for you to say no.

Taking the Superwoman Quiz, which follows, can help you in two ways. First, you will learn something more about Superwoman and who she is. Second, your score will tell you how likely you are to be a victim of the Superwoman Syndrome, the subject of chapter 2.

SUPERWOMAN QUIZ

At the end of this quiz I will give you directions for computing your personal Superwoman score. Answer each question by circling the answer that best describes you.

PART 1: EXTERNAL FACTORS

1. *You were born in the thirties, forties, or fifties.* Most women born in that era were brought up under traditional circumstances. That is, their mothers were homemakers and their fathers worked away from the home as breadwinners. Even if your mother worked, those times were very different.

What was appropriate behavior for men and women then was much more predictable. How old you are now has a major bearing on how much of a traditional orientation you have. The older you are, probably, the more traditional you are, and it is probably true also that the older you are, the more difficulty you have with today's changing sex roles.

	55+	45–54	35–44	25–34	18–24
I am	5	4	3	2	1
	A.	B.	C.	D.	E.

2. *Your marital and parental status* has some bearing on whether you are a Superwoman. You are:

A.	A single parent	5
B.	A married parent	4
C.	Married, no children	3
D.	Single, living with a partner	2
E.	Single, living alone	1

3. *You are married to (or living with) a traditional man.* Times may have changed, but few men have. As is true for women, the older men are, the more likely it is that they have traditional notions of appropriate sex-role behaviors. (If you have no spouse or live-in partner, skip this question.)

A.	My husband/partner is traditional and sabotages every effort I make to do something outside the home.	5
B.	My husband/partner is very traditional.	4
C.	My husband/partner is liberal in word but traditional in action.	3
D.	My husband/partner is aware of nontraditional ways and is struggling with them.	2
E.	My husband/partner is supportive of me in word and deed.	1

4. *Your household responsibility.* Your level of responsibility for family and household chores reflects both how your family participates and the use of household help.

A. With minor exceptions, I have full responsibility for the household.   5

B. My husband and/or children "help" me with the household.   4

C. My husband and/or children share household responsibilities with me. I have no paid help.   3

D. My husband and/or children share household responsibilities with me. I employ a part-time cleaning person.   2

E. I employ a full-time housekeeper.   1

5. *You have one or more children or stepchildren.* There is no single event in a woman's life that has a greater impact than being a parent. The sheer amount of work is enormously time- and energy-consuming. We all know how much time babies and young children require; yet, many of us are surprised at the time and attention adolescents demand. (If you have no children or stepchildren, skip this question.)

A. I have four or more children at home.   15

B. I have three children at home.   12

C. I have two children at home.   5

D. I have one child at home.   3

E. I have no children at home.   0

For *each* preschool child add 5 points   _____

For *each* adolescent add 3 points   _____

For *each* stepchild who does not live with you but visits at least once a month add 2 points   _____

6. *You are dissatisfied with the child-care or after-school programs available to your children.* Perhaps no area is of greater concern to working mothers than that of the absence of good child-care or after-school resources. It is ironic that in this country, where technology is so advanced, we are backward in providing for our children. (If you do not have children or stepchildren living with you, skip this question.)

A. I am very dissatisfied with the child-care or after-school situations for my children.   7

B. I am somewhat dissatisfied with the child-care or after-school situations for my children.   5

C. I am satisfied with the child-care or after-school situations for my children.   3

D. I am relatively pleased with the child-care or after-school situations for my children.   1

E. I am delighted with the child-care or after-school situations for my children.   0

7. *Other-person responsibility.* The willingness to contribute to people and activities outside your immediate family is a typical female need to "do it all" for everyone. If you don't do it, who else will?

I am actively (more than ten hours a week) caring for (circle all that are appropriate):

A. Aging parent(s)   5
B. Grandparent(s)   5
C. Other family member(s) (siblings, etc.)   5
D. Someone else's child (children)   5
E. Friend(s)   5

8. *You are a woman who has a role outside the home.* In addition to wife, mother, and homemaker, other major roles women play today are those of career person, volunteer, or student.

	Work	Volunteer	Student
A. 40+ hours	15	15	15
B. 30–40 hours	11	11	11
C. 1/2-time (approximately)	7	7	7
D. 1/4-time (approximately)	5	5	5
E. Occasionally	1	1	1

Total_____

9. *Your work, school, or volunteer setting is not supportive of you as a woman or your role as a parent.* Many types of work (such as medicine or piloting or traveling salesperson) or work settings are not compatible with a parent role. In addition, most business organizations, including those in the public sector and universities, have policies and procedures that do not recognize their employees' roles as parents. Supportive policies would include leaves for the care of sick children, child-care information and resources, cafeteria-benefits packages, realistic and considerate travel and transfer expectations, and management training for women employees; these are some of the offerings the more progressive organizations have...but there are not many of those.

My work/volunteer/student setting is generally supportive of my role as a woman and a member of a family system:

A.	Rarely	5
B.	Seldom	4
C.	Sometimes	3
D.	Often	2
E.	Always	1

PART 2: INTERNAL CHARACTERISTICS

1. *You are a very nice woman. You are people oriented, supportive, and nurturing.* To say that you have an open-door policy is an understatement. You have an open door, an open telephone, an open refrigerator, and an open car door. You give to all and ask little or nothing in return. You find people coming to you for tasks, support, and advice all the time. You place the needs of others (including your husband, children, co-workers, neighbors, friends, relatives, even needy strangers) before your own. For you, the worst thing someone could say about you is that you are *selfish*.

A.	Always	5
B.	Often	4
C.	Sometimes	3
D.	Seldom	2
E.	Rarely	1

2. *You are very hardworking, yet you never have enough time to do what you would like to do.* Never let it be said that you are a slouch. You work harder than most people you know. Your general level of activity is so high that you don't realize how tired you are until you go on a vacation or you work yourself so hard that you become ill. After all, being sick is the only real, legitimate excuse for not working. With all that you do, it hardly seems fair that there are only 168 hours in a week. You wish you had more time.

I work very hard and I still have more to do:

A.	Always	5
B.	Often	4
C.	Sometimes	3
D.	Seldom	2
E.	Rarely	1

3. *You are very detail conscious.* At home and at work you can be counted on to take care of even the smallest details. Sometimes your finishing touches make the difference between an exquisitely prepared report and a mediocre one. At other times, you work on details far more than is required. It is difficult for you to stop once you get going. It feels good to be thorough and complete. It feels bad not to.

I pay attention to details and I'm very conscientious:

A.	Always	5
B.	Often	4
C.	Sometimes	3
D.	Seldom	2
E.	Rarely	1

4. *You are short-term-response oriented.* The natural way for you is to handle things as they occur. The following sounds very familiar to you: At home you find yourself putting away the groceries, notice the refrigerator needs cleaning, and you do it. The phone rings and you answer it; while at the phone, you notice you haven't RSVP'd to two of the children's party invitations, and you do that. You go back to the groceries, and while you're putting away the canned goods, you straighten up the cupboard. At work, you act similarly. You don't set personal goals for yourself. You try to do everything equally well.

I respond to things when they occur:

A.	Always	5
B.	Often	4
C.	Sometimes	3
D.	Seldom	2
E.	Rarely	1

5. *You are a perfectionist.* You demand of yourself perfection in your work, marriage, home, parenting, entertaining—

everything! It's not just that you strive for it; you expect it of yourself and feel like a failure when you don't meet those stringent standards.

I have very high standards and am a perfectionist:

A.	Always	5
B.	Often	4
C.	Sometimes	3
D.	Seldom	2
E.	Rarely	1

6. *You feel guilty much of the time.* Superwomen feel guilty about something all the time. Like Hester Prynne in *The Scarlet Letter*, Superwomen wear a giant *G* over their hearts (and it doesn't stand for Gucci). They feel guilty about all the things they aren't doing—spending more time with their children, having more sex with their husbands, having their homes neatly organized, spending more time with their friends. Give a Superwoman an inch of reasons and she will feel guilty for miles.

I feel guilty about all the things I'm not doing:

A.	Always	5
B.	Often	4
C.	Sometimes	3
D.	Seldom	2
E.	Rarely	1

7. *You have difficulty saying no to anyone.* Why is it that your response to anyone's request for help is an automatic *yes* whether you mean it or not? You say yes in person, on the phone, on message forms, in the kids' lunch boxes, and on sign-up sheets. Sometimes it's almost as if you can't help yourself.

I agree to all requests and have great difficulty saying no:

A.	Always	5
B.	Often	4
C.	Sometimes	3
D.	Seldom	2
E.	Rarely	1

8. *You find it difficult to delegate tasks.* It is extremely difficult for you to ask others (including husband and children) to do things for you—it's much more comfortable just to do them yourself. As a result, you approach many things as a one-woman band. Even if you have someone to help you, you find it uncomfortable to give directions, make comments, or tell someone a job is not satisfactory. If someone does a job for you halfway, you will probably finish it yourself rather than confront that person. You wish helpers would meet your standards, but you rarely tell them what these are. You think that by setting an example, they'll get the idea.

I have great difficulty delegating tasks to others:

A.	Always	5
B.	Often	4
C.	Sometimes	3
D.	Seldom	2
E.	Rarely	1

9. *You have great difficulty spending money on help.* Other people pay for household help, but not you. In the first place, it's too expensive. In the second place, hiring people to do your "dirty work" is exploitive. Why should someone else (another woman) do it for you? In the third place, you don't want some stranger roaming around your house or personal things. Hiring outside help is a hassle! You have to organize it, look for people, interview them, hire them, train them, and then they don't really do the job the way you want anyway. It's more trouble than it's worth.

I am very reluctant to hire outside help:

A.	Always	5
B.	Often	4
C.	Sometimes	3
D.	Seldom	2
E.	Rarely	1

10. *Your home is an extension of you.* You take pride in how your home appears. It's not just how clean it is. You feel good when the house is nicely decorated and when things are orderly and put away. Likewise, when your house is in chaos, *you* feel chaotic and out of control. You think people will judge you negatively if your home is not "right." The house beckons you; there is always something to do—a smudge to wipe off, a closet to organize, or clothes to mend. It's difficult to relax in your home because the work is rarely done.

I feel bad when my home does not meet my standards:

A.	Always	5
B.	Often	4
C.	Sometimes	3
D.	Seldom	2
E.	Rarely	1

11. *You find it difficult to separate your "work" and your personal life.* At work do you often find yourself worrying about your children or jotting down things you need to do at home? At home does your mind drift into work problems? Superwomen tend to be psychologically "on call" twenty-four hours a day.

I can't separate my work and personal life:

A.	Always	5
B.	Often	4
C.	Sometimes	3
D.	Seldom	2
E.	Rarely	1

12. *You have developed a chronic, low level of anger at your spouse (or partner).* Most of the time you are upset with your husband. He seems to be unaware of your needs. If he is aware he doesn't respond to them. Most of the time you keep your anger inside, but once in a while you blow up and are surprised at the rage you feel. Your friends understand. Why doesn't he? The way it is now, it would almost be easier if he weren't in the house. He doesn't help; in fact, he complains and demands. About twice a year you yell and cry and carry on. He changes for a few days and then reverts to being unresponsive and doing as little as he can. Even if this is only partially true, you still find yourself easily angered.

I am angry with my husband (if you have no spouse or live-in partner, skip this question):

A.	Always	5
B.	Often	4
C.	Sometimes	3
D.	Seldom	2
E.	Rarely	1

13. *You don't take very good care of yourself.* The person who gets what's left over is you. Often you don't get enough food, attention, or sleep. Your eating habits are haphazard and you don't eat particularly nutritious foods. As a result, you're carrying an extra few pounds. Perhaps you smoke. You may drink too much. You don't exercise on a regular basis (Who has the time?). Above all, you find it difficult to take it easy, relax, or have fun.

I don't take care of myself, relax, exercise, or have fun:

A.	Always	5
B.	Often	4
C.	Sometimes	3
D.	Seldom	2
E.	Rarely	1

14. *You don't feel very good about yourself.* Most of the time you feel inadequate. You wish many things of yourself: to be thinner, taller, more assertive, a better mother, a better daughter, a better sexual partner, better educated. Most of what you say to yourself is negative.

I don't like myself:

A.	Always	5
B.	Often	4
C.	Sometimes	3
D.	Seldom	2
E.	Rarely	1

15. *You don't feel that you have any control over your life.* Although you realize that some things need to be changed, you feel powerless. In addition, there is a fear that things will continue year after year as they are now.

I feel powerless:

A.	Always	5
B.	Often	4
C.	Sometimes	3
D.	Seldom	2
E.	Rarely	1

Now go back and add up your points for each section and write your answer in the spaces provided.

Your external score: _____

Your internal score: _____

Your total score (external score + internal score): _____

Scale for Total Superwoman Score:

A. <u>101 and above</u>   You are a full-fledged Superwoman and are likely to be experiencing many of the stress symptoms of "The Superwoman Syndrome."

B. <u>88</u> to <u>100</u>   Things probably are out of control. You need to make some changes.

C. <u>74</u> to <u>87</u>   You have many Superwoman characteristics. Be careful.

D. <u>61</u> to <u>73</u>   You're doing pretty well but need to watch it.

E. <u>60 and below</u>   Congratulations! Things seem to be under control.

1. If your external score is higher than <u>37</u>, you need to make some structural changes in your life.
2. If your internal score is higher than <u>48</u>, you need to look closely at making some personal changes.
3. If your total score is over <u>80</u>, you are likely to be experiencing some, if not all, of the Superwoman Syndrome symptoms described in the next chapter.

If you are a Superwoman, it is unlikely that you have much time to consider what you want, since most of your time is spent meeting others' needs. But perhaps some reflection is appropriate.

DO YOU WANT ANY OF THESE THINGS?

Do you want any of the following?

____ To feel good about yourself

____ To have more time for yourself—for people and things that are important to *you*, for beauty and art, for reflection and relaxation

____ To have more time for your partner or spouse; to have a warm and caring relationship

____ To have happy, independent, competent children who have high self-esteem

____ To have work that you enjoy, where you feel productive and successful

____ To make some money, perhaps a lot of it

____ To be physically healthy and taking care of your nutrition, sleep, exercise, and relaxation needs

____ To have close, nurturing friends

____ To have a home that is a haven rather than a demand list

WHAT THIS BOOK IS NOT ABOUT

Before I go any further, let me tell you what this book is *not* about.

• It is *not about your doing more* of anything that smacks of household chores, meaningless activities, or running around. I will, however, urge you to have *more quality* in your life.

• It is *not about how you can work harder.* You will see, on the contrary, how you can work "smarter" with less effort.

• It is *not about how you can be a Superwoman. I do not want to be a Superwoman. I do not want you to be a Superwoman. Further, I do not want any woman to feel that she needs to be a Superwoman.*

Are you ready to begin making your life simpler, easier, and more enjoyable? Good. I will now take you step by step through the process.

WHAT THIS BOOK IS ALL ABOUT

1. First, we'll identify the major characteristics of a Superwoman.

2. Next, we'll find out what the Superwoman Syndrome is. You see, until you know what the problem is all about, you can't hope to solve it.

3. Then we'll find out why the Superwoman Syndrome is a problem today. We'll review the cultural changes we have experienced over the past ten to fifteen years. In particular, I'll describe the socialization process women and men have gone through that predisposes women to being Superwomen.

4. A special section of the book is devoted to helping you have some quality time with your spouse and your children. Superwomen rarely have quality time with anyone. Not only will I define through *specific behaviors* what quality time is, but I'll tell you how to have *more* of it for your family.

5. In the subsequent chapters I will outline in detail my plan to help you to get control of your life. This includes not only a specific management philosophy, but easy-to-follow, detailed procedures. In the household area, I will itemize what must be done, and, most important, how to get other people to do it. I will provide checklists, timetables, and simple directions for you to implement my plan in your household. I have organized the information for you. All you need do is follow the instructions.

6. We'll also hear from some men—what it's like for them, how they feel about being with Superwomen, and what some of their pressures are.

7. Finally, I'll identify the policies and programs that could be adopted by public and private institutions to deal with the

incompatibility of women's roles in the workplace and the home. Although we live in one of the most technologically advanced countries, our business community provides little support for women (or men) in meeting their family-role needs. We'll deal with that, too.

Neither you nor I bear responsibility for the current dilemma of trying to be everything to everyone. We can't be blamed for the forces pushing us toward Superwomanhood. Having recognized the problem, however, we do have a responsibility to change our nonproductive ways and to help the men and institutions in our lives to do the same.

2

What Is
the Superwoman
Syndrome?

WHAT IS THE Superwoman Syndrome? I see it as a range of physical, psychological, and interpersonal stress symptoms experienced by a woman as she attempts to perform *perfectly* such multiple and conflicting roles as worker or career volunteer, wife, mother, and homemaker.

You do not necessarily have to be performing all those roles at once to experience the Superwoman Syndrome. Some women have stress symptoms as a result of handling just one role and trying to do it perfectly.

The Superwoman Syndrome affects women of different ages, at different career stages, at different economic levels, and with varying intensities. Since we are each unique, we also experience the symptoms of the syndrome differently, but it is usually manifested as *stress*.

Stress is a popular topic these days. It seems almost every newspaper and magazine in the United States has done a feature on it. Television networks have produced "white papers" on it, companies are offering courses to cope with it, yet many people, especially Superwomen, are unaware of their own symptoms. This is not too surprising, because, as Dr. Hans Selye, the guru of stress, tells us, "Depending upon their conditioning, people respond differently to stressful situations...." Further, he says that each of us tends to develop our own particular set of symptoms.[1]

Stress occurs "when we are confronted with an event or a series of events, real or imagined, internal or external, which call for a dramatic response."[2] It is a condition necessary for survival. When our ancestors were confronted, their defense systems went into operation: their heart, breathing, and blood-pressure rates increased; their pituitary glands released adrenaline; their muscles tensed. All this was necessary for them to deal with foes.

Today, however, our foes are different. Superwomen must "fight" the unrelenting demands of insensitive employers, the lack of adequate child-care resources, deadlines, overload, and nonsupportive spouses. Often they feel powerless to do anything about these supposed "enemies." Their bodies, like their ancestors', are readied for the fight, with increased heart, breathing, and blood-pressure rates, released adrenaline, and tensed muscles. Symptoms develop as this state of tension is maintained over a period of time.

Whether you experience one or another symptom will depend greatly on a complex set of factors, including your genetic heritage, personality, age, job, family makeup and support, socioeconomic status, learned coping style, and health status.

THE PHYSICAL SYMPTOMS

The most common physical symptom I hear about from Superwomen is *fatigue*. This, by the way, is more than just being tired. A client of mine describes her fatigue:

> I can't tell you how weary I feel. For the first time in my life, I'm totaled, sometimes weak. I've been trying to get more rest, but that doesn't seem to help.

Another client described fatigue by saying she had lost the joy in life, her "joie de vivre."

Other physical symptoms described by women:

1. Feeling dizzy or weak
2. Headaches, including migraine
3. Grinding teeth
4. Having sweaty palms or perspiring excessively
5. Needing to urinate frequently
6. Pain or tension in the neck, shoulders, or back
7. Heart palpitations or shortness of breath
8. Stomachaches, diarrhea, constipation, nausea
9. Dryness of the mouth or throat
10. Rashes and other dermatological problems
11. Muscle spasms, tics, trembling of hands
12. Menstrual irregularities (While stress may not be *the* cause of all menstrual irregularities, many Superwomen complain of increased premenstrual tension as one of their major symptoms.)
13. Biting of nails
14. Biting of lips

Before I go on, let me tell you one dramatic example of stress leading to physical symptoms. Not long ago I was in a large midwestern city giving a lecture on the Superwoman Syndrome to women corporate executives. While I was there I called an old college friend to congratulate her on a promotion she had just received. Justine, my friend, asked what I was doing in the city, and I told her. She said immediately, "Boy, do I have a Superwoman story to tell you."

One of my co-managers, a woman M.B.A. in her early thirties, just collapsed on our jogging trail, and it has caused quite a stir. The paramedics came and everyone was shocked to hear what happened to this seemingly healthy young woman. The company is looking at the possibility of some kind of environmental pollution as a cause of her collapse, because the doctors can't find anything wrong with her. Actually, the company executives and the doctors are men, but we women *know* why she collapsed. It's really interesting because none of us is talking about

it except among ourselves. She's a woman, working
full time, with two small children, a husband, a new
house and . . . need I say any more? She just simply
used up everything she had.

This story is not the only one of this kind I've heard. More
and more I hear about women pushing themselves to the point
of physical and/or psychological collapse. It is not surprising,
then, to find that clinical studies are linking stress to some of
the more serious disorders such as cardiovascular disease and
cancer.

Needless to say, all the above symptoms can result from
physical illnesses or conditions other than stress. If you have
any symptoms for more than a short period of time, consult
your physician to see if there is an organic cause for your
problem.

THE PSYCHOLOGICAL SYMPTOMS

Psychological symptoms are harder to identify than physical
ones. Physical discomfort either is there or is not there. You
have a cut on your leg or you don't. We have been trained
from an early age to know when we "hurt" physically.

However, most parents are less adept at teaching their children about psychological symptoms—what they are and how
they are experienced. Still fewer teach their children to report
these symptoms. If anything, parents discourage this kind of
reporting because often they feel unable to help. Therefore,
many of us have real problems in identifying what it is we're
feeling, especially if we are hurting "psychologically." And
even if we do identify a "psychological hurt," we have a tendency to want to hide it for fear that it is "bad" or not normal.

Maria, a married hospital administrator who has two
small children, called the other day and began to describe how she had been up until two in the morning

the night before, working on a project (while her husband, Fernando, watched TV and fell asleep). She said she was making plans for a dinner party they were having for *his* business associates. She also talked about their eighteen-month-old daughter, who was getting one ear infection after another. Maria described how often she was getting up at night with her baby and how her husband never seemed to "hear" her. It was always Maria who awakened first and rushed to the baby's crib. A couple of weeks ago, she said, she had developed strep throat and decided to sleep in the den. She asked her husband to be on night call for the baby. Predictably, the baby started crying around three o'clock and continued until three-thirty, when Maria finally got up to comfort her. Her husband never did get up. She was furious with him and really let him "have it" at breakfast. As Maria finished her story, she said that she would really like to chat more but that the laundry needed to be done. Her last statement was something about hoping to get some sleep tonight.

There is no doubt that Maria was experiencing psychological symptoms. The following are some descriptions of other such symptoms:

1. Feeling overextended, overwhelmed, or overloaded
2. Feeling irritable or angry
3. Feeling tense, pressured, or anxious
4. Feeling like running away and hiding from everybody and everything (A colleague of mine experienced this symptom without realizing it. She saw every phone call and every invitation as a burden. She even resented her best friends' phone calls.)
5. Feeling sad or depressed or finding yourself crying without any real cause—perhaps feeling suicidal
6. Finding it difficult to concentrate or keep your mind on what you're doing

7. Finding it difficult to fall asleep or having insomnia, waking to nightmares. (Superwomen keep moving from the time they get up to even after they go to bed. Many complain about waking up around two or three in the morning and feeling so keyed up that they can't go back to sleep. They worry, make mental lists, and get more agitated with each passing minute.)

8. Finding yourself laughing nervously or having difficulty with your speech

9. Becoming accident-prone

10. Losing interest in sex

11. Taking on maladaptive behaviors, such as smoking, increased alcohol or drug consumption, or overeating (Oddly, the opposite—losing one's appetite—is also a symptom of stress.)

Sure, it's normal occasionally to feel temporarily nervous, upset, uptight, or unhappy. The time to be concerned is when one or more of these psychological symptoms become a predominant feature in your life.

THE INTERPERSONAL SYMPTOMS

Damn! I've had it with my husband. I give and give and give, and he never does anything in return. You know, he really believes that if we have sex every other night, *that's* caring! My fuse is getting shorter and shorter with him and that scares me.

Stress can evidence itself in interpersonal symptoms that are even more difficult to recognize than the psychological symptoms. The reason, again, is that few people know when they are stressed and that the interpersonal conflict they are experiencing is a result of it. Most often, they perceive that someone else is to blame for their irritability and unhappiness. The two arenas in which this conflict is most likely to emerge are the home and the workplace.

At home, women often find themselves irritated and short-tempered with their spouses. The complication, of course, is that few husbands are willing to accept blithely such negative behavior for long. Sooner or later (usually it's sooner), they react with anger, and they counterattack. A vicious cycle emerges unless the stressed person gets relief. After a while, who started it is forgotten and a "couple's war" goes on. This is not to say that stressed men can't bring about the same conflict. Obviously they do, and with the same result.

While a husband may contribute to a Superwoman's sense of over-all stress, rarely can he be singled out as the only source. We'll talk about husbands and partners in chapter 5.

In the home, conflicts with children are another way Superwomen express their stress. Babies and teenagers, in particular, are sources of and recipients of stress-related behavior. The following are typical symptoms of stress-related conflict with children:

1. Your children complain about how grumpy you've become.
2. You find yourself becoming more sensitive to the noise and activity of the children.
3. You are yelling at the children more frequently, even finding yourself spanking them more often.
4. The children tell you that you're forgetting to do things for them.
5. There is more conflict among the children themselves.

Stress can evidence itself in personal and interpersonal difficulties at the workplace, too. I am not saying that working women are poor employment risks; on the contrary, there is plenty of evidence to demonstrate that women over-all are good employment risks. However, any employee who is stressed over a period of time can expect stress-related behavior to leak into the work environment. How? Here are some examples:

1. Working harder with less effectiveness
2. Consistently getting to work late, or missing meetings and appointments
3. Feeling always behind schedule—that you will never catch up
4. Conflicts or general irritability with co-workers
5. Increasing difficulty with projects requiring thinking or writing

WHEN THE STRESSES ARE NOT LITTLE ONES

Up to this point, we have been talking about normal women, dealing with normal, everyday circumstances—there is stress enough in doing just that. However, if a woman is handling multiple roles and is also coping with a major change in her life, then we're talking about stress of cataclysmic proportions. As you might expect, Superwomen tend to take on such changes as though they were just one more thing to do. For example, they tend to lose their sense of proportion, responding to divorce, marital separation, personal injury, or pregnancy in the same manner as they respond to everyday problems such as household-appliance breakdowns. This is both inappropriate and destructive behavior. A major life event tends to have multiple effects on one's stress level. Major changes require taking special care of oneself—the last thing a Superwoman is likely to do.

Two psychologists, T.H. Holmes and R.H. Rahe, have identified forty-three life events that cause varying amounts of stress. Each event has been assigned points in proportion to how much stress it is likely to cause. In order to evaluate your stress potential, Holmes and Rahe suggest that you add the points for life events accumulated over a one-year period. If your total number of stress points is 150–199, you are at moderate risk of having a health crisis within the next two years. With 200–299 points, you are at medium risk; an accumulation of 300 or more points puts you at severe risk. Notice that of the forty-three life events, only twelve are truly negative, six are positive, and twenty-five are neutral.

HOLMES/RAHE LIFE EVENTS SCALE[3]

Life-Change Events	Life-Change Units
Death of spouse:	100
Divorce:	73
Marital separation:	65
Jail term:	63
Death of close family member:	63
Personal injury or illness:	53
Marriage:	50
Fired from work:	47
Marital reconciliation:	45
Retirement:	45
Change in health of family member:	44
Pregnancy:	40
Sex difficulties:	39
Gain of new family member:	39
Business readjustment:	39
Change in financial status:	38
Death of close friend:	37
Change to different line of work:	36
Change in number of arguments with spouse:	35
Taking out a large mortgage or loan:	31
Foreclosure of mortgage or loan:	30
Change in responsibilities at work:	29
Son or daughter leaving home:	29
Trouble with in-laws:	29
Outstanding personal achievement:	28
Wife begins or stops work:	26
Begin or end school:	26
Change in living conditions:	25
Revision of personal habits:	24
Trouble with boss:	23
Change in work hours or conditions:	20
Change in residence:	20
Change in schools:	20
Change in recreation:	19

Change in church activities:	19
Change in social activities:	18
Taking out a small mortgage or loan:	17
Change in sleeping habits:	16
Change in number of family get-togethers:	15
Change in eating habits:	15
Vacation:	13
Christmas:	12
Minor violations of the law:	11

As I have said, Superwomen tend just to keep plugging away regardless of the severity of their life's events. They tend to treat everyday crises in the same manner as major life events.

If some of these physical, psychological, and interpersonal symptoms seem to apply to you, you may be one of the victims of the Superwoman Syndrome.

3

"From Ver Did You Came?"

MY HUSBAND, MORT, and I were married in San Diego in early March 1972. Because we had eloped, a few days after the ceremony we took a leisurely drive up to Los Angeles to celebrate our marriage with his family. I remember well walking into the Shaevitzes' Santa Monica home. As we entered the front door I saw a living room filled with lively, Russian-Jewish people, all peering over one another's shoulders to get a look at me.

They were short, dark, curly-haired, and very animated. I was tall and fair, had long, straight blond hair, and was quiet and very soft-spoken. These new Russian-American relatives looked and acted nothing like my Danish-American family.

After all the proper introductions and congratulations had been extended, Mort's eightyish, four-foot-eight-inch grandmother shuffled over to me in her woolly gray slippers, pulled me down into a big, low, overstuffed chair so that she could look me straight in the eye, and said, "And from ver did you came?"

Believe me, I knew well that Grandma Molly did not want to know if I had come from San Diego! By her look, her posture, and her tone, it was clear that she was asking me *a whole lot more*.

She wanted to know who I was. Who my parents were. So if I wasn't Jewish, what was I? Was I nice? Was I going to be a good wife to her grandson? Was I going to be an easy or a difficult member of the family? Was I a good cook? Would I be a good mother?

You may be wondering how this story is relevant to you. Grandma Molly's question, "And from ver did you came?" asked of you, would help to explain how and why the Superwoman Syndrome even exists. It has to do with how you grew up and how you came to be the person you are now.

I believe the Superwoman Syndrome has developed as a result of both historical and contemporary forces, leading us to push ourselves to do and be everything. Until you know what is causing you to act like a Superwoman, you won't be able to stop being so upset. And until you can stop feeling so upset, you won't be able to stop acting like a Superwoman. It is a well-known fact that one's ability to act effectively increases with greater understanding of a situation. So let's take a look at this Superwoman situation.

THE MOST IMPORTANT FORCE IS OUR SOCIALIZATION*

The most powerful force determining our Superwoman status has to do with being brought up as a girl in this culture. In academic circles this process of raising children is called socialization. Socialization is "the process whereby a person [es-

---

*For hundreds of years researchers have been looking at the nature/nurture controversy—that is, whether such things as intelligence, personality, and aptitudes are a result of our genetic predisposition (what we inherit) or of socialization (how we are influenced by the environment). This has been of particular concern to individuals studying the differences between men and women. Most of this chapter has to do with socialization factors. Let me summarize what John and Georgene Seward[1] say about the biological differences between boys and girls:

1. Girls have better verbal skills; boys have better spatial skills.
2. Girls tend to approach things in general ways; boys in analytical ways.
3. Girls are less active than boys.
4. Girls are less aggressive than boys.
5. Girls take fewer risks than do boys.

pecially a child] acquires sensitivity to social stimuli [especially the pressures and obligations of group life] and learns to get along with, and to behave like, others in his group or culture. . . ."[2] Essentially, socialization lets us know what our culture considers proper ways to think, behave, talk, feel, relate to others, and deal with situations.

Before the early seventies, how parents raised girls and boys seemed straightforward. Few, if any, questioned the traditional model of raising girls to be housewives and mothers and raising boys to be breadwinners. From the child's earliest months, parents and grandparents laid the groundwork for these predetermined sex roles to be played out later. Most parents employed both conscious and unconscious techniques for making their girls "girllike" or their boys "boylike." Parental socialization was then reinforced at school and in movies, magazines, newspapers, and books—by the whole of our culture.

Of course, in the eighties virtually everyone recognizes that by giving girls dolls and giving boys trucks one can influence adult behavior and thought.

It has been only in the past few years that social scientists have alerted us to the differences in socialization that men and women have experienced. Because men and women were raised *differently,* they react, think, behave, talk, argue, and deal with situations very *differently.*

By examining the differences between men and women, you will better understand yourself and your behavior; but, even more important, you will also understand some of the conflicts, misunderstandings, and interpersonal difficulties between the sexes.

The twin goals of traditional socialization were for a girl *to become a wife, mother, and homemaker,* and for a boy *to become a successful breadwinner.*

The behaviors we encouraged in girls were supposed to ready them for their future home and family roles. Likewise, the way we raised boys prepared them for the male work world.

What Parents Told Boys and Girls

How did we encourage girls to be good wives and mothers? Above all, *females were raised to be relationship- and people-oriented.* They were supposed to be *other-* rather than *self-*oriented. Here are some of the parental messages women received:

- *"Be nice!"*
- *"Be helpful; above all, don't be selfish."*
- *"Help people feel good about themselves."*
- *"Don't show tension—relieve it."*
- *"Be collaborative, not competitive."*
- *"Be warm, loving, nurturing."*
- *"Be compliant, accepting, understanding."*
- *"Don't say no; it's not nice."*
- *"Don't bother people; if you want something, do it or get it yourself."*

For comparison, let's take a look at some of the messages that boys were given:

- *"Be strong!"*
- *"Don't be helpful; someone might get an edge on you."*
- *"Argue, swear, show tension; it will keep the other guy on guard."*
- *"Be competitive, even combative; nice guys never win."*
- *"Take care of yourself; don't think the other guy is going to take care of you!"*
- *"Figure out what you want and go after it."*
- *"Don't do it if someone else can do it for you."*

Unlike men, women have been trained to be psychologically "there" twenty-four hours a day for their spouses and children.[3] Many women report that they rarely take their minds off their families. Even when they work outside the home, they think loving thoughts about their children, wonder what they are doing, and worry about them. They also report thinking about their husbands, making plans to do nice things for them, or wondering how they are. One patient of mine said she felt like she had an internal beeper that kept her always "on call."

Females have been trained to perform a mental-health function for their spouses that often is not reciprocated.[4] Women traditionally have been very available to their husbands for emotional support, encouragement, and help. Without even thinking about it, they provide an ear, an arm . . . whatever is required for as long as it is required. A University of Michigan study reported that women supply to their husbands twice as much emotional support as they receive.[5] Needless to say, some women feel they never get back what they give, and they're right. At least now we understand why.

Girls have been taught to be keepers of family tradition and ties; boys have not. Who remembers Aunt Minnie's birthday? Who sets up family gatherings? Who buys the Christmas presents? Who sends cards and gifts and flowers to acknowledge important occasions? You know who!

Girls were trained to want and need intimacy in a relationship from courtship to the end of time. Boys are trained to desire moments of intimacy, especially during courtship, but not continuously. This important difference in women and men often results in great conflict. At the end of a long working day, a working woman will still want to connect emotionally with her partner, to talk and to share. However, many a man wants to come home, withdraw, relax, be left alone to his newspaper or TV news, or his computer, because for him, the most important part of his day is over.

Girls were told to "take care" of everybody but themselves; therefore, as adults, they have difficulty asking for help or delegating tasks. Boys were told to take care of themselves and, as adults, do not have as much difficulty in asking or delegating. Most women don't think twice about doing whatever needs to be done. Unlike their husbands, who don't hesitate to accept assistance, women somehow feel that it is wrong to ask. Often, they can't even form the words. When they do, their requests are filled with qualifiers, such as "Would you please"; "If it isn't too much trouble"; "When you have the time"; or, "Oh, never mind, it really isn't that important."

Girls were taught not to express negative feelings. Because it was so important to be *nice*, girls were not to be argumentative, attacking, rejecting, oppositional, or challenging. Boys, on the other hand, were encouraged to be all these things. After all, how could they possibly expect to take care of themselves out in that cruel, competitive work world without these defenses?

Young women were taught to express themselves by being proper, personal, open, emotional, self-disclosing, reactive, indirect, and manipulative. Men were taught that opposition must be shown up or put down, deference must be exacted, directness and solutions are preferable, and face must be saved. (The trouble is that women find these male behaviors confusing at the least, frightening and threatening at the most.)

Girls were taught to be sensitive to nonverbal cues. As a result, women "read" their parents, teachers, girl friends, and, most important, the men in their lives. But men are much less sensitive than women to nonverbal cues.

Everything in a girl's socialization and training was designed around the expectation that she would someday be a mother.[6] Little or no training was given to boys for their future father roles, save their contributions as providers for their families.

In addition to providing her husband and children emotional support, a woman was also prepared by traditional socialization to take care of the family household needs. As a result of observing our mothers and being trained by them, we have emerged with internalized values, images, and feelings about appropriate behaviors and techniques for the household. Similarly, men also have internalized values, images, and feelings about the household; but theirs are based on what they saw their fathers do, and not do, in the home.

HOW TRADITIONAL WOMEN AND MEN "SAW" THE HOME

Women

1. A traditional woman's identity (sense of self and worth) is wrapped up in her performance of household responsibilities. For example, many women feel that people will think less of them if their house is messy.

2. The household represents a major source of the traditional woman's power and control. Her roles as wife and mother are the other major sources.

3. Traditional women have internalized "maps" handed down to them by their mothers of what needs to be done, when, and by what standards. These areas include: over-all household care and maintenance; meal planning, shopping, and preparation; child care; arranging family and social relationships and events; some short-term financial tasks (such as paying bills); laun-

Men

1. Work is the traditional man's source of identity. His identity is in no way determined by his performance in the household. For example, many men may see a messy room, but do not feel responsible for it. Often they just move on to another, less messy room.

2. His job and/or career represent the traditional man's source of power and control.

3. Traditional men are only slightly aware of what's involved in keeping a household functioning. Their fathers have handed down notions of appropriate male behavior limited to the areas of automobile maintenance and repair; outdoor maintenance; heavy carrying or lifting; some household repairs (depending on skill level); outdoor barbecuing; some financial or legal matters

Women	Men
dry and clothes maintenance; pet care; family shopping.	(such as income-tax preparation or investment planning).
4. Traditional women feel all the responsibility for the household.	**4.** Traditional men do not feel responsible for the household, and their actions are dictated by this. If anything, they assist by completing tasks.
5. Traditional women complete 95 percent of all tasks required to keep a household functioning.	**5.** Traditional men complete 5 percent or less of the tasks required to keep a household functioning.
6. Traditional women are highly skilled in the household area.	**6.** Traditional men have developed few household skills.
7. Because the work in a household is never really completed, and because they feel responsible for it, many traditional women find it difficult to relax in their own homes.	**7.** Even when there is a lot of work to be done in a household, because traditional men don't feel responsible for it, they don't have any difficulty relaxing in their own homes. In fact, men use the home as a refuge from work.
8. Traditional women see things in their homes that men don't: smudges, dustballs, spiderwebs, open doors and drawers.	**8.** Men see or hear things related to their own areas of responsibility, such as scratches on car fenders, rattles in engines, insects on plants.

Women	Men
9. Traditional women feel comfortable completing household chores. They might not like certain chores, but there is no discomfort regarding the appropriateness of their doing the work.	**9.** Traditional men feel very uncomfortable, even embarrassed, completing "women's work," especially when they are around other men.
10. Women do not value their time. In many cases, they feel that their time is for everyone else's needs.	**10.** Men set priorities and time limits for each specific task. Men value their time and use it as they see fit for their own needs.
11. Traditional women feel that what they do today has no particular implications for tomorrow. They are very *now* oriented.	**11.** Traditional men feel that what they do today has important implications for tomorrow. They are *future* oriented.
12. Traditional women are short-term-response oriented. This is very much an adaptation to their roles as mother/housekeeper. How can you be long-term oriented in a situation where you are jumping from a crying baby to a ringing telephone to a neighbor walking up to the door to the oven timer letting you know that the dinner casserole is done. They are not taught to take control of their lives, set goals, and have priorities. What would be the purpose?	**12.** Traditional males are long-term-goal oriented. Their work role demands it. They must have goals, must decide where they are going in their work in order to be in control. If men responded only to whatever occurred to them (short term), they would probably not advance in their work and would suffer the financial consequences.

Women	Men
13. Traditional women have been taught to be detail oriented...after all, being in charge of a household requires it. Think of all the situations that demand it: cooking (if you overlook a detail, you may ruin something); entertaining (overlooking a detail may cause embarrassment); noticing small changes in children's behavior (failure to do so may be the difference in detecting illness or not).	**13.** Traditional men have been taught to be macro oriented; often the work world demands that of them. They need to be able to sense "the big picture" in order to make decisions and to plan. To get caught in details might inhibit them from anticipating problems, forecasting budgets, and setting directions.

Most of us have been heavily influenced by traditional socializations. At some level, many of us have accepted one or more of the predicated role assignments of this socialization; that is, we want to be wives or mothers or household managers. With these desires come the traditional ways of thinking, acting, and feeling.

OTHER REASONS WHY WE TRY TO BE SUPERWOMEN

The first challenge probably came from the Women's Movement, and it was a pretty direct one. Betty Friedan started it when she wrote *The Feminine Mystique* in 1963.[7] However, it was almost ten years before large numbers of women got involved with the Feminist Movement or were being affected by it. What Friedan and other feminists deplored was the fact that in our culture, women were defined solely in terms of marriage, motherhood, sex, and service of home. They pushed for two major changes: (1) to have women gain greater control over their lives, including their own physical bodies; and (2) to have women gain greater access to all aspects of the working world.

Since the early seventies, more traditional women have been working outside the home, mostly under circumstances of "until" or "in case." That is, a woman would work "until" she got married or pregnant. She also worked "in case" her husband became ill or unemployed or he died. We hadn't changed much from the forties, when women worked temporarily while their husbands were in the service. That too was an "until" circumstance.

Many women did not rally to the feminist call to change their lives, but joined the labor force anyway. Many went to work because they or their families needed the money. The combined forces of inflation and recession began to put incredible pressures on American families.

The seventies were also a time when divorce became a much more acceptable phenomenon in our society. Many more people divorced, leaving a host of wives/mothers/homemakers to fend for themselves. As women began to see their divorced women friends struggle to make it on their own, many projected that their own marriages might not last a lifetime either. They too went to work, even while in apparently intact marriages. It is these women—the married ones with children—who represent the most rapid increase in the contemporary movement of women into the labor force.

Now, more than 50 percent of the women in the United States are working outside the home. I think the most important change since the early seventies concerns values. While in 1970 there was prejudice against women who worked outside the home, today there is prejudice against women who don't. In less than fifteen years our culture has integrated a new role for women—that of worker and career person. However, our culture has not altered the perception of woman as perfect wife, perfect mother, and perfect homemaker. Now she gets to be perfect employee or executive, too. Performing multiple and conflicting roles has become a fact of life for most American women.

Another Force:
The Contemporary Working Environment

Another major force influencing women to be Superwomen is the nature of the work environment itself. Management consultants Margaret Hennig and Anne Jardim say that in order for a woman to make it in the business world, she has to be more competent, more committed, more efficient, and more effective than any available man at her current job level, at the job above her, and at the job below.[8] This, no doubt, contributes to the current status of "overwork chic." What I'm talking about is my perception that in certain sectors of our population there is status in being overworked.

Think about it. What happens when you run into a friend on the street? After the social niceties, don't you usually begin a blow-by-blow account of all you're doing?

Not much importance is given to the woman who has time to jog or to entertain. Rather, it is supposed that the woman who is *not* overworked doesn't take herself or her job seriously.

A major factor pushing women toward being Superwomen is that they are operating in a work world created by men, for men, with traditional male values.

For most women, entering the work world is like entering a foreign land. There are different rules of behavior, different customs, and a particular style of communication different from women's.

3 + 1 + 1 + 1 = SUPERWOMAN

Let's put this all together. We women have gone through, or have been influenced by, a traditional socialization that has trained us to think, act, and feel in ways that are appropriate for the roles of wife, mother, and homemaker. In addition, the men in our lives have not been socialized to help us in these roles, let alone to share them. Many of us need or want to work, but traditional socialization has not prepared us or our families for that additional role. In fact, such female socialization is an *inhibiting* factor. Finally, there is an increasing need to demonstrate one's ability to overwork in order to prove one's status or acceptability.

UNDERSTANDING THE MEN IN OUR LIVES

We have begun now to understand what is behind our desire to be Superwomen, but the changes that are affecting us are affecting the other people in our lives. Some of us cannot start to restructure our lifestyles without taking into account how men feel and think. That is why I've included at this point a chapter written by my husband that provides some fundamental insights.

4

How Men
Really Feel

Morton H. Shaevitz, Ph.D.

WHAT ARE MEN like? What do they talk about when women aren't around? How do men *really* feel about women, about other men, about work, about sex . . . about you?

Women are curious about the men in their lives. For most women, their father was the first important man, and he spent most of his time at work. Certainly he wasn't nearly as available as their mother. Sometimes what he did and said confused them—and still does.

Women don't understand men very well—and for good reasons. Men don't give women much information. Men don't talk about themselves very often or very openly. As women try to figure out what's going on, they assume men are responding or feeling as a woman might respond or feel. It is a false assumption, and because of this, women are often painfully and unnecessarily disappointed.

So this chapter is, first of all, a way to let women know how men think and feel. Having talked with men as both a friend and a psychologist, perhaps I can give you some understandings that will help you relate to the men in your personal and professional lives with greater effectiveness and less distress.

A second purpose is to let women know that *men want to be understood*. When an interview with Marjorie and me, titled, "How Middle-Aged Men Respond to Their Wives Going Back to Work," appeared in *The Wall Street Journal*,[1] we received phone calls from men all over the country saying how pleased they were finally to have someone let people know how they felt.

We were also struck by how friends and colleagues reacted when they became aware that Marjorie was writing a book on Superwomen in which there would be a chapter about men. Men said, of course, that they wanted to read the book because they felt it would help them understand their wives or partners, but women reacted to the idea of a men's chapter with even greater enthusiasm. Many felt that they had been trying to understand men for years, with only moderate success. What frightened and perplexed them was that as they struggled to balance their own complex lives, they had no idea how their husbands or partners were reacting—and they wanted to know.

Finally, as Marjorie and I discussed this project, we agreed that the inclusion of a chapter about men, written by a man, could add an element of balance. Our publisher and editor agreed and further urged us to coauthor the epilogue, "Where Do We Go from Here?"

Thus, the reasons for this chapter are both personal and professional. It is from this perspective that the chapter is written.

I have been a practicing clinical psychologist for more than twenty years. As a staff member of three university counseling and mental-health services (director of the programs of two), I had the opportunity to talk with younger men who were dealing with issues of separation, intimacy, sexuality, achievement, and career identity. In my private practice I have dealt with men in their thirties, forties, and fifties, who were addressing different developmental issues—commitment, success, disappointment, and the acceptance of what their lives were and would be. At Scripps Clinic I have talked with many men experiencing stress-related disorders, and I have come to understand even more clearly the meaning of work in men's lives.

In the last eight years, since Marjorie and I began doing work in the dual-career area, many couples have come to us— not necessarily in the midst of marital crisis, but for help in dealing with crises related to their dual-career status. We saw men struggling with being part of two-career relationships, often with Superwomen.

Marjorie and I have presented many seminars for couples, helping them to respond positively to the changing nature of the work force and family structures; we have also consulted with major corporations on this topic. We took advantage of these excellent opportunities to distribute questionnaires and gather data about men's responses to various topics, ranging from parenting and housework to supervising female employees. All this has offered me a privileged access to the way many men honestly feel about specific issues.

Finally, I find myself struggling with what I want, what I know to be fair, what I need, and how to respond to what my wife and children need. I am continually struck by the complexity of intimate relationships, and I have come to the conclusion that any assumption that an intimate relationship is other than complex is truly naïve.

The men I am writing about are primarily middle-class, educated, holding white-collar, professional, or managerial positions. I believe that many of my conclusions can be applied to men in general.

MEN AS FRIENDS

The men with whom I have shared moments of verbal intimacy and candor appear in this chapter not as individuals, but as background to what I'm beginning to understand about men. I use the phrase *moments of intimacy* as a way to describe what generally occurs between men. Openness about feelings and personal issues takes place rarely and under very special circumstances.

I have, over the years, brought together groups of men to

talk about themselves, their partners, their successes, and their frustrations. These conversations have proved enlightening, providing a richer sense of how men think, how they feel, and, most important, how deeply they feel—even though they have great difficulty in expressing these feelings spontaneously.

WE ARE DIFFERENT*

In order to understand how men feel, one must first accept the fact that *men and women are different*. As Marjorie showed me early sections of the book, we were both astounded at how differently we perceived situations, approached problems, and interpreted responses. Often, I would say that a certain part simply didn't make sense. But it did to the *women* who read that part.

In saying that differences exist I am not implying that these differences are necessarily good or desirable. The first thing for women to acknowledge, if they really want to understand men, is that often men don't feel the same as women feel. Very often they don't think the way women think and don't do things as women would do them. Men are not deliberately setting out to be combative or obstructive. They are biologically different and have had a different socialization.

Here is a summary of the most accepted findings regarding differences between the sexes. Each finding will not be true for all men in all circumstances, but they tend to hold true for men in general.

1. *Men are more aggressive than women.* They tend to be more combative, more angry, and more territorial. They are more at ease with angry feelings, and this may be the one area where they can express emotion comfortably. When women

*The following authors' works contributed to the formulation of these conclusions: Donald Bell, *Being a Man;* Philip Blumstein and Pepper Schwartz, *American Couples;* Nancy Friday, *Men in Love;* Daniel Levinson, *Seasons of a Man's Life;* Pierre Mornel, *Wild Women, Passive Men;* John and Georgene Seward, *Sex Differences.*

ask why it is that "he always gets so angry," the answer is that anger is a more natural response for men. That is not to say that being angry justifies being physically violent or verbally abusive. It is simply a fact that men are likely to get angrier more often and perhaps more intensely than women.

One of the things women often do is overreact or misinterpret an angry word or gesture. "How could he really love me if he acts that way?" Sometimes a woman will feel hurt for hours or days following an unpleasant interaction, while her partner has forgotten the incident and doesn't understand why she is upset. While for some women the overt demonstration of anger is a very significant event, for men it is often reflexive. When men try to explain this to women, they're often not believed. But it is true.

Men need to be aware of the impact on women of their words and actions. Women need to restrain their tendency to imbue an incident with excess meaning and to give men an insight into their reactions by describing how they feel, rather than by withdrawing or counterattacking.

2. *Men are less nurturing.* It is not yet clear whether the source of the lack of nurturing is biological or learned, but men tend to nurture less. They are not as spontaneously giving. They do not naturally care for, or take care of, others. This is true at home and in the workplace. Women often feel unfairly treated and upset because they don't get back from their partners what they give to them.

Under circumstances where women would *naturally* reach out, such as when men are sick or hurt or upset, men do not automatically reciprocate in the same way. My observation is that men often are uncomfortable with dependency; and that when their wives or partners or children are most in need of support and comfort, their own inability to deal with strong emotions leads them to withdraw, resulting in their partner's feeling rejected, upset, and disappointed.

What women would like is for men to anticipate their needs and respond appropriately. A more effective approach is to request specifically what you want, including being held, being left alone, having your partner take care of the children, or asking that he bring dinner home. Men are much more likely to respond if they know what is desired.

3. *Men's self-esteem is more career related.* Although we now have a generation of women in their twenties and thirties who are also in dedicated career paths, there is a basic difference in attitude in one respect. Most often, men feel devastated and worthless when they have been severely affected by a lack of career success or when they have had a major financial setback. Women can find satisfaction in their lives if they have rewarding relationships with people. I am not suggesting that relationships are not important for men; men's dependence on relationships may be even greater than women's. However, a man's sense of self is linked to what is going on with his career. His marriage may be going well and his children may love him, but if he feels he is not doing well in the world of work, he will not feel adequate or competent as a man.

Often, men's preoccupation with work-related issues is interpreted by women as a rejection of them. This is usually untrue. What may appear to you as an inexplicably intense reaction to a work problem will be more comprehensible to you if you can acknowledge the centrality of career achievement for men's self-esteem. By understanding this, women can avoid feeling unnecessarily hurt and disappointed.

4. *Men are less verbally expressive than women.* Men have more difficulty in identifying and sharing feelings. If they do express feelings to women, they usually do it more at the beginning of a relationship, when the drive for connection is highest. However, for many men this is not a natural behavior, and once the courtship period passes, they often move back to a less open orientation.

Women sometimes believe they have been duped or that their partners are now less devoted than they once were. They interpret the lack of consistent emotional expressiveness as a withdrawal of emotional commitment. What has really happened is that men have returned to being who they were before the courtship began.

Because men are less verbally expressive, they are sometimes viewed as *not having feelings*. This is not true. Some

older men have difficulty in saying "I love you" to their wives
and/or children even though their behavior may demonstrate
their devotion. These men have not been rewarded for being
emotionally expressive. They are now being told that it is all
right to express feelings of tenderness and even of hurt. However, most men, particularly those in their forties, fifties, and
sixties, approach this area with caution.

Among today's younger men there tends to be less difficulty
in talking about feelings. Whether this changes with age we
will have to see. For women, however, being able to look to
men's behavior as evidence of caring is important.

5. *Men have great needs for power and control.* Most men
have great difficulty with relationships in which they perceive
themselves, or they think their partners perceive them, as the
less powerful person. Boys grow up playing games like "king
of the mountain." As they develop, there is implicit and explicit
admiration given to those who become the leaders and take
charge. Even in the most enlightened companies, power and
control are rewarded, and are themselves the rewards.

It is not surprising, then, that men do not instantly accept
relationships based on equal sharing. Most are willing to share
power, particularly if they are able to see that it is also rewarding for them. Men do not feel good about themselves if
they feel they are being thrust into subjugated roles in their
relationships.

As women return to the work world and needed changes
develop in the family system, problems occur. Handling such
difficulties is better accomplished by negotiation than by con-
frontation. Men tend to become more involved if they are asked
to think about a solution rather than faced with having to deal
with a partner in a difficult-to-understand emotional state.
Change is possible, but it usually must take place gradually
for men to feel comfortable.

6. *Men are more vulnerable and dependent on their marriages than women are.* Since men do not have many deep
relationships or many sources of emotional support, they need
more support from their spouses and are more devastated when
they do not get it.

Unfortunately, many men are reluctant to talk about being hurt or lonely. Sometimes they don't really know how they feel. Most often, men react to their perceived emotional abandonment by becoming angry. What women fail to understand is that often when men feel hurt they react by striking out. "Where the hell were you all afternoon?" can mean "I missed you." Men need to learn to be more open, and women need to learn to understand what's really going on.

7. *Finally, most men tend to be more macro oriented than women are.* They are less perfectionist and less responsive to nuances. The problems that arise because of these differences are most manifest when a man is asked to take responsibility for an area that was once his wife's. Housework is the most notable example.

A woman often expects that a man will do the task in the same way she has always done it and interprets a less precise approach as resistance or obstructionism. Sometimes women overwhelm their partners with a list of detailed instructions that is formidable. They don't understand why men recoil.

Most men are likely to be more responsible when they can approach the task as a problem to be solved and devise their own methods. The offer of consultation usually is appreciated—a list of do's and don'ts usually is not. It is also possible that the task will not be done as thoroughly as the woman would have done it, but it will get done.

MEN AND WORK

In my years as a psychologist, I have seen men distressed when a relationship has broken up or when they've had other personal misfortunes. However, the total devastation for men is more likely to occur when they have had a severe and critical setback at work. Many of the suicide attempts I have monitored have been as a result of major career displacement.

When men are in their twenties and thirties their greatest energy is put into making it, being successful, getting ahead.

As they move into their forties and early fifties, there is a general acceptance of what their level of accomplishment has been and is likely to be. As they approach their middle sixties, there is a willingness to cut back and work less. However, most men would continue to work, as long as they could, even if they didn't have to. Retirement for many men is not an opportunity but a sentence.

Blumstein and Schwartz say that men value achievement for its own sake, that they admire the competitive aspect of work and a person who does well in that competition, and that they generally respect work that requires skill and discipline. Men are also aware that work is a stressful place, and in this, they often have great empathy for their working wives.

WORKING WIVES

Men who do not have children seem to experience little difficulty in accepting their wives' working. The extra income is appreciated, and as long as the wife's work does not interfere with the marriage, most men are quite happy about it.

Men have greater difficulty in accepting with equanimity the adaptations necessary if their wives work when (1) their own lives are disrupted, (2) they feel they are not getting the nurturing and the care they want, (3) their wives bring home irritation and anger, and (4) their wives do not take the major responsibility for household and children. Although they know how illogical their reactions are, they still feel discontent.

Men are unhappy when they can't have enough time with their wives. Often, they become angry or they sulk; but they rarely verbalize their feelings of loss, abandonment, loneliness, and perceived lack of importance.

Women's success is a somewhat complicated issue. Many men respond to their partners' success with pure pleasure: "I'm so pleased that Ann's business is going so well. She's excited and so am I."

Some men talk about their wives' success with a sense of

pride and personal ownership: "They made her a vice-president of her company and she's now making almost as much money as I am. She has many options at this point. She doesn't have to be with me, but she really wants to." These men feel proud of their wives, but also proud and secure about themselves.

Men find it difficult, however, to deal with their wives' suddenly becoming significantly more successful than they are financially, achieving greater status and/or visibility. Here the relative disparity beween them tends to be experienced by the man as *his failure* rather than *her success*.

These feelings may be hidden and suppressed because they are embarrassing. A man may acknowledge his partner's success intellectually, but the underlying feelings are still unresolved. In particular, if the success of the woman leads to greater involvement with her career and that means less time for him and their children, he will feel diminished:

"When she first got the position of executive vice-president, I congratulated her but I felt uneasy. Eventually I began feeling abandoned and jealous. It was difficult to go to a company party where she was known and I wasn't. What made it even worse was that I was uncomfortable about what I was feeling. At first I didn't recognize what was going on. When I did, I was too embarrassed to talk to anyone about it."

When a man is incapable of accepting a position of less prominence, or is unable to recognize what is occurring, and is therefore unable to share what he is experiencing, the relationship may be destroyed.

Women should understand that this is a potential problem, but that doesn't mean that they shouldn't strive for success. However, women need to talk openly with their partners before, during, and after their careers become successful. Most important, women must not naïvely assume that everything is okay just because their partners are not saying anything.

Another response to women's success is that men invest themselves further in their work, bringing home projects from the office or taking on a second job. It is as though *her* activity leads to an increase in *his* activity, which makes it even less likely that they will be able to spend any time together. Men feel deserted; and the alternative is to become more deeply involved in the world they know and the world in which they can feel a greater sense of self-esteem: "Even when I figured out what was going on, I couldn't tell her, because to let her know I felt hurt would make me seem less in my own eyes and, worse, in her eyes as well."

Because work is at the core of men's existence, it dictates how they feel about themselves and how they react to and deal with their partners.

MEN AND HOME

For many men, home is a place they anticipate returning to; there they can relax, unwind, and release the day's tensions. If this sounds old-fashioned and/or chauvinistic, it nonetheless reflects most men's feelings.

Men associate home with being nurtured; they do not associate it with housework. Home and housework are quite different things for men and women.

1. Most men want to have a house that is well kept, presentable, and attractive.

2. Most men are willing to "help" in maintaining a reasonable household.

3. Given a choice, most men would rather have housework done by somebody else—their wives, their children, or hired help. (I suspect most women would, too.)

4. Most men resent it when housework interferes with their free time or time with their partners.

Some men think it takes little skill or ability to run a household, and they point to their short-term successes in coping for a day or a weekend as proof that household responsibilities have been exaggerated. Others recognize that running a household smoothly is a complex operation. One man pointed out: "Even though I go shopping, I do so with a list my wife has prepared." Another man said: "In order to figure out all the ingredients that go into doing a wash correctly—what detergent to use, what needs bleach, what needs bluing—I need a list. My wife does it instinctively—it doesn't seem fair that I have to learn how to do this at age forty-five."

In *Making It Together*, Marjorie and I pointed out that many men were subtly encouraged by other men not to participate in housework. Now, men are often inordinately praised for what they do, while women continue to be expected to do it all, with no acknowledgment. A thirty-five-year-old businessman noted: "Not long ago we had some friends visiting, and each time I put away the dishes or took out the garbage, everybody said how wonderful it was that I was helping. No one made mention of the fact that my wife had done the shopping, set the table, prepared the meal, and served it while I played host. In the end, all our friends remembered was that I cleared the dishes and took out the garbage. I must admit I loved it."

For some men, *certainly a minority*, having to participate in housework and in the household is a major burden. They resent it, resist it, feel angry at the perceived imposition, and clearly feel their masculinity demeaned by the request. Their internalized images of what it means to be a man are so fixed that it is unlikely they will be able to do other than the most limited kinds of work without feeling resentful.

"I'm glad she's enjoying her work, but life is getting too complicated. I think about whether this is really the best arrangement for me. If I have to spend my time vacuuming, doing dishes, making beds, as part of my share, perhaps I'm with the wrong person. That's not what I got married for. Maybe I should look for somebody who is more traditional."

A woman married to or living with such a man faces a real dilemma. If she persists in her request for his participation, the relationship is threatened. If she tries to do it all, she will simply wear out physically and emotionally. One solution, if financially possible, is a significant dependence on paid help. Another is to have men do as many non-sex-linked tasks (bill paying, repairs, pickup and delivery) as possible. But there are few easy answers.

Most men approach housework feeling unskilled, uninterested, and uncomfortable. They would rather wax the car than vacuum the rug. It is unfair for women to have to do it all, and it is difficult to get men to do their share. Men can, will, and do participate. Younger men are less uncomfortable with household chores than those in their fifties and sixties. While it is unlikely that equal sharing is about to emerge as the dominant model, attitudes and behaviors are changing, and some movement has occurred.

HOW MEN FEEL ABOUT CHILDREN

Most men will acknowledge that sometime before they got married, or perhaps early into marriage, they thought about "having children." However, the notion of being a *father* or of having to *parent* was a somewhat unanticipated afterthought.

It is not surprising, then, that men feel apprehensive, uncertain, unskilled, and thoroughly confused when they become fathers. What does anyone do when what is happening seems confusing? He goes back to what seems most familiar. Most men were raised in traditional homes. Most men were raised by their mothers. So . . .

A thirty-six-year-old engineer reported the following:

> Everything seemed to be okay until we had Tina. I was really surprised that my wife was so eager to go back to work. We had talked about the fact that she would be working afterward, but she was so ready to leave I got upset. I think kids should be raised by their own parents, not by some stranger. [Translation: I want my wife to stay home and take care of my children.]

The early traditional socialization emerges very powerfully for most men following the birth of their children. Intellectually, they acknowledge that their wives have a "right" to careers. In most instances, they acknowledge the importance of their wives' working because of the financial contribution they make to the household, but they feel vague disquiet about the fact that their children are not being raised by their mother. Since most women feel guilty about leaving their children, their husbands' negative responses may add to their distress. What is apparent is that the plans for child care must be decided on well in advance and that men should actively participate in screening applicants or choosing a child-care setting. Having a sense of involvement often will lessen the anxiety.

For many men, loving their children is an experience that occurs later than it does for women. One successful forty-year-old accountant shared this with me:

> I liked my kids and was beginning to spend more time with them. When they began to really talk and interact, it became more fun. Then one weekend I had them alone because Sherry went back to visit her mother, who was sick. Initially it scared the hell out of me. But after a day or so I began getting used to it; and what really got to me was that by the time she came back, I had feelings for my kids I didn't even know existed.

Some men seem much more capable of disciplining than of being openly loving. Many report that it is awkward for them to hug or kiss their children, even when they want to do so. Their own fathers were not physically affectionate men, and so their expression of love is often lacking, causing confusion to both children and wives.

Men in their twenties and thirties often appear more comfortably participative and involved from an early time. Because they took a more active part during the prenatal stage and in the delivery room, they established an early and natural bond with their infant sons and daughters.

An increasing number of men are now taking the primary responsibility for child rearing or are sharing equally. There are now more men who fully accept the role of single parent. There are a remarkable number of special men who do not need to have the stereotypical proofs of masculinity to reinforce their own male image, and who find less discomfort with balancing home life with career achievement. They tend to be more compassionate, more naturally loving, more naturally nurturing.

Men are capable of and interested in becoming more involved with their children; however, they need to be encouraged to deal with babies. Most men will do better if their initial experiences are time-limited, structured, and children are left in their charge at a time when there is less likelihood of catastrophe. For example, the father takes over a one-hour play period after the baby has awakened and is well fed, while the mother is close by in another room.

As their experience grows and their confidence builds, many men become more involved in their parenting and develop real enthusiasm for it. It's just that getting started is sometimes difficult.

How do men feel about children? Initially, they feel frightened and confused; eventually, loving and supportive; at times, uneasy about their ability to express tender feelings openly; and often, fiercely protective.

RELATIONSHIPS, INTIMACY, AND SEX

Men married to Superwomen complain most about the complexities of their lives and express some sense of disappointment at not being cared for enough. Many men feel that their Superwomen partners are not available to them except when "everything else gets done." I was talking to a couple recently about an upcoming vacation, and in separate conversations they reported the following:

ANN: This will really be a great time to get the house together. His parents are coming in two weeks and I'm going to feel embarrassed if things are a mess. We had planned to go away, but I'm not going to be able to do that knowing all this work has to be done.

TOM: It just drives me crazy. We haven't been away together

in four years. This is the first time we've been able to coordinate time off, and she wants to stick around and paint and polish just because my folks are coming. I sometimes feel she doesn't have her head screwed on right, and when I tell her how angry I am, she just calls me selfish.

Women do not always understand how to respond appropriately to their partners' requests for time and companionship, because they fail to recognize them as signs of caring.

While not spontaneously able to give nurturing, men often need more than their wives do. Since they do not easily express their needs, they may not get love and affection from other sources. If they don't give as much to their children, they don't get it there, either. In some instances, men are capable of being nurturing to one another, but this simply is not the norm. As a result, many men bear pain in isolation.

Often, the *only* nurturing men get is in the intimate relationship they have with their partners. The paradox then is that while men may be less nurturing in their behavior and less intimate in their gestures, they need everything that they don't know how to give.

For many men, being sexual is a way of being intimate, while for many women, intimacy is a precursor to being sexual. It sounds terribly traditional and old-fashioned, but still it is true. When men feel lonely and hurt, they want to hold, be held, and make love. When women feel hurt, they want to be understood and talked to. This difference is very confusing and causes incredible problems between couples.

If sexual contact is decreased to a very low point (fewer than a couple of times a month), the beginnings of sexual aversiveness occur. Sexual aversion dynamically represents some combination of decreased sexual contact along with feelings of anger, resentment, and guilt. The result is increased tension and isolation and the development of sexual distance. I find that sexual aversiveness, as opposed to other kinds of sexual problems, occurs more frequently in couples in which the wife is a Superwoman. A combination of fatigue, unexpressed anger, and lack of effective communication is often at the core.

In counseling couples with this problem, we first explore

the source of anger; second, we see to it that they create time for lovemaking; and finally, we offer explicit guidelines for sexual participation. For example, if the man feels like it and the woman is neutral—it's been a long, difficult day and she's facing another one—my recommendation is that the woman participate anyway. At the end of making love, she will generally feel closer to him, he will feel warmer and more loving, and the likelihood of the aversiveness pattern occurring is diminished. I give the same advice to men: When their partners indicate interest in lovemaking, I urge them to be active and enthusiastic participants. Sexual intimacy allows them to get close and can be a positive and enriching experience for both.

Moreover, men want to be wanted. A frequent complaint among men is that they bear the primary burden for sexual initiation, and they appreciate unanticipated invitations. While Blumstein and Schwartz report a greater balance in "who asks whom" developing, clinical experience indicates that this may be less true for couples in which the wife is a Superwoman. It is my belief that Superwomen are no less ardent, but often are more tired and consequently less interested in making love.

It is obvious that we are leaving the decade of narcissism with its message of "you do your thing and I'll do mine." Men want and need to love and be loved, and most would prefer to share an intimate and sexual relationship with one woman. For this to occur, however, both partners need to realize that they must make the time to be alone together. Without it, and with the complexity that surrounds the lives of Superwomen, these couples' relationships may falter.

WHAT'S NEXT?

While there are significant changes occurring in women's lives, what is happening for men? Although men are changing, there is little societal support for these changes. Most men are expected to go to school, start careers, marry, have children, and live lives not too different from their fathers'. Men still die six years earlier than their wives.

Many are trying to bring more balance to their lives. They would like to spend more time with their wives and children, but they don't know if they can do this and still be successful. They are taking better care of themselves. They jog, order white wine rather than bourbon, eat fish rather than beef, and stop smoking. Still, they feel responsible for the well-being of their families and will work almost all of their lives.

Men would like to change some things and keep other things the same. They would like to have the financial burden shared and their personal lives run smoothly. They want a relationship that is close, warm, and predictable, and a sexual life that is complex and spontaneous. They are aware that things are changing, but they don't know where the changes will lead.

Women are adjusting to new roles in the family, in society, and in the work force. Men are accommodating to changes in women's status and to themselves in new roles. New definitions are developing for the familiar words: *husband, colleague, father, partner.* Just as Superwomen are learning to cope with attitudinal and societal change, men are evolving ways to respond—not only to women's evolution but to their own.

5

Why Today's Relationships Are So Difficult for Us

AROUND EIGHT O'CLOCK last night my husband finished an hour of exercise on his stationary bicycle, took a shower, and discovered that his new watch was not where he had thought it was. When I heard Mort shouting from the bathroom with that all-too-familiar tone of voice, I was upset even before I knew what he was shouting about. He stomped into the bedroom where I was talking with our seven-year-old daughter. The following interaction took place:

"I can't find my watch! Where's my watch?" (*Damn*, he thought, *where is my new, expensive watch? I thought I put it right here on the sink. I'll really be pissed if I lose it; I only took two years to decide to get it. Maybe Marjorie has seen it.*)

"I don't know!" (I thought, *I just hate it when he begins throwing his weight around. How am I supposed to know where his stupid watch is? I didn't take it. He lost it and now he's blaming me!*)

"But I can't find it! Where is it?" (*What's she getting so uptight about? It's my watch that's lost. Why doesn't she help me look for it? There she goes again, personalizing things.*)

(From our seven-year-old): "Daddy, when did you

last have your watch?" (*Daddy's lost his watch. I wonder where it is. Maybe I can help him.*)

I heard our daughter and Mort talking, but by now I was too upset to listen to the actual words.

"I don't know. I had it on when I got home from the office. I thought I took it off in the bathroom when I finished exercising, but it's not there. Where's my watch?" (*Well, that's a helpful response. How come Marjorie can't just get in there and be helpful rather than getting so defensive?*)

"Good grief, Mort, I didn't take your watch. Quit blaming me." (*I can't believe him. He's always losing things and expecting me to find them. I'm tired of it.*)

"That's really helpful, Marjorie. Why don't you just sit there and do nothing!" (*What is her problem?*)

"Daddy, maybe you left the watch in the den by the exercycle." (*What are Mom and Daddy arguing for? Why don't they just go look for the watch?*)

In response to our daughter's unemotional, helpful suggestion, Mort went to the den to look for his watch. He found it on a table near the exercycle. While he was off in the other room, I began thinking about the interaction (typical of many we've had) and about some of the reading I'd been doing about men's and women's different responses to upsetting situations.

I remembered what Donald Bell wrote in *Being a Man* concerning what he had learned from his father and grandfather about emotions: It was acceptable to give vent to frustration and anger—that was masculine—but a man should not allow the full spectrum of his emotions—sadness, elation, despair, joy, pain—to break through.[1]

If Mort was upset about losing his watch, was I? No, I wasn't upset about his watch, but I was upset with Mort. I was upset with his apparent anger. I personalized his upset by feeling that somehow it was directed at me. That observation also made sense because I knew that I and other women tend to have great difficulty in dealing with negative emotions, especially anger.

Then I thought about our daughter's response; she had not seemed upset at all. In essence, what had happened was that Mort was upset with the situation; I was upset by Mort's upset; and our daughter was upset by neither.

When Mort came back into the room, having found his watch, I said, "I guess it would have felt pretty ridiculous for you to have said something like, 'Oh, I'm so upset about losing my watch.' " (I mimicked a soft, helpless voice for emphasis.)

Mort turned to me with a surprised look and said, "Marjorie, in the twelve years we've been together, this is the first time you have ever understood what was going on in a situation like this."

We talked about how it would have been much more useful for Mort to have asked for help rather than acting out his frustration, and how I might have offered some help rather than immediately getting defensive and feeling accused. We laughed about the fact that our seven-year-old daughter was the only person who had acted like an adult in the situation. She was the one who had come up with the unemotional, logical suggestion. Mort then said, "By the way, Marjorie, I apologize for being such an idiot. Sometimes it's not easy, is it?"

INTIMATE RELATIONSHIPS ARE NOT EASY

While at times intimate relationships are wonderful, loving, and rewarding, they are also difficult, confusing, frustrating, and painful. Harvey Fields, in an essay in *The New York Times Magazine,* wrote: ". . . I am afraid for us. Human relationships are delicate affairs. Their circuitry is complex and bewildering.

They jam, overload, and burn out in the most inexplicable ways."[2] Many of us just can't understand this. If a relationship isn't going well, then it must be unusual or bad or, at the very least, inappropriate. We want so much for our relationships to be good, and when they aren't, often we feel betrayed *by our partners*. We have such high expectations that our relationships be always nurturing, always intimate, always smooth.

The 1980s may be the most difficult time *ever* to have a good relationship. The high divorce rates (triple the national total for 1962)[3] may reflect the enormous confusions we all feel about what relationships are supposed to be and how men and women are supposed to be in them. Over the years we have been bombarded with conflicting models. Some of these models are old—such as those our parents portrayed as we grew up; and some are new—such as the equal-sharing ones we hear about from friends and colleagues. They all have the effect of creating our expectations about how women and men should think, act, and feel when they are together.

Let's take a look at some of these models and their messages about appropriate sex-role behaviors, because our expectations are derived from them.

The Traditional Model

Unless they were terribly unusual, your parents are the best example I could give you of the traditional relationship model. From the moment you were born you were surrounded by visible and invisible messages about who did and felt what in a relationship. Every day there was some lesson in appropriate sex-role behavior. From little things like who put the cap back on the toothpaste tube, to big things like who determined what you watched on television—a football game or Ed Sullivan— you inherited your ideas about doing things, and that legacy has a major impact on your life today. Not that you necessarily do everything today exactly as your parents did, but those first impressions are often internalized as the "rights and wrongs" of a relationship. The difficulty for many of us is that our partners, more often than not, learned "rights and wrongs" different from ours, based on their experiences.

The Way Your Parents Were

What did your parents tell you—probably more in behavior than in words—about women and men in traditional relationships?

YOUR FATHER: *My role is to provide financially for my wife and children.*

YOUR MOTHER: *My role is to take emotional and physical care of my husband and children and to maintain the house.*

YOUR FATHER: *I am the senior partner and authority figure in the household.*

YOUR MOTHER: *I am the junior partner and mother figure in the household.*

YOUR FATHER: *I have more power—I am assertive and dominant (or, at least, I act that way).*

YOUR MOTHER: *I have less power—I am passive and submissive (or, at least, I act that way).*

YOUR FATHER: *I don't show feelings (overt expressiveness is weak and feminine); I conceal my inner self.*

YOUR MOTHER: *I show my feelings and I am very expressive.*

YOUR FATHER: *Sex affirms my masculinity.*

YOUR MOTHER: *Sex is what I do for your father; it is my wifely duty.*

Communication in traditional relationships was usually indirect; neither men nor women tended to be very open, although men were more open about their needs and women were more open about their feelings. Men tended to express anger and frustration, which put off and frightened women. Neither could deal very well with conflict.

The Fantasy Romantic Model

This is yet another model that often produces unrealistic expectations. We developed our ideas about this model usually as young girls. Many of us were influenced by the writings of the Brontë sisters, Jane Austen, and George Eliot. More recently, we have been reading the likes of Barbara Cartland. Old television sitcoms like "Ozzie and Harriet" and "Leave It to Beaver," along with the modernday soap operas, contributed to a fantasy image of how relationships work.

Ginger and Fred, Gordon and Doris, and Stephanie and Pierce

We used to see Ginger Rogers and Fred Astaire dancing all the time and Gordon MacRae and Doris Day singing all the time. Today, we see Stephanie Zimbalist and Pierce Brosnan as Laura Holt and Remington Steele adoring each other all the time.

If we are not careful, we find ourselves unconsciously comparing our relationships with those romantic fantasies. We begin wondering why everyone else (we assume) has romance and passion and excitement and good times, and we don't. Even if we don't buy into those fantasies, some of us have our own real-life "being in love" experiences that provide us with yet another romantic model.

The Being-in-Love Romantic Model

Have you ever been in love? How did you feel then? What was it like? Psychologist Georgia Witkin-Lanoil says that being in love is a bit like going into a temporary psychosis. She describes some of the symptoms:

- You distort reality and spend a great deal of time fantasizing about your loved one and your future together.
- You bestow enormous power on him: His phone call produces joy; his absence produces anxiety; his approval is absolutely essential for your self-approval; his disapproval leads to self-blame. You can do nothing until he has phoned, written, or made a date.
- You delude yourself into thinking he is perfect. You imagine that he is irresistible not only to you but to everyone else as well, that he has no faults, that everything he says is right.
- You allow yourself to move temporarily into the childhood world of "magic, fairy godmothers, and happily-ever-afters. Even coincidences take on mystical overtones."[4]

There is absolutely nothing more wonderful than to be in love and to be in-loved back. We feel on top of the world—happier, younger, more beautiful, more powerful. It is bliss—*and it is short-lived*.

You spend most of your time together; you talk; you touch; you do things to please each other; you care and take care; you give and receive gifts; you leave notes; you each do what you think the other wants and needs.

Men, however, see this courting time as a temporary aberration in their behavior necessary to win the affection of the woman they want. Conversely, women often see courtship as a measure of what the relationship is going to be forever, and we feel cheated when our partners curtail the romantic behaviors we expect.

Most women do not realize that courtship is but one phase in the life of a relationship. Many of us feel betrayed when our partners spend increasingly less time courting us.

The Best-Buddy Model

This could also be called "putting all your friendship eggs into one basket." I think it probably evolved from some of the sixties and seventies encounter-group/self-realization movements. The latter encouraged us to move from the polite, distant relationships we had with members of the opposite sex to closer, talking, sharing relationships. We were told that our partners should be not only our husbands and lovers but our best friends.

Today, not only are you and your spouse (or partner) supposed to be best buddies, you're supposed to be the only buddies, female or male. Each of you is supposed to deal with all the other's emotions and needs. If one of you is happy, depressed, excited, upset, aroused, or worried, the other is supposed to respond appropriately. If one has an activity the other doesn't like, forget it! He or she is supposed to give it up because it can't be shared. When people have these expectations of each other, nothing is possible *except* disappointment, hurt, anger, blame, and loneliness.

The Instant Equal-Sharing Model

The instant equal-sharing model, also called the egalitarian model, began to develop in the early seventies as the feminists called for equal rights not only in the workplace but in the home. During the late seventies more and more women entered the work force and were overwhelmed by their quadruple duties as wife, mother, homemaker, and worker outside the home.

An equal-sharing relationship is one in which the partners share *equally* in all the responsibilities and resources of the household. Among the household responsibilities are the physical and emotional care of the people, the earning of income, and the maintenance of the home. Among the household resources are the incomes, time, energy, and abilities of both partners.

It would be foolish for anyone to argue the justice of this model, but there are difficulties in trying to make it work, especially on an instant basis. Usually, it is the woman in the relationship who, because of an inequitable burden of responsibilities, asks for a better arrangement.

Helen, a secretary with a large travel agency, told me about proposing an egalitarian model to her husband, John.

An Equal-Sharing Story

It didn't seem fair to me that I did all the housework and the shopping and the laundry and the cooking and John had access to all our money. The more I thought about it, the angrier I became. One Sunday after the football game, I told John I wanted to talk. He looked at me in a funny way, almost like he knew what I was going to say, but maybe I was just imagining that. I told John how unfair I thought it was that I did all the housework and laundry and cooking and he didn't do anything. Mind you, it was in a cool, calm voice, because I didn't want to upset him. I had practiced this speech for a week before I actually used it on him. I told him about the arrangement a friend of mine, Melanie, had with her husband, Sam. Sam does his own laundry and shops and cooks while Melanie does all the cleaning. As I was talking to John I could see that he was getting very upset. His face started turning red, and I knew it wasn't going the way I wanted it to. As soon as I moved on to the subject of "our" money, he interrupted and said he knew about Sam and Melanie, and that as far as he was concerned, Sam was a wimp and Melanie was a feminist bitch. He stormed out of the house and that was the end of it. I never mentioned the subject again.

This scenario is probably repeated daily in thousands of homes across the United States. The households and people involved may vary greatly, but the dynamics remain the same. A woman feels she has too much to do and too little access to money, leading her to perceive "how unfair it is." She then suggests, requests, or demands an equal-sharing relationship, which often threatens her partner, which then leads to both partners' feeling tension and anger. The result is no change in the status quo and two resentful partners.

Women who espouse an equal-sharing model often dictate that a change take place in the way they perceive it should, with little consideration for the insecurity, uncertainty, resentment, and ambivalence that this request might bring to their partners.

How Men Feel About It

Donald Bell says that the great majority of men feel ambivalent about the changes occurring in presentday relationships. He says that men may "support and sympathize with the women who may have pushed them to reconsider their beliefs and actions, but they also feel divided and uncertain, and at times they resist the changes occurring in their lives. They are caught, in other words, in the paradox of contemporary masculinity, suspended between the world in which they grew up and the one in which they must now live."[5]

To move into equal-sharing relationships now is to move into uncharted territory. We must be willing to work through all the details with our partners. *If* relationships are going to work, there must be changes not only in men but in women. *Whether* they work will depend on the goodwill, patience, and negotiating skills of the partners involved. The most we have today is high expectations; the least we have is knowledge about how to change.

We Are the Transition Generation

As a contemporary woman, it is likely that you expect of your relationship some combination of the old, familiar ways and the new, liberated ways. You are a part of the transition generation, having to develop new ways to bridge your past, deal with the present, and prepare you and younger generations for an uncertain future. It's a hard job, often frustrating and painful. There is a certain guilt and fear associated with rejecting some of Mom's ways of doing and thinking and developing ways of our own.

Here are some findings of my own organization, the Institute for Family and Work Relationships, as well as research conducted by Dr. Virginia Satir, Helen Singer Kaplan, and other relationship therapists, that can help you maintain a good relationship.

THE DIFFICULTIES SUPERWOMEN HAVE WITH RELATIONSHIPS

I want to begin by pointing out some of the specific difficulties Superwomen have with their relationships, then explore some possible solutions.

Not all Superwomen want a relationship; however, I will assume that you either have or want to have a long-term relationship with a member of the opposite sex. This could be with a husband, with a partner in a "live together" situation, or with a partner with whom you are not sharing a household. Throughout this chapter I will use the terms *husband, spouse,* and *partner* interchangeably. Since my knowledge and experience is in the area of heterosexual relationships, the focus will be on these.

Not Enough Time

Women report that more frequently than they would like to admit, their partners get only the time that is left over—*after* the work is done, the kids' needs are met (or they are in bed), the dishes and laundry are finished, and the phone calls are returned. What that usually means, of course, is that partners get the time around eleven or twelve o'clock, when the body is exhausted, the libido is quavering, and the mind is cluttered.

Occupying the same house or sharing the same bed does not count as time with your spouse (although some people mistakenly think it does). *In order to have a relationship with your partner you must spend quality time alone with him on a regular basis*. You cannot leave that time to fate or hope that it will just happen naturally. *You have to make it happen*. And the way you can make it happen is to plan for it, schedule it, and, with all your combined mights, protect it from anyone or anything that threatens it. Treat your scheduled "dates" with your partner with as much respect as you do a medical or work-related appointment.

In addition to *taking* time:

1. Make sure your time together involves just the two of you— without children, friends, or colleagues.
2. Make sure it is pleasurable, free of work, errands, phone calls, or chores.
3. Make sure that it is regular and predictable—one-night stands are as useful as their reputation.
4. Make your time together special and something to anticipate with excitement. Take turns planning the specifics.

Good relationships don't just happen. They require care and attention that can come only from spending time together— time to talk, to have fun, and to be intimate.

Talking Time

Effective talking involves giving of yourself and information.
You look at each other eye to eye; you exchange ideas; you
share feelings; you listen with an open mind to the other's ideas
and feelings. When these elements are part of the conversation,
you will feel more connected with your partner.

Fun Time

When was the last time you had fun with your husband? Yesterday? Last week? A couple of weeks ago? If you responded
to my question with any of these answers, congratulations. You
are *unusual*. Most women answer my question with "When
we were dating," or "Before the kids were born," or "I can't
remember."

When I ask these same women what they do for fun with
their spouses, I usually get empty stares. ("Fun? You have to
be kidding. I don't have time to have fun with him or anyone
else.")

Lois Davitz, a Columbia University psychologist, says that
"The one common link among unhappy or separated couples
... was the absence of fun or shared pleasure."[6]

So, you say to yourself, "I should have some fun with my
spouse? Big deal. What's so difficult about that?" The big deal
is that if it has been a long time since you did share fun, you
might find it difficult to figure out what to do.

Accept the fact that fun is not only necessary for your own
personal health but is essential for your relationship to flourish.
Fun is healthy, not hedonistic, lazy, or sinful. Fun time does
not necessarily have to be organized; in fact, spontaneity often
produces the most fun. Be careful, however, not always to rely
on doing what seems right at the moment; empty, aimless time
will only make you anxious about not getting something else
done. Your time together should recharge your batteries.

How to Make Sure You Have Fun

1. Sit down with your partner and each of you write five things you like to do. Compare lists. If there are any similarities, write them on a master list. Don't worry if you don't have any fun things in common—this happens often.

2. Now each of you write five fun things you used to do before you got so busy. You might have to go all the way back to high school or college. It's easy to forget that you love jazz concerts or gardening or whatever. Again, compare your lists and note on the master list any entries that are similar.

3. After you and your partner check any of the following activities you enjoy or think you might enjoy, put similar interests on the master list.

FUN THINGS FOR THE TWO OF YOU TO DO

Arts: Dancing (ballet, modern, jazz); acting/dramatics; painting/drawing; singing; playing musical instrument; photography; writing (poetry, stories, journal)

Crafts: Ceramics; sewing; carpentry; leather working; metalwork; needlework; jewelry making; weaving; flower arranging

Hobbies: Auto racing; cooking/baking; collecting (stamps, coins, etc.); amateur radio; pets

Cultural/educational: Visiting museums/arts-and-crafts exhibits; taking lessons in something unfamiliar; taking college courses; attending lectures (not college); viewing documentary films

Exercise: Aerobics; calisthenics; jazzercise; jumping rope; jogging/running; weight lifting; yoga

Games: Chess, checkers, backgammon, Parchesi, Monopoly, Scrabble, and other board games; computer games; jigsaw puzzles; word puzzles; card games (poker, bridge, etc.); billiards or pool

Indoor activities: Reading newspapers/magazines; reading books (fiction/nonfiction); reading plays or poetry; browsing in library; listening to records; listening to radio (music, news, sports); television viewing

Outdoor activities: Walking (city walks, nature walks); hiking; mountain climbing; camping; horseback riding; bicycling; motorcycling; gardening; panning; kite flying; sunbathing; going to the beach

Social: Visiting (family or friends, by phone or in person); partying; entertaining; dining out; going to night clubs; social dancing; attending small social gatherings (dinner parties); attending large social functions (balls, benefit programs); exchanging ideas with others

Spectator: Viewing wrestling/boxing/tennis matches; whale watching; birdwatching; watching sunrise/sunset; window shopping; attending ball games (basketball, hockey, football, baseball, soccer)

Sports (competitive): Volleyball; football; basketball; baseball/softball; tennis; badminton; table tennis; golf; raquetball; squash/handball; judo/karate; bowling

Sports (water): Swimming; snorkeling; water skiing; surfing (body/board); windsurfing; scuba diving; inner-tube floating; sailing; sandsailing; windsurfing; canoeing; boat drag racing; motorboating; fishing

Sports (other): Skiing (downhill, cross country, hot dog, skibobbing); bobsledding; ice skating; ice hockey; ice danc-

ing; roller skating; hang gliding; sport parachuting; sky diving; hunting; flying/gliding; curling; gymnastics

Travel: Touring (organized or individual); sightseeing;
exploring; freighter trips; steamboat cruises; raft trips; going
for a drive (city/country)

Miscellaneous: Gambling; playing the stock market;
business/professional organizations; charitable organizations; social/cultural organizations; human-growth groups;
political activities; attending conferences/conventions

---

4. Try each of these activities to see if you both enjoy any
of them. Just trying will be fun. Note other activities as they
emerge. This is an ongoing process, not a stagnant one. You
are likely to enjoy some things for a while and then move on
to others.

What you want to do is to seek out the activities and people
who make you laugh and have a good time.

Intimate Time

PRIORITIES

We're working too hard
Accomplishing a lot but . . .
The time to play is passing us by.

We're in our separate worlds
Of creative concentration
It's wonderful but . . .
The time to be is passing us by.

We meet for meals
And speak of work

It's helpful but...
The time to know is passing us by.

We meet in bed
And go to sleep
It's restful but...
The time to love is passing us by.

Natasha Josefowitz[7]
Is This Where I Was Going?

When was the last time you had good sex with your partner? My bet is that your answers will range from "a few weeks ago" to "a few years ago."

If I made bumper stickers, I would make one that says SUPERWOMEN DO IT LESS! I say this not because they are less sexual, less interested, less capable, or less loving. Superwomen do it less because they are more tired! Fatigue is the major deterrent to an active sex life.

Difficulty in finding time to have sex is compounded by feelings of inadequacy or guilt about not having sex often enough. Usually, the problem involves finding the right time or the right place or the right mood to make love. Too often, Superwomen and their partners leave the question of when to make love up to fate, waiting for the magic moment when having sex just happens. How often are both partners ready and "magical" at the same time?

When You Leave Sex to Fate

When busy people leave their sexual activities to fateful, spontaneous interactions, they are often disappointed. Because everyday distractions—such as fatigue, work, children, and even an interesting television program—can easily interfere, you need to plan for sexual contact.

I don't mean for you to set a clock for seven o'clock on a Saturday evening and say, "Ready, set, go." Rather, suggest to your partner that you get together tonight (or tomorrow night or whatever night makes most sense). Suggest eating dinner early, getting the kids to bed early, and spending time alone. To have more intimate time in your relationship, you must identify those times and conditions that are good for each of you, and then use them. Excitement can be generated just in the anticipation of making love.

Not Enough Care

The second thing I hear from Superwomen about relationships is they don't get enough love (not sex), care, or support from their spouses. Perhaps the best way to describe this dilemma is to tell you about Margot, the manager of a local bookstore, who, in addition to her regular job, edits books for local authors.

Another Superwoman Story

Educated at a midwestern Catholic women's college during the sixties, Margot is a bright, hardworking woman in her late thirties. Like her husband, Bill, Margot works outside the home to help support a family of three teenagers, two of whom are in private colleges. This is what she said to me about her fatigue and neediness:

> There is no question that I'm tired—not only am I tired, but I'm exhausted. I've been working extra hard lately because next year we'll have three teenagers in college—it's absolutely overwhelming. But that's not what's really bothering me. What bothers me the most is how Bill is treating me. I'm working so hard and need his support so much, but what I get is a "quickie" at night a couple of times a week. He seems to think that's all that is required of him. Most of the time I'm

too tired for sex anyway, and what I'd really like is for him to just hold me and talk to me for a while. In fact, the more tired or needy I feel, the more he seems to move away from me.

Sometimes I wish I were back in college with all my friends; they were always there when you needed them. Everyone is so busy these days. There doesn't seem to be any time for that kind of thing anymore.

What Really Was Going On

Because Margot feels so overwhelmed and stressed, she probably needs more support and more care than does the average woman.

Because she has gone through a traditional socialization, Margot does not understand the necessity of explaining to her husband what she needs in affection and care. She incorrectly assumes that because she knows what he needs, he knows what she needs.

As with most women, Margot is looking to her partner for nurturance. But as Eichenbaum and Orbach, the psychologists who wrote *Understanding Women*, point out, men rarely are as nurturant as women would like them to be, which causes women "to feel tremendous pain, confusion, disappointment, rage, and guilt. . . ."[8] Margot described to me what I hear from so many other women: "Perhaps the most difficult time of all is when I am really feeling low, have a painful need for concern, crave affection, really desire some understanding, and Bill tells me that I'm being silly, childish, or narcissistic."

I think it is possible that men get so discomforted by raw emotions that they need to put distance between themselves and the emotional person. They sometimes use negative expressions such as ridicule to distance themselves.

Women Give and Give and Give. Men Give.

My colleague Dr. Veronica Welch says that women "take care" of people all the time; it is an ongoing *process*. They take care of people when they feel like it, when they don't, when it is required, and when it is not. Men, on the other hand, tend to engage in a "taking care" behavior and then move on; for them, it is a time-limited *task*. These different behaviors can be the basis for great misunderstandings between the sexes. For example, if a woman asks for affection (using her own model of relentless giving) and gets one hug from her husband (his response based on what he thinks is required), she is likely to feel ignored or unimportant. He is likely to feel that he responded to the situation appropriately, and if charged with not giving enough, he is likely to see her needs as too great for him to fill.

What Margot Could Do to Feel Better

First, Margot could take some steps to deal with her exhaustion and feelings of helplessness. This is her responsibility, not Bill's. She needs to get better control of her work schedule — putting limits on work hours, taking time for fun and relaxation, getting regular sleep and exercise, employing stress-reduction techniques, and eating regular, nutritious meals. She might get a physical checkup to make sure she doesn't have an illness that is contributing to her fatigue.

Margot also might talk with her husband and children about the financial situation. Are they all handling it in the most reasonable and effective way? Could the children themselves take on more of the financial burden? Have the financial-aid resources been fully explored?

Second, Margot might take a look at how her own behavior could be affecting Bill's. Is she doing anything that might provoke anger or rejection or withdrawal? Is she employing ineffective methods of communicating with Bill: giving him orders, giving him advice, criticizing, blaming, or withdrawing from him? Is she playing a victim role with him? A victim feels powerless, helpless, and at the mercy of another person. A victim's vocabulary is filled with "shoulds" and "it's not fair." A victim complains and feels overwhelmed and does not engage in mature, coping behaviors. Margot must honestly ask herself if she is playing the victim's role.

Third, Margot could talk with Bill about specific ways in which he could demonstrate his love for her. She must be as descriptive and detailed as she can, leaving little for him to guess or work out on his own. She will probably have to do this more than once. One cannot assume that behavior will change as a result of one interaction. Bill is likely to need regular, nonmoralizing reminders and plenty of reinforcement.

Fourth, Margot might want to lower her expectations of Bill's nurturing. It is unrealistic to expect any one person always to meet all our needs for care, attention, understanding, and affection.

She might want to get reconnected with some of her female friends and/or develop new ones. Traditionally, women have provided one another with much care, affection, concern, and understanding. When we cut ourselves off from these important resources, we become isolated and needy, and we begin to look to our partners to fill those needs.

Finally, if the situation does not improve, Margot might consult with a mental-health professional—a marriage-and-family counselor, a psychologist, or a psychiatrist. Sometimes we are just too close to a situation to do anything to correct it on our own. Mental-health professionals can sometimes give us information, perspective, and useful techniques for bringing about change in ourselves and others.

Too Much Success

The third concern I hear from Superwomen about relationships is how success at work affects the men in their lives. Success—the attainment of wealth, fame, or prestige—is something we often dream about, but once attained we find it difficult to live with.

Until women moved into the workplace, success was a phenomenon we rarely experienced. How many women were called successful because they were great housewives? It was difficult, if not impossible, to attain wealth or fame in our roles as wives, mothers, and housekeepers. Generally, we were considered successful if we were cunning enough to "catch" a successful man and marry him. Success was reserved for men who were earning better-than-average salaries, attaining advanced degrees, rising to executive levels in the business world, or becoming persons of influence.[10]

Things have changed. Women not only are working in greater numbers, but some are beginning to equal if not surpass their partners' successes. Since traditional upbringing called for men to outrank their wives in income, education, status, and power, many women today are feeling uncomfortable with their newfound success. For some Superwomen, to be successful is to be ambivalent. For example, consider the case of Susan, a budding artist in the San Francisco area.

> When Jason and I went to New York to sell my artwork, I was eager for some long-awaited acclaim. I was hoping that some of the galleries would be interested in my work, but was really taken aback when several were ecstatic about it. By the time I reached the last gallery, some of the owners were actually competing with one another to give me a show.
>
> I couldn't believe it! I would have thought that this would be one of the most wonderful days of my life ... that I would feel exhilarated, high, happy, and

excited, and I did. But I also felt scared, alone, depressed, and vulnerable. I wanted to run away.

All I could think was: *It might really happen!* What if it does? What will Jason think? He says he'll be proud, but I think he might be threatened. How will he handle *my* success? What will the artists back home think? They'll be so excited for me! No, maybe they'll be jealous, even ostracize me. How will our lives change? What will I do with the money? Why am I feeling so awful?

Susan's anxieties are shared by many other women who have or are facing success in their work. These anxieties involve fear of the success itself and fear about how that success will affect their partners.

How Women Feel About Success

The following statements represent other varied and complicated fears expressed by successful women:

"I really don't know how to handle it. I've always been an underdog."

"I don't like being in the spotlight."

"Somehow it feels inappropriate and unfeminine."

"I'm afraid of the changes it'll make in me."

"My comfortable routine has been dashed forever."

"Success breeds success. With every new interview comes another interview, invitation, or trip."

"I don't want the responsibilities that come with all this success. So much is expected of me now."

"I really feel set apart from my colleagues. I'm no longer one of them."

"Now people seem to be either afraid or in awe of me."

"He's going to start competing with me. I can feel it already."

"What if he doesn't keep up with me? Both of us will be uncomfortable."

"I'm afraid he's going to leave me."

"The more successful I am, the more guilty I feel about him. I do have less time and energy."

"I worry about 'us.' "

"My feelings about him have changed. As I get more successful, he seems smaller."

The fears about success are real and heartfelt, not imagined or counterfeit. It seems incongruous to have negative consequences of something we initially thought so positive. Success can be upsetting, isolating, disruptive, and demanding. In other words, success can be stressful.

Men's feelings about their successful partners are often ambivalent. They report feeling great pride and outright irritation, occasionally at the same time. My husband discussed this in greater detail in chapter 4, "How Men Really Feel."

In *Making It Together,* my husband and I describe some of the circumstances under which the success of a woman is most likely to affect her partner negatively. They are:

• When the man in the relationship reaches a low point or feels confused or suffers defeat in his own work just at the moment his partner achieves success

• When the man is directly affected by a woman's success, as, for example, when the woman's success requires him to move with her to another community; when the man must assume more responsibility for the home or children or both; when his partner becomes less available to him because of her travel schedule or her added work responsibilities

• When the woman's behavior changes markedly because of her success

• When her success is sudden and unanticipated[11]

What You Can Do

Some of the ways we suggest that you can prevent or handle problems with your success are:

1. Anticipate that your success will have an impact. Discuss thoroughly with your partner the implications of success before it happens.

2. Keep cool until the first blush of success passes and you have an opportunity to evaluate what is happening.

3. Search for women who have already experienced some success. Ask them for information and advice about their experiences and how their success affected their spouses.

4. Make every attempt to share the success with your partner, all the way from involving him in projects (talks, books, whatever is appropriate) to sharing the financial rewards. Be sensitive to what he needs and is comfortable with.

5. Talk frequently about your feelings and his.

6. Follow, even more closely, the techniques described in chapter 6 on having a good relationship.

Success will affect a relationship, and for it to become integrated lovingly, you will need time, effort, understanding, and care.

Today's relationships are difficult, but they are more important than ever in our stress-filled lives.

6

The Key to Having a Good Relationship

LET US NOW move on to some of the elements of a good relationship, to what you and your partner can do to communicate more openly, better deal with the negative aspects of your relationship, and focus on the positive aspects. While these are not the only important elements—I couldn't hope to cover all in one chapter—they are some of the most important in having a good relationship.

GOOD COMMUNICATION IS ESSENTIAL FOR A GOOD RELATIONSHIP

One of the most crucial elements in having a good relationship is *to be able to express your own needs and feelings to your partner, and to be willing to listen to his.*

Virginia Satir says that "communication is to relationships what breathing is to life...."[1] Further, she says that "communication is the largest single factor determining what kinds of relationships (one has) with others."[2]

Satir has studied hundreds of families who are "somewhere along a scale from very nurturing to very troubled."

Communication in Troubled Families

The atmosphere in a troubled family ("family" meaning anywhere from two to ten people) is uncomfortable, cold, and extremely polite. Family members appear to be bored. There is an air of foreboding, like the lull before a storm. Sometimes the air is full of secrecy. The bodies of family members are stiff, tight, or slouchy. Faces look sullen, sad, or blank. Voices are either harsh and strident or barely audible. There is little evidence of friendship or joy. More often than not, humor is caustic, sarcastic, or even cruel. The whole appearance is one of "hopelessness, helplessness, and loneliness."[3]

Communication in Happy Families

This is how Dr. Satir describes nurturing families:

> How different it is to be with [them]. Immediately, I can sense the aliveness, the genuineness, honesty, and love. I feel the heart and soul present as well as the head. I feel that if I lived in such a family, I would be listened to and would be interested in listening to others; I would be considered and would wish to consider others; I could openly show my affection as well as my pain and disapproval; I wouldn't be afraid to take risks because everyone in my family would realize that some mistakes are bound to come with my risk-taking—that my mistakes are a sign that I am growing. I would feel like a person in my own right—noticed, valued, loved, and clearly asked to notice, value, and love others. One can actually see and hear the vitality in such a family. The bodies are graceful, the facial expressions relaxed. People look at one another, not through one another or at the floor; and they speak in bright, clear voices. There is a flow and harmony in their relations with one another.[4]

Troubled families communicate poorly and infrequently—they withhold; nurturing families communicate openly, frequently, and unselfishly—they never hold back.

Satir reports that there are many troubled families in the United States, but she also maintains that troubled families can become nurturing ones. She says that because troubled families learned their ineffective ways, they can also unlearn them. She suggests that the process of unlearning involves the following three steps:

1. Recognizing that you have a troubled family (or relationship)
2. Having some hope that things can be different
3. Taking action to become nurturing

The first two steps require nothing more than your awareness. The last requires some specific changes in behavior, which we will now examine.

How to Communicate Better

A. *Before you can communicate your needs and feelings to your partner, you have to know what they are.* Women have been raised to recognize others' needs and to deny their own. But they are not reluctant to express their feelings of happiness, enthusiasm, anxiety, guilt, worry, being moved or touched, hurt, sadness, joy, love, admiration, shame, humiliation, compassion, sympathy, et cetera.

Men have been raised not to be emotional; emotionality, or the expression of feelings, is deemed a feminine characteristic and is greatly discouraged. Some men and some women have difficulty expressing both their needs and their feelings.

In chapter 9 we go through a lengthy process to help you determine some of your longer-range needs—who is important and what is essential in your life. Those items will be helpful;

they are windows to some of your basic needs. However, what I am referring to now are your moment-to-moment needs. These are often more difficult to identify because you have spent years putting them aside, not paying attention to them, denying them.

To become aware of your needs and feelings, ask yourself the following, right now—at this moment:

- What am I feeling?
- What do I really need?
- What do I want?

Let's apply this formula to a real-life situation. My husband calls me at noon and suggests going out to dinner with friends. (This is Thursday; we were out Sunday, Monday, and Wednesday nights; I am tired.) I ask myself: What am I feeling? (Very tired and anticipatory—I like going out with these friends.) What do I really need? (There is not much question about this. Sleep and rest.) What do I want? (To go home and go to bed early.)

As you can see, I am ambivalent about going out tonight. But my needs are very clear. I would like to point out that just because I am clear about my needs does not necessarily mean that my husband will meet them. A solution will have to be negotiated, taking into consideration both my needs and his.

It would have been very easy for me immediately to respond to what my husband wanted, and not even to consider my feelings. In many ways, this would have been a convenient way for me to respond to his suggestion—no fuss and no bother. But taking the easy way out could have resulted in my blaming my husband because I "did something for him" that I didn't want to do.

B. *After determining what your needs and feelings are, you must express them to your partner.* I'd like to share with you four skills that have been helpful to me and to couples we have worked with at the Institute for Family and Work Relationships. Not every skill will work for you, nor will each skill work every time you use it.

Virginia Satir says, "Absolutely clear communication is impossible to achieve because communication is, by its very nature, incomplete. But there are degrees of incompleteness. The dysfunctional communicator leaves the receiver groping and guessing about what he has inside his head or heart."[5]

The following four skills will help you to express what is in your "head and heart."

1. *Using "I" language.* "I" language is a way of assuming responsibility for what you say about your thoughts, feelings, and desires. You may recognize the term from things you have heard about parent-effectiveness techniques. Thomas Gordon and others say that "I" language is a nonjudgmental way of speaking to another person. Most of us used "I" language when we were very young. Take a look at three-year-olds as they talk about what they want: "I want ice cream! I want juice!" There is no mistaking their desires. As we move to adulthood, however, the "I's" in our vocabulary slowly disappear. Perhaps it began with a parent telling us not to be selfish: "Don't ask for things; that's selfish." Maybe we learned to get what we wanted by being manipulative: "Wouldn't *you* like to go to the beach today? I bet *you'd* enjoy relaxing in the sun." The clearest example I remember is the time my English teacher filled my papers with red marks anytime I used "I" in a sentence. I'll never forget some of his remarks: "Who cares what you think or feel? Who do you think you are, some authority?"

In place of "I" we learned to use other pronouns, and we became increasingly vague and unclear.

2. *Giving information by using descriptive language.* Most of us don't give people enough information for them to understand what we intend. We think that because we love someone or have lived with him for a long time, he should know how we feel or what we think. Right? Wrong. When it comes to communicating with someone, you must not take anything for granted, no matter how long you have known each other.

Journalists use the questions *who? what? where? when?*

why? as a formula for developing their news stories. While it may seem cumbersome at first, I suggest that you use these questions to make yourself clear to your partner. They will help prevent misunderstandings, confusion, and hurt feelings. After a while you will automatically give all the information spontaneously.

Instead of saying, "John, pick up your clothes!" try saying, "John [who], would you please pick up your clothes [what] in the bathroom [where] before you go to work [when]. I'm having a friend over after work and I would feel embarrassed to have her see the bathroom so messy [why]." This does not guarantee that you will get what you want, but your chances are increased and the communication is clearer.

3. *Making an effort to be honest.* To communicate honestly means that at any given moment you speak the truth about yourself or a situation. Your whole body will exude your real feelings—your voice, your words, your facial expression, your movements.

Many people are dishonest because they fear rejection by others. Virginia Satir says that to thwart the rejection, we say to ourselves some of the following:

1. I might make a mistake.
2. Someone might not like me.
3. Someone will criticize me.
4. I might impose.
5. He will think I am no good.
6. I might be thought of as imperfect.
7. He might leave.[6]

Satir's responses to these fears:

1. You are sure to make mistakes if you take any action, especially a new action.
2. You can be quite sure there will be someone who won't like what you do—not everyone likes the same things.

3. Yes, someone will criticize you; you really aren't perfect, and some criticism is useful.

4. Sure! Every time you are in the presence of another person, speak to him, interrupt him, you impose!

5. Maybe he will think you're no good. Can you live with that? Maybe sometimes you aren't so hot. On the other hand, the other person may be putting his trip on you. Can you tell the difference?

6. If you think of yourself as needing to be perfect, chances are you will always find imperfection in yourself and others.

7. So he leaves. Maybe he should leave, and anyway—you'll live through it.[7]

4. *Eliminating the negative ways of expressing thoughts and feelings.* Just for a moment, let us fantasize that you are Simona Legree, the meanest, most despicable woman alive. You decide in your own nasty way that you want to bring unhappiness and discomfort to your husband. When he talks with you, you want him to feel

judged	blamed
defensive	unloved
fearful	rejected
inadequate	worthless
guilty	lazy
ridiculed	stupid
criticized	thoughtless
shamed	inconsiderate

Now you need to figure out your methods. You decide to use an insidious combination of direct and indirect methods.

You order and command: *"Damn it! Clean up your mess!"*

You threaten: *"If you can't give me any more support than that, you'll just have to find yourself another wife!"*

You lecture or moralize: *"Do you think that was a mature way of handling the situation?"*

You name-call: *"You are nothing but a chauvinist pig!"*

You blame, criticize, or accuse: *"You are the most thoughtless, inconsiderate person I've ever met!"*

You compare: *"Why can't you be more like Jeff? He's always helping his wife!"*

You use sarcasm: *"You think that's help? I can't believe it. You put away two dishes and you think you've done me a great big favor."*

You lay a guilt trip: *"Do you see these wrinkles? Do you see these gray hairs? They're there because of you!"*

You withdraw: *"Never mind, forget about it."*

Unfortunately, this is how we often treat our partners, even though we may not *want* them to feel rejected, inadequate, blamed, worthless, et cetera; but these behaviors elicit precisely those feelings.

To communicate effectively with your partner, you must listen to what he says about his needs and feelings, recognizing that many may be very different from yours. You cannot assume that your partner's needs and feelings are the same as yours. You are, in fact, inviting disaster when you presume that because you are feeling warm, he is too; or that because you don't want to have sex when you are angry, he doesn't either; or that because you are excited about your new job, he will be just as thrilled.

WHAT MEN AND WOMEN WANT

Let us examine what men and women say they want in their relationships. In a 1983 survey conducted by *Marriage and Divorce Today* (a professional newsletter for family-therapy practitioners), men and women agreed on some needs: fidelity, affection, open communication, intimacy, and appreciation by their spouses.

Women expressed a need for sex as a loving experience. Men expressed a need for good and frequent sex. All other responses were different.

What women sought in a relationship were security (emotional and financial); responsibility; respect; honesty; equality; sensitivity; softness; kindness; someone who cares; someone who talks about feelings; someone who pays attention; support; dependability; trust; companionship; understanding; acceptance; freedom from violence; love.

What men sought in a relationship were obedience; some amount of inequality; to be in charge; an understanding of the importance of their work; warmth; freedom to pursue individual interests; freedom to go out with the guys; for her to be there (home) when he wants her; not to be controlled; a good wife and mother; someone to tend the house; for her to be content and loyal; low pressure (fewer demands); fair sharing of expenses; help in recognizing feelings; validation of the breadwinner role; commitment; quality time; marriage and family as priority rather than her career.

The survey revealed that women have generally accepted the goals of the Feminist Movement, but men have not, regardless of location in the country. And this dichotomy is the cause of conflict. The people who were surveyed commented repeatedly that women are seeking not only equality but respect.

Men still want a woman whose sole function (or major function) is to satisfy his needs and support him in his career. A number of respondents emphasized that men view the "independent woman" as bossy and nagging. They also say men want more time to pursue their own interests. A few noted that some men really are sharing roles, but they need help in learning how to achieve this equality. They also reported that men realize that they must be more aware and expressive of their feelings, but are just not sure how to achieve this goal.[8]

What We Can Do

Obviously, men's and women's needs are so different that when we communicate we must be as clear as possible—both when we speak and when we listen. It is easy to misunderstand our partners by presuming to "know" what they mean when they say something. Women, particularly, guess or assume their partners' thoughts and intentions.

To "hear" our partner we must give him our full attention. We need to see him—his eyes, face, and body—as well as listen to his words.

We also must acknowledge his feelings. We have our own opinions about whether they are right or wrong, legitimate or illegitimate, logical or illogical. The fact is that feelings "are what they are" for the person experiencing them. You can be helpful by increasing the accuracy of your partner's perception or description, but you have no right to judge the feeling.

Dorothy Corkille Briggs, an eminent marriage-and-family counselor, says that "when you share personal feelings, you don't want judgment, logic, reasons, or advice. You don't want your feelings brushed aside, denied, or taken lightly."[9]

What most of us want are acknowledgment and a sense that it is safe to talk further. We want to feel understood.

To "hear" another person, you must use your own words to let him know that he is understood. One of the best ways of doing this is to paraphrase what he has said. Some examples of this are:

"You sound..."

"If I am hearing you correctly, you are saying..."

"Do you mean that...?"

"That must have been..."

"You seem to be..."

"Is this what you are trying to say...?"

Sometimes the information we receive seems incomplete, confusing, or unclear. Under these circumstances, ask the sender *who? what? when? where?* or *why?* Or you can simply say, "I don't think I understand," or, "I feel confused," or, "I am unclear about what you are saying." You can also go back to the questions you used to become aware of your own needs and feelings: "What are you feeling?"; "What do you need right now?"; "What do you think you want?" All this is not to interrogate, intimidate, or avoid; rather, it is to arrive at the "truth" of the situation at that moment.

WHAT ABOUT CONFLICT?

Every relationship has its conflicts—that is both predictable and normal; yet, most people want to avoid conflict at all costs, because they think conflicts are bad and not normal. It is only common sense that two people in a relationship will have conflict: After all, they bring to the relationship differences in sex, background, experience, personality, needs, wants, and feelings, among other things. It may even be unhealthy for a relationship *not* to have open conflict. Denial or avoidance of conflict can have powerfully negative stress consequences on the individuals concerned. The real questions about conflict are: What are they about? When and how often do they occur? How quickly are they resolved?

Marriage and Divorce Today reports that couples "fight" about the following issues:

Distance: Every couple needs to establish a "distance" they feel comfortable with. Arguments occur over how much physical closeness they have and how much time they spend together.

Power: Power issues in a relationship have to do with the dynamics of influence and control between partners. Who makes what decisions? Who has responsibility for what? What rights does each partner have? Who has authority over finances, career, children, housekeeping, and sexual matters?

Trust: To trust one's partner means one can rely on his character, ability, truthfulness, and care without fear or misgivings. How much personal exposure is possible? How vulnerable can you let yourself be without fear of being hurt?

Unrealistic expectations: Very often, problems arise when one spouse tries to get the other to play a role that seems foreign or unnatural. This occurs when one or both spouses have unrealistic expectations of the other based on an idealized notion. For example, a husband might want his wife to meet his "playboy" notion of women; a wife might want her husband to meet her "equal sharing" notion of men.

Sex: In every relationship there are questions and differences of opinion about what kind of sex to have, how often to have it, who initiates it, and under what conditions it should occur.

Priorities: Couples argue about how important each is in the other's life. The arguments are more frequent as each partner perceives that he or she is low on the other's priority list.[10]

In our work, we have found that "what" couples argue about (the content) changes all the time, while the psychological themes (trust, power, et cetera) remain very much the same. More often than not, the conflicts arise in relation to content issues ranging from money management to work commitments, children's upbringing, and housework arrangements. Each couple's potential range of topics to argue about is limitless. While couples can always solve content issues, others will surface until the core issues are resolved. What is the commitment? What is the level of trust? Who feels powerless? Sometimes, an objective outsider is needed to facilitate such understanding.

What can you do to resolve inevitable conflict? First, you can do some of the things we have already discussed that prevent conflict:

1. Make your relationship a priority.
2. Spend regular time alone together.
3. Demonstrate your affection and care.
4. Communicate openly and directly.
5. Negotiate your differences on issues.

(More detail and explanation of negotiation is offered in chapter 11.)

Second, you can employ a "win-win" model of resolving conflicts, one in which no one loses. The two of you arrive at a solution that is acceptable to both.

For example, you and your husband disagree about what kind of restaurant to go to for dinner tonight. Let's say he wants to eat at a soup-and-salad-bar place, and you want Chinese food. How do you resolve this simple conflict?

1. First, you must agree on a joint search for a mutually acceptable solution to the conflict.

YOU: *Obviously we disagree about what to have for dinner tonight. Let's see if we can come up with a place that we will both enjoy.*

HE: *Sounds good to me.*

2. Second, each of you should clearly describe your initial preference, including the reasons you chose it and any feelings you have.

YOU: *What I was thinking about when I suggested Chinese food was the Kung Po shrimp at Sun's. I really feel like having something hot and spicy. I'm not too keen about soup and salad because that's what I had for lunch today.*

HE: *Oh, I see. Well, I'm trying to lose a few pounds, so I wanted something light, like the spinach salad at Frenchie's. I'm not interested in Sun's because whenever we go there we seem to overorder and I overeat.*

3. One or both of you offer possible solutions to the conflict.

YOU: *Well, I have an idea. How about going to Sal's? They have great salads there and they also have good hot Mexican food. I don't have to have Kung Po shrimp but I really want something spicy.*

HE: *Yeah, that's an idea. We could do the same thing at El Paseo or La Puerta. Actually, we haven't been to La Puerta in a long time. I'd like to go there.*

4. You agree on a final solution that is acceptable to both of you.

YOU: *Fine, I like La Puerta.*

HE: *Good, we both agree that it's La Puerta. I'll make the reservations.*

Your goal in this kind of problem solving is to come up with a solution that is fair—taking turns, doing a little of both, doing something completely different. The solutions are limited only by your energies and creativity. The major ingredients in conflict solution are goodwill, the absence of trying to get "your way," and a willingness to consider your needs and feelings and those of your partner.

FOCUS ON THE POSITIVE

The last element in having a good relationship is to focus on what is important and positive about your partner and in your relationship.

Every relationship is fraught with irritations and difficulties. We all have habits and ways of doing things that annoy and irritate our partners. It is easy to allow trivial matters to become the barometers of our relationships. If you can think only about what went wrong this morning, not what went right; if you can remember only that he leaves hair in the sink, not how good-looking he is; if you can remember only his bad mood last Saturday, not his good one Sunday; if you can think only about your birthday he sort of celebrated, not the ones he remembered with something special, you are likely to have a negative view of him and of your relationship.

If *you think* negative, you are much more likely to *have* negative. If you think positive, if you say positive things, if you reward his positive qualities and gestures, you are focusing on the "right" things in your relationship. It's a matter of being aware of faults but not dwelling on them.

Researchers in Canada have isolated one crucial ingredient in having a good marriage: "an accurate and realistic perception of your spouse's important traits."[11] Another researcher has said that "one of the reasons marriages often become better and better as couples grow older is that husband and wife acquire the knack of focusing on what is significant. The trivia, the day-to-day details and mechanics of life are put in their proper perspective—as subordinate to fun, secondary to pleasure."[12]

More than anyone else, I think, Donald Bell expresses best the dilemmas of contemporary relationships.

> I have learned that love relationships are creatures of evolution and change. They are built not so much on hope for an idealized future as upon the ability to deal with the survival needs of the present as well as the

daily permutation of our emotions. A partner is not a parent; she is a lover, a friend, a helper, and a counselor, but I cannot expect her to be there always to take care of my needs. I've come to realize, as well, that our time here is too short to sweat the small stuff—so arguments should be clean, and one should be prepared to surrender the most impregnable positions for the good of the relationship.

[My wife and I] are still uneasy about the new expectations which confront men and women today, but we have found some ways to overcome our ambivalent and divided feelings.

Specifically, I have learned, first, that one can ensure some degree of continuity in relationships by being willing to negotiate about everything. Second, I have learned to hide neither appreciation nor resentment, but to give voice to as many of my feelings as possible and to listen to those of my partner with as little defensiveness as I can muster. Third, I have found that I must continue to negotiate, discuss, and listen every day of my life with [my wife], and that I must be available to share and divide the mundane and indispensable tasks of daily living. I have learned not to avoid confrontations in the name of an idealized perfection, but to enter into such struggles in the hope that they will produce resolution and change. Finally, I have learned that when the above resolutions fail to bring relief and when two people can no longer move forward together, then it is worthwhile to get some professional therapeutic help and not to be reluctant to admit this need.[13]

I DO NOT WANT TO CHANGE YOU

I do not
want to change you
You know what is best for you
much better than I

I do not
want you to change me
I want you to
accept me and respect me
the way I am

In this way
we can build
a strong relationship
based on reality
rather than a dream

Susan Polis Schutz[14]
Yours If You Ask

7

Motherhood:
What Has Changed
and What Has Not

Mom
beautiful nice
helping sharing understanding
I love her so much
Mom

Third grader,
La Jolla Country Day School

THERE IS NO event in a woman's life that has greater impact than having a child. There is no image in our culture stronger than that of mother.

As sociologist Jessie Bernard says, "Motherhood is more than the biological process of reproduction. It is an institution consisting of customs, traditions, conventions, beliefs, attitudes, mores, rules, laws, precepts, and the host of other rational and nonrational norms which deal with the care and rearing of children."[1]

While 55 percent of all children under the age of eighteen (32 million in all) have mothers in the labor force,[2] most of our notions and assumptions about motherhood are based on the nonworking mother. What we expect of mothers today is based largely on who they were and what they did yesterday. And that yesterday was fifteen, twenty, or thirty years ago.

YESTERDAY'S MOTHER

First, yesterday's mother was just about everywoman. It wasn't long ago that women didn't feel they had much choice about motherhood, let alone motherhood and a career. Second, conventional wisdom dictated that the time to have your children was when you were in your twenties—when you were supposed to be the most fertile, the strongest physically, and the most energetic. If one or two children happened to come in your thirties, that was okay—but it was pushing it a bit. Finally, it was assumed that motherhood was part of the package of being a wife and homemaker: If you married, you "mothered."

What was expected of yesterday's mother and what did she expect of herself? She might have said the following:

> *I am first and foremost a mother. The commitment to my children is forever. I am responsible for their over-all care—physical and emotional. I am on call for their needs twenty-four hours a day.*
>
> *I attend school and community events on their behalf. That means I go to school programs, am present at teacher conferences, help with class parties and field trips, participate in parent organizations, volunteer in the classroom, lead children's activities such as Brownies and Cub Scouts, and attend their sports or other performing events.*
>
> *I provide them with such varied things as cookies for school parties, costumes for Halloween and school plays, and clothing for special events.*
>
> *I organize and supervise play with other children.*
>
> *I remember and organize celebrations for such important occasions as births, birthdays, graduations, award ceremonies, and religious events.*
>
> *I provide transportation to places and events including school, sports practices and events, play days, lessons, shopping, haircuts, and social events.*

*I buy educational toys and books, create an atmos-
phere of learning, help them with their homework,
and find outside resources when there are educational
needs or problems beyond my scope.*

*When they are sick, I take care of them and seek
out the best medical care available.*

*On those rare occasions when it is necessary for
me to be away from them, I locate, hire, and supervise
baby-sitters.*

*I organize and supervise chores and family re-
sponsibilities.*

*I organize and supervise times when they are not
in school—afternoons, vacations, holidays, and
weekends.*

*With their father's assistance, I discipline when
necessary.*

*More than anything else, I love them and provide
them with physical affection.*

It was assumed that if mothers of yesterday did all these
things, their children would turn out all right. If they didn't
do these things, their children would be deprived. To abdicate
maternal responsibilities provoked the harshest internal and
external judgments. After all, there was and is nothing worse
than a bad mother.

WHAT HAS CHANGED?

There have been some dramatic changes concerning the issue
of motherhood in the past ten to fifteen years. For example,
one can now choose *whether* to have a child. There are more
options as to *when* to have children. The time to have children
is not only the twenties, but now the thirties and even the early
forties are considered "healthy." The most dramatic change
over the past few years has been the necessity for, and ac-

ceptability of, large numbers of mothers entering the labor force.

WHAT HAS NOT CHANGED?

What has not changed are expectations of mothers. The culture, many fathers, and even many women themselves expect mothers today to be responsible for all the same functions as yesterday's mothers were, in spite of the fact that mothers today also have jobs outside the home. If you are at the workplace, how can you be at home, or at school, or at the doctor's office, or at soccer practice, or driving to any of these places? You can't—even though you and others think you should. And the younger your child is, the stronger are your feelings of maternal worry and guilt.

University of California Professor William Michelson acknowledges that "married, working mothers report feeling greater tension and more pressure . . . than any other group of men and women. . . ."[3] How much pain is involved is shown in the comments of this thirty-four-year-old single parent:

> Every time I leave Jimmy, I just die. I worry about what my leaving is doing to him. I worry that he'll miss me. I think about what could go wrong. I wonder if his child-care person is going to change him often enough, love him enough, play with him enough. I feel so guilty.

What has not changed are the expectations of business organizations regarding the nature and needs of their employees. The policies and procedures of many businesses were formed at a time when most employees were male and free from child-rearing responsibilities. Consequently, most organizations have little or no concern for the parent roles of their workers, male or female. (I will discuss these issues at greater length in chapter 12.)

What has not changed are societal expectations that a parent, usually a mother, is available anytime to

- care for preschool children
- attend school and community events
- provide "things" for children that require both time and energy
- furnish transportation to places and events
- make, meet, and wait during medical and dental appointments
- organize and supervise nonschool time

Because some things have changed and some haven't, the combination of being a worker outside the home and a mother causes tremendous stress: the expectations are great; the supports are minimal; the needs are unremitting; and the propensity for worry and guilt is enormous.

Children of all ages, particularly young children, have needs that must be met so that they can grow and mature. Unlike housework or career demands or husbands' needs, these needs are difficult, if not impossible, to simplify, eliminate, or postpone. For good reasons, few mothers are willing to lower their child-raising standards. The consequences are just too great. As one patient pointed out: If the living-room carpet doesn't get vacuumed for a day or a week or two weeks, what difference does it make? But if the baby's diaper doesn't get changed when it needs to be, her health could be jeopardized. If you forget a business appointment, it is likely that your colleague will be annoyed or angry with you. However, if you forget to pick up a child from school, you may cause an unnecessary trauma or your child may feel abandoned, second-rate, and unloved.

CONTEMPORARY CHILD-REARING MODELS

Working mothers have developed four basic child-rearing models. In the first model, mothers or fathers have "dropped out" of the work force to provide full-time care. I mention fathers here because this pattern is occurring, albeit infrequently. Most dropouts are mothers. In the second model, mothers and fathers have rearranged their work schedules so that they can share full-time care of their children. In the third model, mothers and/or fathers have hired someone, some organization, or some combination of both to provide child care while the parents work. Because of very limited resources, a fourth model has developed: Some mothers must work full time and cannot afford or arrange child care. Children of these mothers must care for themselves and for their younger siblings. These are the so-called latch-key kids.

Dropout

The "dropout" parenting model is based on yesterday's view of mothering, even when it is the father who is providing the care. Parents who choose this model acknowledge the unrelenting nature of it and the negative consequences of their being out of the work force. Many feel that the loss of income and career options is worth it in comparison to the uncertainties of substitute care.

Shared Parenting

Shared parenting means that both parents provide care for their children in equal or unequal amounts, without depending to a great extent on outside care. This arrangement is growing in popularity among younger, well-educated couples whose professions allow them a certain amount of flexibility. Although an employer might consider a request from a mother for a part-time position legitimate, that request from a father would conjure all kinds of negative connotations. Such attitudes don't help mothers or fathers. Still, more and more couples are accepting the challenge, feeling that the time, energy, and care they give their children are worth all the other hassles.

Substitute Care

The vast majority of parents choose the third option—hired outside care—because they either cannot or prefer not to live on one income or have flexible work schedules. Substitute child care is a problem particularly for working mothers of preschool children, because of the lack of quality care available and the guilt associated with delegating this function.

This delegation is usually a tenuous decision because of the uncertainties of child-care resources. To be blunt: *Child care in the United States is a national disgrace*. Unless you have exceptional skill at choosing a child-care resource and are lucky, the chances of your finding quality, long-term care for your children are slim. Even wealth and skill and luck may not guarantee success in this area.

In many cases, child care simply is not available. One has somehow to create it out of whatever or whoever is around. There are 23 million children in our country who need child care because their mothers work, but there are only 1.2 million licensed daycare slots available.[4] No one has dared comment on the quality of these slots.

Each of us must act alone in determining our children's needs, sorting out the available resources, setting our standards, choosing a situation or person, training or evaluating that choice, and monitoring our children and the situation on a daily basis. Who or what provides our child care is a critical decision because of the length of time our children spend with them and the impact they have on our children.

Can you imagine finding schools for our children using the same processes we employ for finding child care? The comparison is a useful one. Let's apply it.

As you go through the following comparison of school and child-care resources, remember that *the most important time for a child to develop physically, intellectually, and emotionally is between birth and the age of five.*

1. AVAILABILITY

School resources for children ages 5–18:

There is a "place" for every school-age child. In fact, it is legally mandated.

Child-care resources for children ages birth–5:

Depending on the age of a child, the availability of resources (no comment about quality) ranges from none to limited. Clearly, there is not a place for every child who needs it.

2. FACILITIES

School resources:

Each state is responsible for providing safe, accessible, well-maintained educational environments for school-age children.

Child-care resources:

The environments are as varied as the children in them. Safety, accessibility, and maintenance are regulated only under certain circumstances.

3. STAFF

School resources:

Teachers and administrators of schools are college graduates at the very least, trained in the field of education, and required to serve an apprenticeship prior to becoming licensed by the state.

Child-care resources:

Anyone can be a child-care person, regardless of age, health, mental health, experience with children, or even criminal record. Some training is available, but it is not required. Licensing is required of individuals in limited, special settings. Licensing sometimes is just a matter of filling out a form.

4. COSTS

School resources:

Fees are indirect through taxes. Out-of-pocket expenses are not required except in cases of private schools.

Child-care resources:

Fees are direct costs for parents. Even tax deductions for child-care expenses are limited.

5. SALARIES AND BENEFITS

School resources:

Although one could argue for higher teachers' salaries, teachers do have minimum salary and benefit standards; and their needs are represented by professional teacher associations and unions.

Child-care resources:

No standards for salaries and benefits exist. Most parents try to pay the smallest amount possible, regardless of their financial capabilities. No professional associations and unions represent child-care people.

These are just some of the issues. Add to them the lack of government agencies concerned with child care, the sparsity of child-care lobbyists concerned with the needs of children under the age of six, and the scarcity of research in the areas of child-care needs, child-care training, child-care programs, and child-care transitions, and you can see where our children stand in terms of national priorities. The criminals in our prisons get more time, attention, and money allotted by the government than do young children.

Many working mothers are leaving the care of their young children to individuals and/or organizations that are usually unlicensed, untrained, understaffed, and underpaid. No wonder working mothers are agitated, overworked, and feeling guilty.

Latch Key

The latch-key model is one of no care at all. The child is alone, unsupervised, and uncared for. This model is inappropriate and bespeaks physical and emotional neglect.

WHAT WORKING MOTHERS HAVE TO CONTEND WITH

First, working and mothering call for very different orientations. Typically, a worker is supposed to be self-centered, assertive, and work oriented in order to succeed. However, a mother is supposed to be other oriented (selfless), passive, and, above all, concerned about her child. Obviously, there are inherent conflicts in wearing those two hats at the same time.

Second, women themselves and others still expect working mothers to be responsible for all the functions nonworking mothers perform.

Third, most business organizations have policies and procedures that in no way support an employee's role as a parent.

Fourth, society in general has neither acknowledged nor supported (via action) the fact that many mothers work.

Finally, there is no organized child-care profession, nor are there high-quality, affordable child-care institutions for women who must work.

There is one other factor that affects working mothers: participation by the fathers. Fathers are just now beginning to take part in family child-rearing functions. However, researchers tell us that "regardless of a family's work situation, the traditional pattern of the wife playing a more dominant role in child rearing remains constant."[5] Reasons for this go beyond individual male stubbornness or recalcitrance. Our society, most particularly the business sector, discourages men's participation in child rearing. Add to that the fact that men come into parenting disadvantaged. While everything in a girl's socialization was designed around the fact that someday she would be a mother, boys' socialization did not train them to be fathers except in the breadwinner aspect. As one man said: "Sure I wanted to have kids. But I never thought about what it meant to be a father, and I sure as hell didn't think about 'parenting' them." Thus, fathers appear to be changing, but their changes are slow and hesitant.

Amazing as it seems, researchers report that working can be "good" for women and "not bad" for their children. Let's take a look at some of the evidence.

A SUMMARY OF THE RESEARCH
ON WORKING MOTHERS

1. "Among women expressing major stress in their lives, merely being employed, regardless of the kind of job, helps protect women from developing psychiatric symptoms. We would argue that this is because work can provide a sense of self-esteem, meaning, and control often hard to come by in the thorny area of human relationships."[6]

2. Role strain is high among women who have children and who work outside the home. It's being a mother, rather than having a job, that is most likely to make a woman feel pulled apart and overloaded.[7]

3. "The real issue turns out to be how a woman manages the roles and resources she commands. A working woman who feels she has to be a 'superwife' and whip up three-course dinners after work or keep the kitchen floor gleaming with a new coat of wax may feel role strain while a more relaxed woman may not."[8]

4. "The women who scored highest on all the indices of well-being were married women with children who have high-prestige jobs."[9]

5. "The nature of the job a woman has may have more impact on her well-being and on her physical health than the simple fact that she is working. . . . [The Framingham Heart Study shows] that women in clerical jobs, which are usually low in both prestige and salary and high in frustration and insecurity, showed higher rates [of increased coronary risk]. Among these workers, the women who were at highest risk were those who had husbands in blue-collar jobs and several children. The inference is that these women had a heavy load at home on top of a dead-end job. For women, it's not having a job that's bad for your health, it's having a lousy job with inadequate support for at-home responsibilities."[10]

A SUMMARY OF THE RESEARCH ON CHILDREN OF WORKING MOTHERS

1. "There is a great deal of evidence to show that . . . the children of working mothers are no less and no more stable and happy than those with mothers at home."[11]

2. "Over-attachment to children is a zone of vulnerability for women who are mothers. Homemakers may be especially vulnerable to the trap of living for the kids, but working women are far from immune. In fact, some working mothers who feel guilty about being away from their children overcompensate by throwing themselves headlong into their children's lives and catering to them."[12]

3. "Conflict with children has a greater negative impact on employed women than on women at home. . . . The woman at home may find it difficult to cope with problems with children, but just because she is at home, she may see herself as doing all she can to resolve the problems and may therefore be less vulnerable to automatic self-blame than is the employed woman. The working woman may be quick to see any problems with children as her fault because she isn't as available to them."[13]

4. "The amount of money a working woman earns is related to the quality of parenthood [she provides]. . . . Earning her own money makes a woman feel competent and in charge of her life, and this, in turn, can make it easier to tolerate daily ups and downs with children."[14]

5. "The available data indicate that high-quality nonmaternal care does not appear to have adverse effects on a young child's maternal attachment, intellectual development, or social-emotional behavior."[15]

6. "Employed mothers tend to spend as much—or even more—time with their children, on a one-to-one basis, as do nonemployed mothers."[16]

7. "Sons and daughters of working mothers tend to have higher educational goals."[17]

8. "The daughters of working women have higher career aspirations than do daughters of nonworking women. And the

former more often choose careers in male-dominated fields than do the latter."[18]

9. "Children of working mothers are less inclined to discriminate between masculine and feminine roles."[19]

Though there have been some studies of working mothers and their children in the past few years, the evidence is incomplete. Frankly, we haven't had enough time to see what the over-all, long-term effects will be.

Most of the working-mother issues we have dealt with up to this point have been external ones: that is, organizational or societal issues outside women's locus of individual control. Let's address the two internal issues over which they do have some control.

WHETHER OR NOT TO HAVE A BABY

As the authors of *Lifeprints* say, "The question of whether or not to have children may be the most emotion-laden one a woman faces [today]."[20] It's so very confusing. On one hand, we hear about the glories of motherhood and fulfillment. We fear that our decision not to have children is an abdication of a sacred duty. People tell us that without children our lives will be empty and lonely.

On the other hand, we hear that our decision to have children is the beginning of the end—of our happy marriages, of our career aspirations, and of our freedom and independence. We see other friends with their "bratty, noisy, demanding kids" and wonder if this is what we want.

As Baruch and Barnett say, children are not the sina qua non of a woman's happiness, nor are they millstones around her neck. There are both joys and problems in having children.[21]

In *Making It Together*, my husband and I describe a process you and your spouse can go through to make this decision. There is, of course, no surefire way to avoid mistakes in making such a crucial decision. However, there are certain steps you can take that may help you with the decision.

1. *Talk*. Don't sidestep the issue. Talk about your hopes, images, fears, preconceptions, and fantasies about babies and having babies.

In your imagination, what is parenthood like? How do you see yourself, in your mind's eye, as a father or mother? How do you see your spouse, in your mind, as a parent? If the true-life actions of your partner do not match your daydream images, then disappointments and frustrations are inevitable.

Consider the rewards of parenthood: getting and giving love; watching a child's development and guiding that growth; self-fulfillment; companionship; challenge; achievement.

Consider the costs of parenthood: economic cost; restriction on freedom, time, mobility; increased responsibility and worry; noise, hassle, frustration; interference in relationship with husband and in career; doubts about adequacy; fear of pregnancy and childbirth.

Talk about everything.

2. *List your questions about having a child*. Consult books, classes, friends, and professionals for answers to these questions.

3. *Practice parenting*. You may decide, before having children, to get some firsthand experience with the children of others. Margaret Mead once said she thought couples should experience "trial parenthood." Offer to baby-sit for a couple over a weekend. Develop a special relationship with a favorite niece, nephew, or young cousin. Join Big Sisters or Big Brothers. Practice parenting with children of all ages.

Talk with couples who already are parents. Be sure to question them about both the rewards *and* the problems.

These experiences cannot, of course, duplicate all the circumstances of real parenthood, but they may help you decide whether parenting is for you. If you find yourselves at a stalemate, set the question aside for the time being, seek help from a skilled third party as a negotiator (a well-informed friend whose judgment you trust, or a professional—psychologist, psychiatrist, or marriage-and-family counselor or social worker) and negotiate a change in your attitudes.

If either partner really does not *want* to have a baby, he or she must be brave and honest enough to say so unequivocally. At least both partners then will know exactly where they stand.

4. *Keep talking*. Experience has demonstrated clearly that people tend to avoid unpleasant and difficult topics. The mere act of talking—as opposed to thinking about or postponing— usually brings an issue to resolution.

Enjoying children is not the same as parenting them. The conceiving, bearing, and rearing of offspring give much joy to some, much grief to others. You cannot afford to make a mistake on this key decision. Children are for keeps.[22]

For those who want more information and assistance in making a decision, see appendix A for books and organizations you can consult.

When the Answer Is Yes

For many women, the question is not whether, but *when* to have a child. Although the traditional time to marry *and* to have a child was in our twenties, those are also the prime years in which to launch a career—and that launching is no easy task. As I mentioned in chapter 3, Hennig and Jardim's study of corporate women found that "a woman could move upward through the ranks of management only if she were more competent at her current job, at the job above her, and at the job below her than any man available. This took enormous amounts of energy and concentration."[23] And MIT professor Lester Thurow confirms what many of us have feared—that if we leave the job market completely during those twenties years we may never catch up.[24]

While I would not presume to advise you on this very important question, given the mores of the current work world, the case is strong for postponing children until your career is well launched. We have already seen some expert findings relevant to this issue:

• The higher the prestige and salary of a job, the happier and healthier a woman is.
• Having a job and being a mother of young children may lead a woman to feel pulled apart and overloaded.
• The amount of money a woman makes may affect positively the quality of parenting she provides.

Consider the expert information offered by eminent sociologist Jessie Bernard:

> . . . The age at which a woman enters the world of motherhood—the birth of her first child—is almost determinative of all the rest of her life. If she enters it as a teenager, the prospect is bleak. The chances are that her schooling will be cut short, that she will bear a large number of children, that they will come earlier than her peers' offspring, and that her marriage will be unstable. Her disadvantaged opportunities in the labor market will mean lifelong poverty . . . All in all, early childbearers seem to have experienced more difficulties and endured more unhappiness and as a group have ended up less well off than people who delayed childbearing. Moreover, although we have not looked at the consequences from a child's point of view, we think that their children would have had easier lives if their parents had been older at the beginning of parenthood and marriage.[25]

The authors of *Parent Test* agree with Jessie Bernard. They even suggest that people under the age of twenty-five shouldn't have children. Further, they state that in their research on parents, the most satisfied were those who had their first child after they were thirty-five, because the delay allowed both partners to "grow up" before having kids.[26]

I add to this the suggestion that if you and your spouse postpone your first child until you are *both* firmly established in your careers, you will have finished the grueling experience of going through training and perhaps apprenticeship (this is particularly true for young doctors, young attorneys, and young corporate executives). You will have advanced to higher levels at your job and be earning better incomes with which to pay for child care, housekeeping, and countless other services. You will probably have more flexible work schedules so that you can spend more time as parents, and more job "perks" such as longer vacations, more flexible leave time for parenting functions, and more power to "change" the work rules.

After you have answered the *if* and the *when* questions, another often pops up: How many children do you want? Again I refer you to the comments we made in *Making It Together:*

> Small families tend to be happier than large ones. "An inverse relationship exists between marital adjustment and family size—the more children, the less adjustment. . . ." There is widespread denigration of the one-child family, which is not supported either by common sense or by fact. With the addition of each successive child to a family, there is an increased burden in household and caretaking tasks, not to mention the added financial load. One researcher cites a nationwide study that found that a mother's housework load may double with the arrival of her first child. The same study found that mothers of preschool children spend some fifty to sixty hours a week on household chores. Other research in the same field came up with these findings:
>
> ●If there are no children, 1,000 hours of housework are required per year (an average of 2.74 hours per day, 365 days per year).
> ●If there are no children under the age of six, 1,500

hours of housework are necessary (an average of 4.11 hours per day, 365 days per year).

●Where there are children under age six, 2,000 hours of housework are needed (an average of 5.48 hours per day, 365 days per year)—and it *seems* much more.

Finally, other studies have shown that "even taking into account differences in social class . . . intelligence measures [of children] progressively decline with family size."

Couples who have children in close succession will lessen the total number of years devoted to the heavy demands of babies and young children. Though the immediate load may be greater on parents who elect to have children in close succession, in the long run there is a net gain, because the years needed for intensive child care are telescoped into a few. This leaves more time in which the parents may pursue careers or other activities.

There is evidence that siblings help one another in rough, stressful situations. If two children are enrolled in a child-care center, for example, the stress on both will usually be less than on a single child. Children also are company for one another in the parents' absence (working, vacations, business trips).[27]

> Don't poets know it
> Better than others?
> God can't be always everywhere: and, so,
> Invented Mothers.

> *Sir Edwin Arnold*[28]
> *"Mothers"*

But "He's" not making it easy for us these days, is "He"?

8

Raising Happy, Productive Kids

IF YOU ARE reading this chapter, you probably are a Superwoman mother. You probably feel pulled and pushed and drained and overwhelmed, and, above all, guilty. Under these circumstances it really is difficult to find the energy to meet a child's needs.

I understand what it's like to come home from a hard day at the office feeling you have nothing left to give to anyone, let alone a child or children. If this happens once in a while, your children are not greatly affected. But if you come home every day or every week feeling exhausted, irritable, resentful of your children's neediness, and unable to "give," you are putting yourself and your children in an untenable situation.

Some relief is available if you have a child-oriented spouse, but many women don't have that luxury, and others are raising children alone.

WHERE DO YOU GET THE TIME TO BE AN EFFECTIVE MOTHER?

Where *do* you get the time, energy, and skills to be an effective mother?

You get the time by declaring your children an important

part of your life. You make them a priority not only in your mind but in your actions. Above all, you *don't allow* unimportant people or events to get in the way. You have the ability to make this decision.

You get the energy to be an effective mother by making sure that your own physical and emotional needs are met.

Finally, you get the skills to be an effective mother by educating yourself about good parenting methods.

The process of becoming a mother seems relatively easy compared to the requirements of being a good parent. If you are thinking of having a child, how are you going to prepare for parenting? If you are already a mother, how do you know your parenting methods are effective?

Experts say that while many future parents spend a great deal of time preparing for childbirth, which lasts a number of hours, they spend relatively little time preparing for child rearing, which covers at least eighteen years. Our society is very lax in training its adults to be good parents. Why do we train for jobs but not for parenting? Why do we suppose we'll know what to do?

Dr. Fitzhugh Dodson says that to parent "is to use, with tender loving care, all the information science has assimilated about child psychology in order to raise happy and intelligent human beings."[1] He also says that there is no harder job in our society.

How you parent is probably a mixture of a number of influences. No doubt, your memories of being parented are a very strong influence. Some of us want to duplicate what our mothers and fathers did; others want to do things very differently. Still others parent with a combination of what their parents did and didn't do. Since most of our parents were traditional, it is difficult to apply some of their techniques to our very different realities.

Even the contemporary kid experts are biased. Dr. Spock, Dr. Salk, and Dr. Dodson don't have much advice for working mothers.

Most of us are doing the best we can with methods that

include two parts memory, one part expert advice, one part wishful thinking, one part observation, and one part hope for the best—and we're doing it with a limited amount of time.

The latter factor—limited time—is a source of great concern to Superwomen mothers. We want to make sure that the most is made of the time we have with our children. How do we do that?

THE OUTCOME MODEL OF PARENTING

One approach to use is what I call the *outcome model*. This model begins with the final goal of your parenting: *what kind of adult you hope your child will be*. It views the process of parenting as a means to an end, the end being a fully functioning human being who is able to actualize his or her unique self.

As long as you are going to be a parent, you might as well have an end in mind. Your behaviors affect your child anyway. Why not try to have them affect him or her positively, in the direction you want? While no one mother can fully determine how her child will turn out, this model offers you a way of giving your behaviors a purpose.

What kind of adult would you like your child to be? I asked this question of a group of local parents. I asked them to describe in a word or two the characteristics they hoped their children would have as adults. Here are their answers:

What Parents Want Their Children to Be

happy	self-confident
independent, self-reliant	loving, caring
responsible	intelligent, competent
successful	poised
hardworking, productive	creative, exploring
outgoing, comfortable socially	communicative
someone with high self-esteem	sophisticated

involved, excited about life   assertive
patient, tolerant, accepting   calm, relaxed

You can probably add quite a number of your own.

THE BASICS OF GOOD PARENTING

If these or other outcomes are what you want, then which behaviors from you will help produce them? What behaviors in you are least likely to produce the outcomes you want? As an example, let's see what various child-development experts suggest you do to increase the chances of your child's having high self-esteem.

Dorothy Corkille Briggs says that "if your child has high self-esteem, he [she] has it made." Further, she states that self-esteem is "how a person feels about himself [herself] . . . a quiet sense of self-respect, a feeling of self-worth. . . ." Sometimes parents are afraid of developing *too much* self-esteem. They are concerned about producing conceited children. But, according to Briggs, "conceit is but whitewash to cover low self-esteem. With high self-esteem you don't waste time and energy impressing others; you already know you have value." She emphasizes that self-esteem forms "the core of [a child's] personality and determines the use he [she] makes of his [her] aptitudes and abilities."[2]

How can you as a parent help or hinder your child's potential for high self-esteem? Let's consider the positive and negative effects of what you do.

DEVELOPING HIGH SELF-ESTEEM

1. **Helpful:** Helping your child to *feel* loved through your words and actions—hugging, touching, smiling at your child.
   Unhelpful: Loving your child but somehow failing to get

the message across—not being demonstrative, keeping your feelings to yourself.

2. Helpful: Treating your child with warmth and sensitivity—supporting her when she's worried, rejoicing with her when she's happy.

Unhelpful: Ignoring your child's feelings, treating her with disinterest and insensitivity.

3. Helpful: Respecting your child by listening to her opinions, negotiating differences, and taking the time to resolve conflicts.

Unhelpful: Rejecting your child's opinions when they differ from yours, using power to deal with differences, being abrupt.

4. Helpful: Sending honest, positive word messages to your child, such as, "You're great, you're neat, you're wonderful."

Unhelpful: Sending negative messages, such as, "You're bad, you're impossible, I can't wait for you to leave home for college."

5. Helpful: Giving your child your time and attention.

Unhelpful: Giving your child material things in place of your time and attention.[3]

Gene Hawes and Helen and Martin Weiss have written a wonderful book, *How to Raise Your Child to Be a Winner.* Here are some of the things they see as constructive or destructive to a child's self-esteem.

1. Constructive: Emphasizing your child's strengths and competencies while helping him or her to overcome areas of difficulty.

Destructive: Dismissing or ignoring what is positive while emphasizing areas where he or she is deficient.

2. Constructive: Encouraging a child to do things and helping him or her to do them.

Destructive: Doing things for a child; discouraging him or her from doing things independently.

3. Constructive: Expressing disapproval of inappropriate or inconsiderate acts. Example: "I am really upset that you didn't clean up the yard today."

Destructive: Criticizing your child. Examples: "You're lazy, you're a slob."

4. Constructive: Encouraging your child to express his or her opinions and ideas and to disagree with yours.

Destructive: Putting down your child's ideas; not allowing him or her to disagree with you; responding with rancor and punishment.

5. Constructive: Helping your child to express his or her emotions openly.

Destructive: Discouraging or denying strong emotions from your child; telling him or her that emotions are silly, childish.[4]

If You Want Them to Have High Self-Esteem

You must love your kids, reward them, set limits for them, teach them, adore them, reason with them, cherish them, like them, empathize with them, understand them, accept them, respect them, and encourage them if you want them to feel good about themselves.

You *must not* ignore them, lecture them, order them, control them, demand obedience from them, hit them, reject them, put them down, withdraw from them, or dominate them. Rather than leading to high self-esteem, these behaviors lead to anger, frustration, anxiety, withdrawal, self-doubt, fear, insecurity, defiance, rebellion, self-hate, alienation, resentment, dependency, hostility, submission, compliance, and failure.

You Are the Key to Helping Children Feel Confident

Some parents may respond to suggestions by saying something like, "But I don't want to have all that power or all that responsibility." Or, "My kids don't listen to me anyway; none of this is going to make any difference." To this, the authors of the "Raising Winners" book say:

> What you do and say over the years has more impact on the child than anything—more than friends, relatives, community, teachers, schools, colleges. When very young, the child literally sees life and the world through you. For the infant, you are the largest and most important part of the world. And while the child grows up, you provide the central vantage point from which your child views life inside and increasingly far beyond the home. Moreover, your actions first decisively shape the child's key capabilities.[5]

Take the opportunity to make a real difference in your child's life. Dorothy Briggs has noted that "therapists' records are filled with reports of children [and adults] who, with only one hour of 'sunshine' [positive reflections] a week, make enormous changes in their self-images."[6]

Psychologists and child-development experts tell us that, in addition to developing high self-esteem, certain other parenting behaviors are likely to produce full-functioning adults. Those that are most relevant for Superwomen mothers are (1) quality time; (2) effective communication; (3) dealing with children's inappropriate behaviors.

QUALITY TIME

The first element of effective parenting is taking the time to be with your child. Time—that precious element we Superwomen mothers seem to have so little of—is the most important ingredient in building a relationship. Without it, you cannot employ any methods of good parenting.

In order for this time to count, you must give it happily, joyfully, and eagerly. Children are very quick to pick up the signals when your time is given unhappily, reluctantly, hesitantly, or halfheartedly.

1. *Quality time is being alone with and interacting with a child.* Children love to have you all to themselves. So often time is spent with other family members, other kids, or other adults. To make it special, give your child time away from everyone else. It's also important that you be an active companion. Be physically and emotionally involved.

WHAT YOU CAN DO

A. Talk with your child.

B. Play a game.

C. Go to a sports event.

D. Participate in an activity such as bicycling or tennis.

E. Have lunch or breakfast or dinner "out."

2. *Quality time is engaging in child-initiated or child-sanctioned activities.* How easy it is to use your parental power and have your child do whatever you want to do. While this is often appropriate, don't confuse it with having quality time. You will want to participate in activities your child initiates, for they satisfy expressed desires, and those that are sanctioned by the child, because when you suggest an activity and the child accepts eagerly, it means that you have taken the time to think of something you both can enjoy.

DO THE THINGS YOUR CHILD SUGGESTS

A. Accept an invitation to play Monopoly.

B. Agree to build a Lego house.

C. Play hide-and-seek with your two-year-old.

D. Consent to go on an afternoon mountain hike.

E. Agree to read your child's favorite book, again.

DO THINGS YOU SUGGEST AND YOUR CHILD WANTS, TOO

A. Ask your daughter to play tennis—she eagerly accepts the invitation.

B. Ask your son to join you in making peanut butter cookies—he jumps at the chance.

C. Invite your daughter to go shopping for her—she is delighted with the idea.

D. Ask your child to go skiing with you—he loves the idea.

E. Invite your eight-year-old daughter to attend a special concert—she feels good about going to such a grown-up affair.

3. *Quality time is demonstrating through words and/or actions that you love a child.* Some people feel that too much affection will "spoil" a child. Nothing could be further from the truth. Children of all ages have a deep need to be loved and cherished. But do be sensitive to how much, when, and what kind of affection different children desire. For example, overwhelming a child with hugs and kisses he does not want is an act of insensitivity, not an act of love.

DEMONSTRATE YOUR AFFECTION BY

A. Hugging

B. Kissing

C. Snuggling

D. Telling your child that you love her

E. Writing an affectionate note

F. Holding your child's hand

G. Smiling appreciatively at your child, often

4. *Quality time is the time you spend with a child when it has a special impact.* There are certain routine times, such as just before you leave home, when you return, and bedtimes, that are important to children, especially young ones. How easy it is when you are rushing off or rushing into your home to look first at the day's mail or check phone messages or react to a messy room than to give special attention to your children. They, however, have a need to "connect" with you at your comings and goings. A few minutes of talking or hugging or playing can go a very long way. In fact, the more you can meet a child's immediate need to be with you, the less needy she is likely to be in the long run.

WHAT CAN HAVE A SPECIAL IMPACT

A. Sitting down with your young child and talking about where you are going and when you will return

B. Giving your daughter or son a hug and kiss, or quite a few

C. Listening to what your child has to say

D. Paying "special attention" to your child

E. Telling phone callers that you are now occupied and will return their calls later

There are other times when "being there"—events, games, or performances—has special meaning for your child. Even more, your presence makes the event complete. Ask your children to let you know what is special and what is ordinary for them. Very often we think we know what is important, but we really don't.

SPECIAL BEHAVIORS FOR SPECIAL EVENTS

A. Attending a school athletic day in which your child is competing

B. Taking your young child to his or her first day of school and staying there until he or she feels comfortable

C. At bedtime, reading or snuggling or talking with your child

D. Going to some school parties or field trips

E. Celebrating your child's birthday in the way he or she wants

How Much Time Should You Spend?

How much time you "should" spend with your child is very difficult to determine. It depends on many things—how much time you have available, your child's age and needs, the number of children you have, everyone's health, and the amount of time your spouse and other important people spend with your child.

The younger the child, the more time he or she needs and deserves from you. Remember, the first five years of a child's life are critical in physical, emotional, and intellectual development. Children of all ages, including adolescents, need and deserve regular and routine time with you. In chapter 10, I'll make some recommendations that may help you set aside those very important hours.

Finally, children need and deserve priority in your life. So often, career demands, social invitations, and other people's requests make you forget that priority for a while. To assure your children plenty of time, put some weekday and weekend limits on how much time you will spend away from them. For example, you might want to limit yourself to one evening out Monday through Friday, and one evening out on the weekend. Because they have such limited time available to their children, many busy people include their children in as many events and invitations as is appropriate and possible. When you give your children such quality time, you give them the feeling that they are loved, important, connected with you, valued, and significant in your life.

EFFECTIVE COMMUNICATION

The second element of good parenting is using effective communication techniques. Somehow, when we become parents a weird thing happens to us. We begin to act and talk like parents instead of normal, ordinary people. We find ourselves using a special language for children, with unnatural locutions ("And how are we feeling today?"); special words ("Does Jimmy want a yum-yum?"); and restricted topics (school, homework, "their" behavior, "their" appearance, "their" friends). Our conversations are stilted and superficial. Our references are cryptic ("I understand something happened at school."), and our comments are preachy ("Don't you think it's time you learned how to be more responsible?").

Many of us feel compelled to tell our kids all the things they are doing wrong: "You didn't say thank you; you didn't pick up your clothes; your elbows are on the table, that shirt is a mess; your hair is too long [or too short]; your music is terrible; you're too noisy; you're too fat [or too thin]; you're too talkative [or too withdrawn]; you don't spend enough time with us; your friends drive us crazy," and so on.

Also, there is an unreal quality about our conversations with children. We feel a need to put up a front of perfection. The unspoken rule is that we are never wrong, never make mistakes, will never change our minds, and are never in doubt or confused. We don't want our children to be privy to our weaknesses, vulnerabilities, or inadequacies.

I think we confuse and mislead our kids most of the time. So, what can we do to "clean up our act" and communicate more effectively with them? Except for minor modifications when dealing with infants or toddlers, we need to use the same communication methods with our children as those that we use with adults.

Express your needs and feelings to your children and listen to theirs; use "I" language; use descriptive language so that your thoughts are understood; be honest; eliminate the negatives in your language; listen carefully; acknowledge feelings; deal with conflict; and focus on the positive.

It is likely that your child will then feel understood and respected, become more open and communicative, and more aware of you as a person.

CHILDREN'S INAPPROPRIATE BEHAVIORS

The third element of effective parenting is knowing how to deal with your child's inappropriate behaviors. This is often a difficult area for mothers because it usually involves conflict. Because of their discomfort, some mothers leave all or most of the discipline to fathers. By doing this, women give up an important opportunity to effect behaviors they want in their children. Some mothers and fathers think that the most important parental function is to punish children for inappropriate behaviors. Punishment, in fact, sometimes produces behaviors exactly opposite what we want. Haim Ginott says that punishment doesn't work because rather than helping children to improve it pushes them to become preoccupied with revenge fantasies.[7] There are many other things we can do that are more effective.

1. *Behaving toward our children as we would have them behave.* Very often "what we do" has much more impact on children than "what we say." If we want our children to be honest, we must be honest with them; if we want our children to be kind and polite, we must be kind and polite to them; if we want our children to be responsible and trustworthy, we must be responsible and trustworthy with them. While our actions with other people count, our actions with our kids count for everything.

2. *Explaining and describing behaviors we expect.* How easy it is to assume that someone, particularly a child, "knows" what our expectations are. Don't expect your child to read your mind. Again, I urge you to use the five-*W*'s model for making yourself clear—who, what, when, where, and why. For example, "Johnny, so that you can enjoy your weekday evenings and I don't have to worry [why], I would like you [who] to do your homework [what] at your desk in your room [where] before seven o'clock each night [when]."

3. *Focusing on what is important and positive, not on what is unimportant or trivial.* It is too easy to pay attention to what our kids are "not doing" or to trivia. Think about the *outcome* you desire in answering these questions: How important is it for your child to keep her room clean? Why? How important is it for your child to wear certain clothes? Why? How important is it for your teenage child to join you in family outings or trips? Why? How important is it that your child eat everything on his or her plate? Why? How important are these things in comparison to lying, cheating, taking drugs, stealing, running away, failing in school, or doing something dangerous to herself or others? These larger problems are the ones to be concerned about.

4. *Rewarding appropriate behaviors.* Behavioral psychologists have come a long way in helping us learn how to get our children to behave more often as we would like them to. They describe their method as using "positive reinforcement." I call it rewarding appropriate behavior. Dr. Spencer Johnson encourages us to "catch our child doing something right."[8] That means you praise, you encourage, you thank, you show your appreciation, you notice when something is done right.

Johnson tells us to give a "one-minute praising" and describes this as follows:

1. I tell my children beforehand that I am going to praise them when they do well.
2. I catch my children doing something right.
3. I tell my children specifically what they did.
4. I tell them how good I feel about what they did.
5. I stop and let a few seconds of silence pass to let them feel how good I feel.
6. Then I do what genuinely matches my feelings right then. I tell them I love them or give them a hug, or both.
7. I later encourage my children to do the same for me. To catch me doing something right and to give me a praising.[9]

If you want good behavior to occur, you must reward it.

5. *Attacking the actions, not the child.* Unless you are unusual, you don't want to get rid of the child (although you may feel like it sometimes), you want to get rid of the inappropriate behavior. So, focus on it immediately as it occurs. Talk about what it is and why it is inappropriate. Then, either suggest a better way of behaving or ask your child for her suggestion.

For example, let's say that at the dinner table your daughter put her glass of grape juice at the edge and has knocked it over. What do you do? Using our model, you might say the following:

Mary, I am really upset that you knocked over that glass of grape juice. Remember how we have talked about not putting your glass on the edge of the table? Let's quickly clean it up and then I want to talk with you about it.

Okay, thank you for helping me.

You see how the grape juice stains the carpet. It's really a mess. That's why it's so important for you to keep your glass in front of you in a place where you or someone else can't knock it over.

From now on it is really important that you remember to do that. If it happens again, then you won't be able to drink grape juice at this table for a while.

All right, let's get on with dinner.

6. Teaching your child about the consequences of inappropriate behavior. Everybody makes mistakes. Children tend to make more mistakes because of their inexperience and immaturity. You can use these mistakes, or inappropriate behaviors, as opportunities for punishment or as opportunities for learning by applying the concept of consequences.

You have two options—the consequences can be parental displeasure or parental suggestion about other, more appropriate behaviors. You can also create consequences for the child when you feel they are required.

For example, let's say your son has just jumped on his new bike and whizzed out of the driveway without checking for oncoming cars. How can you use the consequences principles to handle the situation? You might call him back immediately and say:

Jack, you just went screaming out of the driveway and never looked once to see if any cars were coming. I'm really upset. You could easily have been hit— really hurt or killed. [The five W's.]

You must never do that again. From now on, I want you to walk your bike down to the edge of the driveway, look both ways for traffic, and then if the street is clear, get on your bike and go. [The appropriate behaviors.]

This is the first time you have done this, so I'm just letting you know how dangerous it is. But if I see it happen again, I'm going to ask you to not ride your bike for a week. If it happens a third time, you won't be able to use your bike for six months or until I can feel certain about your bike-safety behavior. [The consequences.]

See how it works?

CHOOSING THE BEST CHILD CARE AVAILABLE

The final element in being a good parent is choosing good care for your children when you cannot be with them. As I indicated earlier, this is easier said than done. I described in detail in my previous book, *Making It Together as a Two-Career Couple,* what the current options are and how to choose one. Also, Rebecca Sager Ashery and Michele Margolin Basen cover this topic in their new book, *The Parents with Careers Workbook.*[10] Other resources are listed in the bibliography.

WHAT ELSE CAN YOU DO?

At the beginning of this chapter I discussed some of the difficulties we face in dealing with societal and organizational expectations about our roles as mothers. Conditions don't improve unless we do something to change them. I urge you to begin talking with school administrators and teachers about making changes. I urge you to speak with physicians, dentists, and other professionals about your needs, i.e., information you need, attitudes you expect, hours that make sense for your work schedule. Choose professionals who are not only competent but available and responsive to your needs as a working mother. If you encounter professionals who ignore or belittle your requests, go to other, more sensitive people for services, and let the others know by letter why you left.

Someday, circumstances will change so that it will be easier for women to be financially secure and be good mothers. Someday, fathers will be more involved in parenting. Someday, organizations will change and societal expectations will change too. Until that time, as responsible women, we can do our best to raise our children to be the most they can be.

9

Who Is Important, What Is Essential in Your Life?

DOES YOUR LIFE feel chaotic and out of control? Is there too much to do and never enough time to do it? If your answer to these questions is a resounding yes, know that you are not alone. Millions of women join you in these sentiments.

In my therapy practice, patient after patient asks: "Why can't I get control of things?" But before I can answer, they offer their own self-deprecating answers: "Something is obviously wrong with me. I've tried to get control so many times but it never seems to do any good," or, "Maybe I'm not working hard enough." A few will blame the men in their lives for not helping more. However, the majority find great fault with themselves.

But what are the real reasons that Superwomen feel their lives are out of control? There are four key factors:

- Great capacity for feelings of guilt
- Lack of assertiveness skills
- "Here and now" orientation
- Resistance to change

ARE YOU GUILTY?

Let's first take a look at guilt. Everyone feels it. Psychologists and psychiatrists love to write about it. The best definition of guilt that I have seen comes from the *Dictionary of Psychological Terms*. It says that guilt is "a realization that one has violated ethical or moral or religious principles, together with a regretful feeling of lessened personal worth on that account."[1] In other words, someone who feels guilty has a sense of having done something wrong or having been unfaithful to one's most ardent beliefs. Superwomen are masters at that.

As I said earlier, one of the most fundamental functions of women is to nurture others. For Superwomen this is a critical factor in their guilt. Because they have been socialized to put the needs of others first, *Superwomen feel guilty if they don't take care of everybody else's needs.* Superwomen attend to children, husbands, friends, parents, in-laws, employers, employees ... anyone who happens to enter their lives.

In *Understanding Women,* Luise Eichenbaum and Susie Orbach describe how a woman "must care for others and help them to express what they need, particularly at the emotional level. Once she has understood what others need, she must help them satisfy those needs. Part of her social role as caregiver and nurturer of others involves putting her own needs second."[2] Of course, the upshot of this is that not only do Superwomen feel guilty if they don't take care of the needs of others, *but they feel guilty if they take care of their own needs.*

A thirty-year-old community volunteer, Merrill, told me how far down on the totem pole she puts herself:

> When I get up in the morning I am so concerned about helping my children and my husband get dressed and fed that I don't even bathe myself properly. I rush into the shower; soap up and off before three minutes is up. The critical areas are hit, but believe me, I wouldn't pass a cleaning inspection. I brush my teeth in the

same way. I am embarrassed to tell you how infrequently I actually floss my teeth.

Like this volunteer, Superwomen are always at the beck and call of those around them. They never really know how their days will go because there are all those potentially needy people lurking around their homes and offices, or waiting to catch them on the phone. Superwomen ignore their own needs in favor of meeting the momentary needs even of mere acquaintances. They have no limits for what they will do for you, yet they do the minimum for themselves.

Why is it that you do the following?

_____ Stop an important writing project to talk to someone on the phone

_____ Agree to pick up your friend's child for a school play (after all, it will take only a few minutes more)

_____ Run errands for your boss during your lunch hour

_____ Attend a seminar with a friend because she wants company

_____ Agree to have houseguests during a particularly hectic time

_____ Accept a luncheon invitation, even if it's inconvenient

_____ Listen to a friend's laundry list of problems with her husband and kids when you'd rather be doing something else.

It's our great capacity for feelings of guilt that makes us do these things. When you put everyone else's needs before your own to avoid feeling guilty, you lose control of your sense of worth. And . . . *you lose control of your life*.

ARE YOU ASSERTIVE?

A second factor in feeling out of control is lack of assertiveness. What do I mean by *assertiveness*? The dictionary says that to assert oneself means to "compel recognition of one's rights." Many people confuse assertiveness with aggression, but aggression is "the practice of making attacks or encroachments; or hostile, injurious, or destructive behavior or outlook." Obviously, I am not endorsing this kind of behavior.

There are many assertiveness skills, including telling someone about something that bothers you, responding to a put-down, or receiving a compliment. But there are two skills that are of particular importance in gaining control over one's life. They are (1) *saying no to requests for your time or effort;* and (2) *asking for help.* Superwomen have great difficulty with both of these.

"I Can't Say No"

Because of their "other" orientation, Superwomen often feel that they *can't* say no even when they *want* to say no and feel that *it is appropriate* to do so.

In talking about this issue before a women's group, I asked the audience to give me their reasons for *not* saying no. I think you will find their answers very interesting.

_____ *"I'd feel guilty if I did."*

_____ *"I don't want to offend someone; I couldn't stand that."*

_____ *"I'm afraid the other person won't like me."*

_____ *"Actually, I'm afraid of someone getting angry at me. If there is one thing I can't stand, it's anger."*

_____ *"They expect me to say yes. I think it would shock the socks off someone I knew if I said no."*

_____ *"I'm afraid I'll lose their friendship (or love, if it's someone like my mother or my husband)."*

_____ *"Just thinking about it makes me feel anxious."*

_____ *"It's just really uncomfortable, that's all."*

_____ *"Actually, I really don't even think about it . . . I just do it automatically. It's kind of like a reflex."*

You see, what we're really talking about is your inability to set limits. If you can't say no, *you lose control of your life*.

"I Can't Ask for Help"

If Superwomen have difficulty saying no, then what they experience in trying to ask for help is close to paralysis. Part of this comes from a lifetime of being told not to bother other people. Part comes also from a long history of not wanting to feel the hurt of someone's rejecting a request. Unlike men, women tend to take very personally someone's saying no to them (which may tell you something more about why women themselves find it difficult to say no). Eichenbaum and Orbach say that "some women have to be absolutely desperate before they can ask for help and be helped."[3]

Jane, a graphics artist in her early thirties, talks about how difficult it is for her to ask friends for "anything."

> You know, before I went back to work, I think I had less difficulty asking my friends for something. I was a much better friend then. I was always doing something for them; or taking little things over to their houses. I'd do something for them; and they'd do something for me. Give and take. But now that I'm working I can't do as much for them . . . so I don't feel comfortable asking them anymore.

Jane's dilemma is one that is expressed by many Superwomen these days. Eichenbaum and Orbach help us to understand the situation by explaining that "only after a woman has given something to the other person does she feel justified in taking. If someone is kind, concerned, and receptive, the woman feels the urge to repay a hundredfold. Being given to purely because she is deserving is often confusing and moving for a woman because she does not conceive of herself in this way."[4]

So the Superwoman not only has some anxiety about asking

people for help, but the internal "catch-22" is that she probably feels she's going to have to repay that help in some multiple way. *And that is also losing control of your life.*

ARE YOU ON TWENTY-FOUR-HOUR CALL?

The third way in which Superwomen lose control is by having a "here and now" orientation to time, which means that they are focused mostly on the present. Superwomen have learned to react to the things and people around them. In a sense, they are always in a passive state of readiness to respond to whatever comes their way. They are physically and psychologically on call twenty-four hours a day.

You know you have a here-and-now orientation when

_____ you live day to day

_____ you confuse activity with results

_____ your time is cluttered with details and interruptions

_____ you substitute the momentary needs of others for your own needs

_____ you misconstrue the disorganization and chaos in your life as spontaneity and flexibility

_____ you don't have the satisfaction of reaching personal goals

_____ you get seduced by many possibilities

_____ you give equal time to important and unimportant details

_____ you don't know if you are progressing if you have no goals

_____ you find it hard to make decisions because you don't have a sense of your priorities

_____ you feel frazzled and overworked much of the time

_____ you lack purpose and direction in your life

_____ activities become ends rather than means to ends

_____ there are no limits to the amount of time you commit to "work"

_____ you try to do too much at one time, and you easily get overcommitted

Of course, the trouble with a here-and-now orientation is that *you lose control of your life*.

ARE YOU RESISTANT TO CHANGE?

Resistance to change is the final factor contributing to Superwomen's losing control. Actually, Superwomen have not captured the market in this area, because almost everyone has difficulty dealing with change.

Anne, a thirty-seven-year-old marketing specialist, describes how hard it is for her to deal with change:

> I really love my job. It's so exciting . . . especially after spending so many years at home. I know I'm being a little hard on myself, but I really am trying to keep our home pretty much the same as it was before I went to work. It may sound silly in this day and age, but things can never be neat enough. I love having elegant evening meals with all the trimmings . . . cloth napkins, candles. That's the right way, right? I really love having fresh flowers in the house. It makes me feel so good. Some of my friends at work tell me that I'm crazy for wanting things that way. I kind of resent that. I should be able to run my life the way I want it. Right? Anyway, even if I did want to change, I don't think my family would appreciate it very much. Who has time to figure out "what" to change, or how to do it. So what if I have to work a little harder. . . . Like my Dad used to say, "Hard work never hurt anyone."

We are creatures of habit. We tend to like whatever we've been doing in the past. Change—doing something new or different—is strongly resisted. Why? It's quite simple. It takes more effort to change than to do the same old thing in the same old way. It's easier.

Like Anne, we "love" certain ways of doing things even if

the situation has changed or it's no longer good for us. We resist change when we fear repercussions from the people around us. We resist change when it comes as a recommendation from someone else. And we resist change when we don't really know what it is we want to change or how to do it. An unwillingness to change also means that *you lose control of your life*.

GET CONTROL OF YOUR LIFE

So, how do you begin to get control of your life? First, you have to deal with the natural tendency to resist change. If you don't face the challenge of change in your life, everything will be more of a problem.

Psychologists have written so much on behavior and how to change it that I won't try to summarize the work in this area. From a practical standpoint, however, I have found that keeping in mind a few major points helps me to be more effective in making changes in my life. These points have been helpful to my patients as well, so I'd like to share them.

1. People often want things to change but are unwilling to *do* anything to effect the changes. So, the first thing you must know is that *change requires action on your part*, not just your thinking about it, or your hoping things will change, or your wanting others to make changes for you. It really is up to you.

2. Often I hear women say that they will begin to make changes when they "feel right about it." That's not the way it works. *Feelings change when you act differently*, not the other way around. So, the sooner you begin to make the changes you want, the sooner you will feel more comfortable with the new behavior. In fact, putting things off is what really doesn't "feel good." You probably have at least thirty-two ways of punishing yourself for not doing what you think you should.

3. In the past, when I was about to undertake some change in my life, I would throw myself into it, abruptly and totally. For example, if I began an early-morning exercise program, I would bend and stretch enthusiastically for forty-five minutes and really give it all I had. I can just hear you saying to yourself, "Yeah, and I know exactly what happened: She got so sore after a couple of days that she ended up quitting the whole thing." You're right. That's exactly what happened. But eventually I learned how to do it more effectively.

Whether it is starting an exercise program or beginning to pamper yourself in the evenings, *change is most likely to occur when it comes slowly, gradually, and systematically.*

Let's say you decide to begin reading books for pleasure two or three evenings a week. The first week you might establish that between nine and ten-thirty on Sundays you are going to cozy up in an overstuffed chair with a cup of tea and a good book. You also determine that during that time you will not answer any phone calls or be interrupted. The second week, you might increase the frequency to twice a week; and the third week, increase it to three times. Are you beginning to see how this works?

4. *Change is more likely to occur if it is specified in writing and organized into a schedule.* It may seem silly to write out a statement about how you're going to take more time for yourself. But do it anyway. It's important. You must know exactly what you are going to do. Without specifying the changes you want to effect, the whole thing will probably remain a vague idea that will be difficult to carry through.

For example, if you decide to spend that hour-and-a-half three times a week reading your favorite novelists, write that down on an index card. Then look at your calendar, determine a reasonable time, and block it out. If you have a family calendar posted someplace (if you don't have one now, you probably will by the time you finish reading this book), write it there too. Then write down where you're going to read and what supplies you will need (your books, your glasses, a cozy chair, good lighting, perhaps a thermos of tea or a glass of your favorite wine).

Also, determine how you are going to deal with possible infringements on this time. What will you do about the phone (take it off the hook, or put on an answering machine), or unexpected guests (don't answer the door, or put a note on it that says you're unavailable until a certain time)? If you have children, rearrange activities or child care for them. Or schedule your reading time when they are already occupied, being cared for, or asleep.

5. Sometimes our efforts to change are thwarted by the people around us. Not only do individuals resist change, but so do the systems they live in. *Changes that will affect the important people in your life should be discussed with them in advance.*

Consider the example of a woman telling her husband that she would like to go away with a friend for a weekend. What do you suppose his response would be? "You're going to do *what*?" That's right. To help him understand the situation, she might say something like this: "George, I'm really feeling overwhelmed these days. The project at work is getting to me. Ann has asked me to join her in the mountains next weekend and that sounds like just what the doctor ordered. Would you mind holding down the fort for a few days?" By discussing plans or ideas in advance, you can avert a lot of hurt feelings.

6. Each time you engage in a behavior change, *reward yourself*. Sometimes, the behavior itself is reward enough, as in taking time alone for yourself. In other cases, the rewards are more elusive. In those cases, it's very important that you reward your efforts to change. Let's say you're trying to say "no" more often to invitations that are of little significance to you. Each time you do that, say something like, "Congratulations, I did it!" or, "Good try!" or, "Boy, I really am changing!" Give yourself a pep talk; be your own best rooting section.

This may not feel comfortable at first. Many women feel that it's important to be modest about their achievements, even to themselves. Ignore those feelings of modesty; in this case, they are inappropriate. Please believe that it is very important for you to reward your own efforts. It will help to support the behavior changes you are making.

Another way of rewarding yourself is to get support from

the people close to you. Tell them what you're trying to do and why you're doing it, and ask them to encourage and reward your efforts. Ask them to join your rooting section. Tell them, please, *not* to put you down for failed efforts and/or lost opportunities. You want and need support, not retribution. And that goes for you, too. You must not punish, put down, or humiliate yourself.

7. Sometimes people resist change because they are afraid of the consequences. Often they experience a general feeling of anxiety when confronting the issue of change. The best way of dealing with this is *to face the fears head-on by writing out all the possible negative outcomes*. What is the worst thing that could happen to you? Most of the time, your fears become less intense if you articulate them, particularly if you write them out. So, write down all the things that bother you or frighten you about a particular change. At the same time, write out some of the possible *positive* outcomes. This will give you an opportunity to evaluate the pros and cons of a situation. And it will help you to face your fears.

8. Finally, once you have begun to implement a change, *evaluate it* to see if you are accomplishing what you set out to do. Ask yourself, "Is this change working out?" If your answer is yes, give yourself a cheer. If your answer is no, figure out what you need to do to make it work.

FOR EVERYONE'S SAKE—TAKE CARE OF YOURSELF

Now I must state directly and openly what I believe to be the most critical issue of this book:

It is in your family's best interests as well as your own that you take care of yourself and your own needs.

I was reluctant to express this fundamental belief at the beginning of the book for fear that readers would dismiss me as another remnant of the narcissistic "me" generation. Nothing could be further from the truth.

I hope by now you see that I am concerned not only about

you as a woman, but about those who are closest to you. I believe in good relationships; I believe in the family. But I also believe that the strength of a relationship or a family depends on the strength of all the people involved. And that depends on each person's having her or his needs met directly. This means that you, too, must have your needs met.

Let me be clear about one other thing: By urging you to take care of yourself, I am in no way implying that you should stop caring for others. Believe me, I see no surplus of nurturing and caring in this world. I ask only that you *include yourself on the list of people for whom you care so well*.

Psychologists Say It's Important for Your Health

The brilliant psychologist Abraham Maslow said that "a new conception of human sickness and of human health"[5] is now emerging. We are coming to understand that each of us has an inner nature that is good or neutral rather than bad. It is best to bring out this inner nature and to encourage it rather than to suppress it. If it is permitted to guide our lives, we grow healthy, fruitful, and happy. But if this essential core of the person is denied or suppressed, he or she gets sick, sometimes in obvious ways, sometimes in subtle ways, sometimes immediately, sometimes later.

This inner nature is not strong, overpowering, and unmistakable, as are the instincts of animals. Rather, it is weak, delicate, subtle, and easily overcome by habit, cultural pressure, and wrong attitudes toward it.

"Even though weak, it rarely disappears in the normal person—perhaps not even in the sick person. Even though denied, it persists underground, forever pressing for actualization."[6]

Maslow also laments the fact that for many people, using the word *self* "seems to put people off" as they inevitably associate it with "the powerful linguistic of selfishness."[7]

To summarize, Maslow is saying that all of us, women and

men alike, have basic needs. When these needs are met, we are healthy, fruitful, and happy. But when these needs are not met, sooner or later we get sick, physically or emotionally. Our unmet needs may be expressed as painful feelings of dependency, anger, guilt, competition, envy, neediness, disappointment, despair, and depression.

Psychologists Grace Baruch and Rosalind Barnett point out:

> . . . The woman who feels good about herself and her life, who has high self-esteem and is able to see that her own needs are met, as well as those of others, is more able to relate to others in a healthy way. The woman who feels that she is nothing unless she is constantly giving, who is in constant need of reassurance, or who falls into the martyr role—getting what she wants by stirring up guilt in those around her—creates misery for others as well as herself.[8]

I repeat, it is in your own and your family's best interests that you take care of yourself.

HOW TO GET CONTROL OF YOUR LIFE

If you want to start caring for yourself so that you can continue to care for others, you must make some changes. *Change*—there's that word again. Remember the points I made earlier about confronting change head-on. It really does feel better to change than to keep on doing things that make you unhappy. You can change if you go about it in a gradual and systematic way. Now I will detail some skills that can help you to change. It is likely that you already have some of these skills but have just not used them. In the simplest, least complicated way, let's see if you can

- establish who is important and what is essential in your life

- set some personal goals
- develop a plan of action
- organize your time and resources
- delegate responsibilities and tasks to others

(The first three skills are detailed in the next section. The latter two are discussed at length in chapter 10.)

Knowing who is important and what is essential in your life is the first step in gaining control. This must be worked out first in order for the rest of your life to make sense. You need to know who and what comes first so that your life is not controlled by chance or by others.

How do you know who and what are essential and important in your life? The answer is quite simple. You know it when you state it. Most people don't take the time to do this.

I suggest that you write out your answers, and I have good reasons for asking you to do this. First, your ideas will become clearer. Very often, "who and what are important" remain in your head as vague notions, easily lost in the hustle and bustle of a busy life. Second, when you write down your thoughts, you have a permanent record that can be referred to over and over. Finally, the very act of writing down your ideas reinforces your commitment to them, and that often feels good. Some people are concerned that when they list ideas on paper, they will have to stick to them no matter what—they become etched in stone. Of course, that doesn't have to be the case. These ideas, like others, can and should be reevaluated and updated from time to time to reflect the changes that occur in your life.

Who Is Important?

Who is important to you? Spouses, children, and parents will be at the top of many lists.

Others about whom you care might include a "special" person of the opposite sex; a grandparent; a sister or brother; an aunt or uncle; a friend; a stepparent or stepchild; a long-term employer or employee; an in-law; your mentor or teacher; your therapist or counselor; a minister, priest, or rabbi.

On an index card, list the special and important people in your life. Please don't be tempted to skip this part or to do it later. This is some of the most important work you will be doing in this book—you need to have these thoughts as guides for later decisions and actions.

I hope you didn't forget to list yourself. Given our previous discussion, do you think I would allow you not to put *your* name on this list?

What Is Essential?

Now let's discuss a more difficult question: *What is essential in your life?* Until a few years ago, people in our culture assumed that the "who" in a woman's life were so important that virtually nothing else counted. This message was so well internalized that many women today still have difficulty in saying "what" is important to them.

The "what" question is difficult to answer for another reason—it's so broad. Where do you begin? Here are some general categories to consider: health; relationships; work; personal growth; home; lifestyle; financial and material needs. In addition, I will give examples of how other women have answered the question of *what* was essential in their lives. This by no means implies that their "whats" should be yours. They are here only for illustration. As you will see by the examples, it is all right for you to be general in your answers. We will get down to specifics when we get to the goal-setting section.

1. Health. It is easy to take one's health for granted, especially when you're in your twenties, thirties, and forties. However, if you are ill, even temporarily, all of the other parts of your life are shot. And as much as we might want to deny it, how well you take care of yourself during your twenties, thirties, and forties will affect how healthy you are in your fifties, sixties, and seventies.

EXAMPLES OF HEALTH STATEMENTS

A. *"I want to live the longest, healthiest life I can have."*

B. *"I want to have control over my alcohol consumption for the rest of my life."*

C. *"I want to lose fifty pounds without losing my health in the process."*

2. *Relationships.* We all know that throughout the ages women have been relationship oriented. But, as we have seen, women have given much more than they have received. In this category, please consider your needs as well. Who is going to give back to you some of what you give?

EXAMPLES OF RELATIONSHIP STATEMENTS

A. *"I want to have a good marriage with a partner who loves, respects, and encourages me."*

B. *"I want my children to grow up to be loving, confident, independent, competent people."*

C. *"I want to have close relationships with my parents."*

3. *Work.* Let me be clear about one thing. Whether or not you have a paid job, you work. However, for purposes of this exercise, let us focus on paid and/or volunteer work, leaving consideration of the household to another area.

EXAMPLES OF WORK STATEMENTS

A. *"I want work to be an integral part of my life."*

B. *"I want to be very competent in my work."*

C. *"I want to help improve my community through my work."*

4. Personal growth. Do you have a vision of yourself? What do you need in order to feel really good about yourself? What, for example, is important and essential for you about your body, your mind, your psyche, or your soul?

EXAMPLES OF PERSONAL-GROWTH STATEMENTS

A. *"I want to be comfortable with and proud of my physical body."*

B. *"I want to be respected for my mind."*

C. *"I want to be a direct, open, self-confident, focused person."*

D. *"I want to be able to speak French fluently."*

5. Home. Traditional socialization had women identify with their homes. If their homes looked good, they felt good. This may not be as true for the modernday woman, but it is still true that one's home can be an essential part of one's life.

EXAMPLES OF HOME STATEMENTS

A. *"I want my home to reflect my taste in design, color, art, and music."*

B. *"I want my home to be a place for gathering people together, talking, laughing, and having a good time."*

C. *"I want my home to be a comfortable place for my children and their friends."*

6. Lifestyle. A lifestyle is the way and the manner in which you spend your time and money. It includes all that you do— for yourself, with others, in your home, at work, and as leisure activities. It involves a particular way of doing things—relaxed, hectic, involving, or reclusive. It can also be expensive or austere.

EXAMPLES OF LIFESTYLE STATEMENTS

A. *"I want a balance of time between the people I love and my work."*

B. *"I want to have some time alone to think, plan, and relax."*

C. *"I want to have friends who lead exciting lives and do unusual, worthwhile things with their time."*

7. Financial and material needs. Many women feel uncomfortable about managing finances or handling money. While it may come as a surprise to men, many women also feel terribly uncomfortable spending money on themselves. They can easily spend money on others, but to do so for themselves brings on oceans of guilt. What is essential for you in this area?

EXAMPLES OF FINANCIAL STATEMENTS

A. *"I want to be financially successful in my work."*

B. *"I want to be financially competent—to understand and operate effectively in the financial world."*

C. *"I want to buy things for myself without feeling guilty."*

Now It's Your Turn

At this point, take an index card and title it WHAT IS ESSENTIAL TO ME. Now try to write something for each of the seven categories. Then check yourself in each of the categories to make sure that you can answer yes to the question: "Is this really essential to me?" Make sure that you answer for you, not for your husband, your children, your mother, or whomever. You might also want to check back to the "Who Is Important" section to see if there are any inconsistencies between the "who" answers and the "what" answers. Finally, check to see if there are any incompatibilities. For example, let's say that the attainment of your work goal involves working long hours and weekends and traveling extensively. Does that conflict with any of your other personal or relationship goals? You want to work out now the aspects of any goal that might undermine or deter the others. Of course, this does not mean that you cannot be working on more than one goal at a time. On the contrary, you will probably be doing just that. But if you see any serious inconsistencies, you may have to rethink, rewrite, or alter one or more of your goals at this point. But that's all right. That, too, is part of this process.

Now look at all your answers. Doesn't it feel good to know what's essential? Some women with whom I have worked have told me that they gained a real sense of power from completing this exercise. As one woman said, "I can't tell you how great it feels to know me. It all seems to make sense now. I wish I had done this years ago. I'm going to show this exercise to my husband and see if he will do it, too. It will be really interesting to see what he comes up with."

You will want to keep your lists of who is important and what is essential in a place easily accessible, such as on the first page of your work calendar or on a visible place at your desk (or both). You'll probably want to refer to these lists often, such as when you're making decisions or scheduling your time.

Let us now move on to the next phase of your gaining control of your life: goal setting.

WHAT ARE YOUR GOALS?

According to Webster's dictionary, a goal is "the end toward which effort is directed."[9] Goals, like destinations, give us information, help us to plan, and let us know whether we've accomplished anything. Without goals (or destinations), we tend to wander aimlessly and get lost.

Goal setting tends to be a problem for women. It's easy to understand why, when you consider that (1) women traditionally have been brought up to be reactive, but goal setting is an active process; (2) women have been brought up to be here-and-now oriented, but goal setting is future oriented; and (3) women have been taught not to be selfish, but goal setting requires one to be focused on the self. No wonder we have been such basket cases in this area! That's the bad news. The good news is that goal setting is a skill that can be learned quickly and easily. Start with your list titled WHAT IS ESSENTIAL TO ME. Rewrite this list in terms that allow you to develop a plan for action. The procedure I am suggesting goes like this:

Goal-Setting Steps

1. Take your list of "whats" and select the statement that you want to concentrate on first.

2. Write this statement at the top of an index card.

3. Then rewrite this statement as a lifetime goal. Include the elements of *who, what, when, where,* and *how much.*

4. Under the lifetime goal, write a three-year or four-year goal that is as specific as you can make it.

5. Then write one-year and three-month goals that will carry you to the three-year (or four-year) goal.

6. Finally, write an action plan using your three-month goal.

Repeat these six steps for each of your "whats." To clarify, let's look at an example.

Myra, a clinical social worker, has determined that she wants to be competent and financially successful in her work. Therefore, she wants to be a fully licensed clinical psychologist. In order to do this, she must go back to school in two phases.

First, she must return to school to take some prerequisite courses. Second, she must take the Graduate Record Examination and then get accepted into a doctoral program in psychology. It is now spring; Myra has learned that if she takes certain courses during the coming summer-school session and the upcoming fall and winter quarters, she will be eligible to apply to the graduate program in psychology a year from this coming fall. If all goes well, she should be able to complete the doctoral program four years from now.

This information is crucial to Myra's being able to set goals using the six-step procedure. You may find, as Myra did, that you must gather some information before you can list your goals. That's fine. Don't hesitate to do that. But please don't let this be an impediment to your continued work in this area. Now let's look at how Myra used the six-step procedure.

In Step 1, Myra selected the statement she wanted to concentrate on first.

What's Essential and Important in My Life: *I want to be very competent in my work* (category: work). *I want to be financially successful in my work* (category: financial and material). Myra decided to combine two of her statements here.

In step 2, Myra wrote these statements at the top of an index card.

In step 3, she rewrote the statements as a lifetime goal, including the elements of who, what, when, where, and how much.

Lifetime Goal: *At the end of my career, I want to be a highly respected, licensed clinical psychologist who earns the equivalent of today's $85,000 a year. I want to see about twenty-five clients a week and consult with hospitals and schools concerning my specialization in learning problems.*

In step 4, Myra wrote a four-year goal.

Four-Year Goal: To have completed a Ph.D. program at the California School of Professional Psychology, and to have met the requirements for licensure.

In step 5, Myra wrote one-year and three-month goals. She added a six-month goal because it was obvious that she needed it. You can adjust the time frame according to the kind of goal you've set.

One-Year Goal: To have completed the course prerequisites for the clinical-psychology program, taken the Graduate Record Examination, and made application to the doctoral program.

Six-Month Goal: To be accepted at San Diego State University as an unclassified student in order to take the prerequisite courses in psychology.

Three-Month Goal: To enroll in the summer session at San Diego State University in order to take prerequisite courses in psychology.

You can see that the important thing about goals is that they must be specific. That is what I mean when I say you should include the elements of who, what, where, when, and how much. As Michael LeBoeuf says: "If you find that you cannot quantify it, measure it, rate it, or describe it, you probably can forget it as a goal."[10]

Developing an Action Plan

Once you have set down a series of short-term goals to work toward, the next task is to spell out exactly what you will need to do in order to reach these goals. This is step 6, writing your action plan. Let's see what Myra did in this area.

First, she listed the things she had to do before she could enroll in the upcoming summer school. Her list included the following:

1. *Call college for summer school registration materials.*
2. *Get information from "Y" on their summer camps* (for her children, ages eight and twelve). *Enroll children in camp.*
3. *Create a study space and create study time on calendar.*
4. *Talk with John* (her husband) *and children about my plans.*
5. *Get the car serviced and new tires put on before the session begins.*
6. *Buy books and supplies.*
7. *Plan and arrange summer vacation.*
8. *Call local girls in neighborhood to see about their availability for summer baby-sitting.*

Then she took the list of activities and organized it according to (1) what must be done; (2) who will do it; and (3) when it must be completed. This is an absolutely critical part. Myra took on this last task with great vigor. This is how she arranged for her activities before summer school.

Things to be done	Who	When
1. Call college for registration materials	Me	This week
2. Get information from "Y" about summer camp	Me	This week, by phone
3. Enroll children in camp	Me	As soon as materials are sent
4. Enroll in summer session	Me	By mail, if possible; if not, find out how, when

5. Create study space; create study schedule	Me	Create space two weekends from now; talk with family about study schedule as soon as class schedule is known
6. Talk with John and children about plans to go back to school	All of us	At next family meeting
7. Get car serviced	John	Week before school starts
8. Buy books and supplies	Me	First day of school
9. Plan and arrange summer vacation	Ask John to do this	Now
10. Call baby-sitters about summer availability	Me	End of May

When you have written your action plan, the only thing that remains to be done is to mark on your calendar those activities that must be accomplished on the dates that you have assigned them. And that is what getting control of your life is all about.

10

Better Manage Your Time—It's All You Have

You know, it just isn't fair. There aren't enough hours in the week to do everything I have to do.

A MAJOR COMPLAINT I hear from Superwomen is that they don't have enough time. We all have 24 hours a day, 168 hours a week, in which to do everything we must do and want to do. People use or manage their time in greatly different ways. Some devote 2 hours per day to physical fitness, or to playing with the children, or to a second job, or to socializing, or to reading. If you are a Superwoman, you are probably squeezing all those activities into the same 2-hour period—and wondering why you can't get it all done. That is what we will discuss in this chapter. I want to help you take the information we have just generated—who is important and what is essential in your life—and show you how to make it work. What I hope to do is teach you how to take control.

As you are undoubtedly aware, there are plenty of books about time management. Some of the better ones are listed in the bibliography. Obviously, I can't cover in one chapter what others say in ten or twelve; so I have pulled together the ideas and techniques I think make the most difference in managing time. This is an area where the 80/20 rule applies. I'm referring to the Pareto Principle, which states that 80 percent of the value of something is generally contained in only 20 percent of it.[1] If we apply the Pareto Principle to time-management concepts, we would have to say that 80 percent of what is valuable and useful is contained in 20 percent of the information. I've pulled together that 20 percent of valuable information on time management.

Think about all the proverbs you have heard about time:

"Time is money." "Lost time is never found again."
Franklin
"Wait for that wisest of all counselors, Time."
Plutarch
"Time is the most valuable thing a man can spend."
Diogenes Laërtius

One would think that with time being such a scarce and important commodity, people would employ all kinds of techniques to manage it. The truth is, it's a rare person who successfully manages time; most of us don't even try. We "spend" our time in ways that end up wasting it. Most of us are a lot more cautious about spending money than about spending time.

WHY PEOPLE DON'T USE TIME-MANAGEMENT TECHNIQUES

People don't use time-management techniques because they don't think they have the time to do it, or because they are waiting for the "right time" to do it. Doesn't that sound familiar? Many of us believe that "someday" we're going to make our lives less chaotic. That "someday" often takes the form of—when the next project gets done, when the kids go to school, when the weight is lost, when the holiday season is over, when it stops snowing, when hell freezes over. The list of "whens" is endless. The time to do it is now. There will never be a "right" time; you will always have one more project or ten more pounds to lose or just one more thing to do first. The "right" time is now.

Another reason people don't use time-management techniques is that they don't like the idea of being controlled. Plainly said, people *hate* to be controlled even when *they* are doing the controlling. Whenever I talk with patients about managing their time, they become visibly resistant and sometimes even hostile. They tell me how they don't want to become compulsive clock watchers or list makers. The thought of managing time makes most of them very uncomfortable. Control connotes binds, hindrances, "have to's." The kind of control I'm discussing, however, is neither compulsive nor obsessive. Effective time-management techniques put you in charge of all aspects of your life. They give freedom and control. The techniques themselves are only as dictatorial as you allow them to be.

Occasionally I run across someone who is not willing to do some work now in order to reap the rewards in the future. He or she wants things to get better without taking responsibility for the actions required. This is the person who reads the "How to Have Everything You Want in Five Days or Less" books. Things will get better only if you put in the effort to make them get better. This is one area where you don't have to wait months or years for the fruits of your efforts to be obvious. In the area of time management, it takes very little to bring about immediate, positive changes. Let me show you how easily it can be done.

First, I will summarize some of the most useful time-management points made by one of the leading authorities on time management, Michael LeBoeuf. Second, I will teach you how to structure your time more effectively, especially for those important people and things in your life. Finally, I will offer techniques for dealing with everyday demands in your life, such as social invitations and telephone interruptions.

A SUMMARY OF TIME-MANAGEMENT POINTS

Before anything else, remember that there are only 24 hours in a day (actually, only 16–19 hours of actual waking time, depending on how much you sleep). In a week's time those figures add up to 168 hours total time; 112 waking hours if you sleep 8 hours a night; 133 waking hours if you sleep 5 hours a night. *Please* do not see this as a subtle challenge to get you to sleep less so that you can be awake more hours!

Michael LeBoeuf is the author of my favorite time-management book, *Working Smart.*[2] He makes the following important points.

1. Most of us work harder than we have to to reap the benefits life has to offer.
2. Time is irreplaceable. We are all given a finite amount of time, but the irony is that we never know how much we have until it's gone.
3. We hear a lot about hard work and success, but hard work and failure probably occur just as often.
4. A good rule of thumb is that there are always at least two good ways to do anything.
5. Whenever you need to concentrate, make it a habit to think with a pencil in your hand. As ideas come to you, jot them down. (Another version of this method is to keep a small tape recorder next to you in your car.)
6. Many of us spend our lives fighting fires under the tyranny of urgency. The result is that we ignore the less urgent but more important things in life. It's a great effectiveness killer.
7. Your success at working smart depends on knowing what not to do.
8. Everyone talks of hard work and the pressures of living in our society, but the fact is that when we are

talking about pressure we are talking about what we do to ourselves. It's much like Pogo once said: "We has met the enemy and they is us."

9. Before you rise in the morning, resolve to do two things with each day: Enjoy today, and do something that will make for a better tomorrow. Every day is a treasure.

10. There simply isn't enough time in one lifetime to do everything.

HOW OPTIMAL PERFORMERS USE THEIR TIME

Charles Garfield, a clinical psychologist in the San Francisco area, has spent the past fifteen to twenty years studying what he calls "optimal performers." These are people who achieve literally at the top of their form. He has studied people in such diverse occupational groups as education, sports, health, business, industry, and the arts. Garfield has studied top-performing people as divergent as Winston Churchill, Nadia Comaneci, Saul Bellow, and Eleanor Roosevelt. Garfield has determined that optimal performers share some characteristics, some of which have to do with the use of time. Among his findings are the following:

1. Unlike "workaholics," who are motivated primarily by fear of failure, optimal performers derive their motivation from commitment to "a very personal set of goals."

2. Optimal performers understand the need for systematic relaxation and consider vacations the source of much creative thinking.

3. Optimal performers are extraordinary delegators, dividing their tasks into three categories: those tasks that they reserve for themselves; those tasks that can be handled by others; and those tasks that are interesting possibilities but take too much time. Optimal performers tend not to be seduced by possibilities.

4. Optimal performers set high standards for their work but are free from trying to be perfect.

Finally, Garfield says that optimal performers "work smart": that is, they use their time efficiently and focus their efforts where they will produce maximum results.[3]

All the points covered thus far are important background information for you. They offer a kind of philosophy of time management that underlies the techniques and procedures I will now describe. Remember, it is just as important to know why you are doing something as to know how to do it.

HOW TO STRUCTURE YOUR TIME

The first thing you need is a week-at-a-glance calendar. Choose one that pleases you aesthetically, but make sure it will fit into whatever purses or briefcases you carry. Then carry it with you *at all times*. It will be your major reference point in keeping control of your life.

Next, I'd like you to take a look at the Weekly Schedule Worksheet on page 168. You can use this sheet, copy it in longhand, or photocopy it.

You will need a pencil and the index cards or the sheets that list your Important People and Essential Things. Now, get settled in a comfortable place. This exercise should take fifteen to thirty minutes.

Your Weekly Schedule

1. So that you know the time parameters of your workweek, *record on the Weekly Schedule Worksheet the time you get up and the time you usually go to bed*. Do this first for your usual workweek. Then mark the weekend times. Obviously, the

weekend times will be more flexible than the workweek times.
But put down what is usual.

2. *Now indicate the hours you spend at your workplace* (or
volunteer job or college).

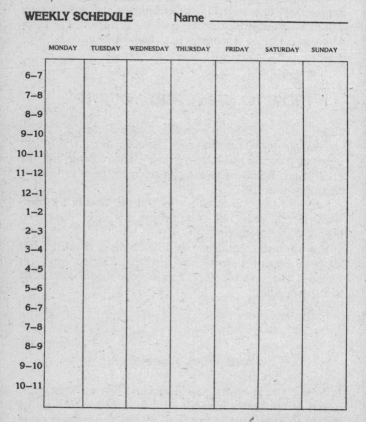

WEEKLY SCHEDULE   Name _____

	MONDAY	TUESDAY	WEDNESDAY	THURSDAY	FRIDAY	SATURDAY	SUNDAY
6–7							
7–8							
8–9							
9–10							
10–11							
11–12							
12–1							
1–2							
2–3							
3–4							
4–5							
5–6							
6–7							
7–8							
8–9							
9–10							
10–11							

Shaevitz & Associates
1981

3. Look at the list of people who are special in your life. *Schedule on your sheet two to three hours for each important person.* I am suggesting a few hours as an arbitrary starting place. As you progress through this exercise, you may find that you want to spend more (probably not less) time. (Myra has five people on her Important People list: herself; her husband; her son, Larry; her daughter, Allison; and her mother, Elaine.) Remember: You are an Important Person in your life— you also deserve time.

Planning Time

4. *Designate at least a half-hour of over-all planning time for yourself once a week.* Take into consideration all personal and work activities. Record all regular items such as we are doing now. Establish what you want to accomplish in meeting short-term and long-term goals. Ask your family if they have any appointments or activities of which you should be aware.

While you're scheduling activities, keep in mind two questions: *Why am I doing this particular activity?* and *Is this activity necessary or important?* Most of the women I have worked with found that Sunday or Monday evenings are the best times for them to do this kind of planning.

5. *Establish a ten-minute daily planning time for yourself at your workplace.* Some women like to do this at the very beginning of the day; others prefer to do it at the end of the day, anticipating tomorrow's needs. This planning time should take place quietly with no interruptions. I can just hear you saying something like, "Good luck—that will never happen." Don't worry, we'll deal with that in the next section.

Developing a Daily To-do List

This is a good time to develop a daily To-do List. Actually, you can call it your plans, action sheet, or whatever you choose. You don't have to be a natural list maker in order to do it; just get a sheet of paper that fits into your calendar/address book.

I should warn you that some people resist making To-do Lists for the same reason they resist structuring their time: They think it will control and restrain them. But I can tell you that most people find that it unclutters their minds of a lot of little details. We all have more important things to remember than to pick up toilet paper on the way home from work, right?

The To-do List can include activities that relate to your goals; errands; telephone calls to make; toilet paper to pick up; projects you want to work on. My list looks like this:

WORK	PERSONAL
1. Write thank you notes to interviewers	1. Get birthday gift for Jeff
2. Return typewriter (ask secretary) for repair	2. Pick up picture frame
3. Begin report	3. Buy light globes for patio
4. Rewrite resumé	4. Drop off dry cleaning

Write down what you would like to accomplish today. Then indicate just how important each activity is in relation to the others. You can make whatever designations you prefer for this—underline the items, star them, or put check marks beside them. When you have completed your priority items, give yourself a little cheer. Instead of berating yourself for all you didn't do, try applauding yourself for what you did accomplish. Don't worry if you don't complete all the items on your To-do List. Simply transfer whatever you don't do today onto tomorrow's list. If you find a few items getting transferred regularly, day after day, take a look at them. Perhaps they don't really need to be done. But if they do, put them on your priority list for today, and for goodness' sake, *do* them now.

Making a To-do List is another way of ensuring that you are involved with what you want, not with what comes your way by fiat. Just one last suggestion: Before you begin, *figure out if it really must be done*. Later in this chapter I will give you a formula for getting other people to do things for you. It involves asking yourself a series of questions and then seeing if you can ask someone to do the task, pay someone to do it, or delegate it to someone. Give this method a chance—what you've been doing probably hasn't worked, so why not try something different? It can work.

Putting Limits on Chores and Errands

6. In any woman's life there are all kinds of housekeeping chores, shopping, and errands that eat up a great deal of time. Current research indicates that women who work outside the home put in, on the average, thirty-five hours a week on housekeeping; full-time homemakers work fifty hours a week on these same activities.[4] In chapter 11 we will discuss how to get other people to do a fair share of the housekeeping chores and errands. However, realistically, there will still be a certain number of chores and errands you will need or want to do. What I suggest is that you *designate a certain amount of time for these activities and then* **do no more.** Schedule certain times on your worksheet and leave it at that. How much time is involved in any given household depends on a number of factors: how large a house you have; how easy it is to care for; what your standards of upkeep are; how effective you are in delegating or buying tasks and services; whether you have children and how old they are. For now, limit what you do in the household! Does that sound impossible? I think you will be surprised at the results. There are too many important people in your life and things for you to do to be wasting your time on chores and errands.

7. In any person's life, man or woman, there are personal services that are required in order to feel and look good. I am talking about such services as medical, dental, hair, and other kinds of care. These are easiest to handle if you can lump your appointments together at routine, specified times on a particular day. *Each week give yourself a two- or three-hour block of time for professional personal care.* Actually, you probably won't use it every week, but it will be reassuring to have it prearranged. I try to schedule all personal-service appointments between three o'clock and six o'clock on Fridays. I don't always have appointments on Fridays, but it is easier to arrange things knowing that there is time set aside. This is also time that could be used for other family members if they need you.

Taking Time to Relax

8. Most women are ridiculously lax about taking time for fun and relaxation. They seem to be waiting for the magical day when the earth stops, the heavens open up, and they have time to play. Fun and relaxation are essential for good physical and mental health. You can have fun alone or with family or friends. *Right now, schedule it—at least a couple of hours a week.* If you have doubts about the importance of this time, consider what Garfield says about optimal performers: They have passionate interests outside of work and they understand the need for systematic relaxation.[5]

9. One other area that you need to account for is commuting time. For some of you this will be significant. Regardless of the amount of time, *block out commuting time* so that you can see it in relation to the other parts of your life.

How About Some Open Time?

10. Every woman needs to feel that her life has some spontaneity to it. Therefore, *the last designation is for open time.* This is time to do whatever seems right at the moment. It can be time to spend catching up or it can be time to do nothing. It needs to be unplanned, unhurried, and open to spontaneous events.

Now, look over the blocks of time you have scheduled. Are they reasonable? *Do they reflect how you want to spend your time?* How does the time for important people and things compare with the less essential parts of your life? Have you committed yourself to some activities that have little importance to you? If so, take them out. What can you eliminate from your schedule? Have you scheduled too much time in one area and not enough in another? Use your eraser: Change things. Move things around until you achieve a balance that makes sense. Sure, things will change. Sure, it might be a little difficult to follow this schedule. Of course, there are exceptions and emergencies and things over which you have no control. This schedule does not control you; rather, you author, you adjust, you control the schedule. You have nothing to lose by trying. What you stand to lose by not gaining control is *time*.

Remember, this is a technique that makes possible more time for the people and things you hold dear or important. It will help to keep you focused and not to be seduced by possibilities. It will help you in being selective and in making a statement about the value of your time.

To make this scheduling work, you now must transfer the blocks of time you have organized onto your weekly calendar. Check the illustration on pages 176–177 to see what Myra did for this. What you put on your calendar and how really is up to you.

TECHNIQUES FOR DEALING WITH EVERYDAY DEMANDS

Before we launch into some techniques to deal better with time, I urge you to read and reread these five statements often:

- I *can* get control of my time.
- My time *is* valuable. It is as valuable as my husband's, my boss's, my doctor's, or my friends'.
- I *am not* on call to everyone to do everything—people will respect me because I respect my time.
- I *don't* have to be perfect at everything—in fact, it is neither effective nor possible for me to try.
- I *don't* have to say yes to all requests for my time.

The time-management hints I will now offer apply as well at the office as in your home. After all, that is what this book is about—getting a balance between the two. *Please* pick and choose from the ideas offered. I do not mean for you to implement each and every one. Different people find that different techniques are useful for them. Change is best handled incrementally; if you find all the ideas useful, begin using them a few at a time. They are more likely to be effective for you that way. You don't have to do everything at once.

Dealing with Time Robbers

Time-management experts, such as Alec MacKenzie, have conducted research about the activities that actually waste or rob us of time. As MacKenzie says in his book *About Time!*, a time robber is "anything preventing you from achieving your objectives most effectively."[6] Time robbers can be both internal and external. Internal ones are self-generated. External time robbers occur as a result of other people or things imposed on you. However, whether they actually impose or how much they impose depends very much on the way you respond to them.

I. TIME ROBBER: Lack of goals and planning
   SOURCE: Internal
   FEELING: *"I just don't know where I'm going."*
   DESCRIPTION: When you are unclear about your goals, it is virtually impossible to know if what you are doing is a waste of time. You set yourself up to be more vulnerable to a wide range of other time wasters. If you don't know what your goal is, even for a day, you can easily become interrupted, overwhelmed, overcommitted, and disorganized.

SOLUTION

Go through chapter 9 to determine your priorities and goals.

II. TIME ROBBER: Interruptions
   SOURCE: External
   FEELING: *"If I get one more phone call I'm going to scream!"*
   DESCRIPTION: Superwomen describe interruptions as their most serious time robber. This is certainly true for me. Interruptions come in the form of telephone calls, drop-in visitors, and other people, particularly children, asking for or demanding immediate attention. Many of us take for granted that we are going to be interrupted many times a day. At times we don't mind this. But there are other times—such as when we are seriously working, thinking through a problem, in an important conference, planning the day's events, sitting down for some quiet reading time, putting together the last ingredients for a special dessert, or having some quiet snuggle time with the youngest child—when it is *so* annoying!

Most interrupters are unaware that they are interrupting you. They call or come because of their needs. Some interrupters just want to talk to you. Others want you to solve a problem, do something for them, buy something, invite you, or schedule an event. Some just happen to catch you because you are conveniently located (like in a busy hallway). Circumstances,

WEEKLY SCHEDULE Name _____

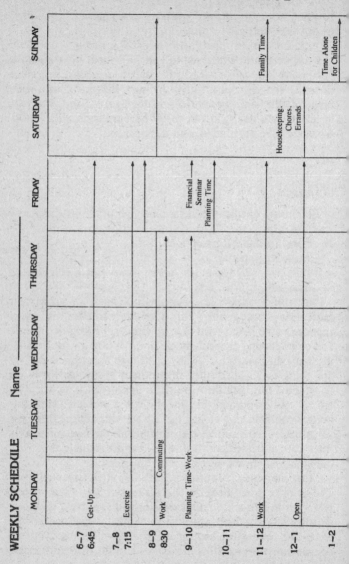

	MONDAY	TUESDAY	WEDNESDAY	THURSDAY	FRIDAY	SATURDAY	SUNDAY
6–7 6:45	Get-Up						
7–8 7:15	Exercise						
8–9 8:30	Work — Commuting						
9–10	Planning Time–Work			Financial Seminar Planning Time			
10–11							
11–12	Work					Housekeeping, Chores, Errands	Family Time
12–1	Open						
1–2							Time Alone for Children

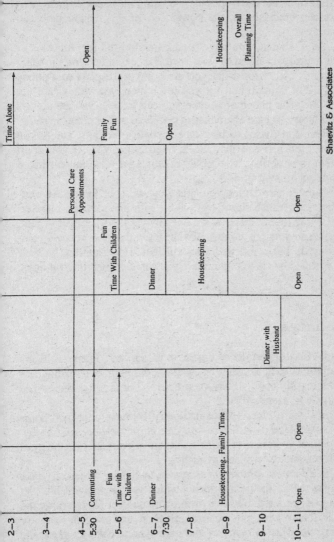

Shaevitz & Associates
1981

too, can create interruptions. Dictating machines or dishwashers can break down; the power can go off; a light bulb can burn out.

As a woman, you have been trained to put the demands of an interrupter ahead of your own. For example, you probably automatically drop what you are doing to respond to a phone call. If it is important for you to be nice, you won't dare not answer your phone or ask them to call later. If you are always available, you are encouraging people to call or come anytime. If you don't want to hurt other people's feelings, surely you won't tell a friend that she is interrupting you. If you don't want to be selfish, you probably won't set aside uninterrupted time to finish a project.

But let me assure you that you will not become a self-centered, selfish shrew by dealing with interruptions more effectively (not unless you are one anyway)! As a matter of fact, the more you gain control of your time, the more relaxed, self-assured, and competent you will feel. How can that be bad? Let's discuss some of the ways you can deal with interruptions.

SOLUTIONS

1. *Create periods of uninterrupted time.* There are many activities, such as planning, writing, thinking, and reading, for which you need uninterrupted time. Allot time for them. You can do it. Here's how.

A. *Find a place* (office or library, room in your own home or someplace else) *where you can close the door and be left alone*. If you are in an open-office situation, then find the most remote and quiet place available.

B. *Eliminate phone interruptions* by having a secretary take messages for the period during which you are unavailable. Set aside a specified time two or three hours later for returning the calls that require your personal attention, and ask your secretary to respond to as many of the other phone calls as he or she can, giving you a written or oral summary when you come out for air. If you do not have a secretary, or if you are at home, you can avoid taking calls by using an answering machine; acquiring the services of an answering service; not answering the phone (although that can drive you crazy); taking the phone off the hook (that will drive the phone company and potential callers crazy); unplugging the phone; asking a colleague or family member to answer the phone; pooling the resources of employees around you.

C. *Declare to everyone around you that you are not to be interrupted.* Actually, it's a good idea to explain how long you will be taking and even something about what you are doing. People need to be informed. If they are not, their resentment or your guilt could result. In my office, I tell everyone that I am going into "Pope Status" when I don't want to be interrupted. They know that, with the exception of emergency calls from my children, I will accept calls only from the Pope. This means I accept calls from no one, including my husband, mother, or close friends.

Sometimes this causes a problem because a number of my friends think they should be exceptions to this rule. But if I made exceptions, I wouldn't have uninterrupted time. A few were miffed at me for a while, but they got used to it, and now there aren't any problems. In fact, some of them are trying the method themselves!

D. *Eliminate drop-in interruptions* by having a secretary, colleagues, or family members tell people that you are unavailable until a specified time. Another way of handling phone or people interruptions is to arrange uninterrupted time when no one else is around or likely to call you—for instance, in the early morning or late at night or on the weekends. By suggesting this, I am not implying that you should necessarily be working overtime. I mention this alternative for those who are unable to arrange the other circumstances I have described.

E. *Use assertive language.* It is so difficult for many women to say things that might offend others that they often end up not saying anything at all, even when it is appropriate to do so. Here are some things you might say to people who interrupt you:

"*I really am very busy now; can we set a time to talk later?*"

"*I am working on _____ now; could I call you Wednesday?*"

"*I can't see you now; would you check with my secretary to set up a mutually convenient time?*"

"*I'd love to hear more; how about getting together for breakfast Saturday morning?*"

F. *Arrange care or activities for children if your uninterrupted time is spent at home.* First, let me say that children are much less likely to interrupt you if their needs are being met. Before establishing time for yourself at home, think about how to arrange for the kids while you're occupied. It's a good idea to give them some uninterrupted time before you have your own. Also, explain to them how long you need and what you're going to be doing. Kids need to know these things too. Here are some ways of getting care or activities for the children:

• If your children are young, ask your spouse or child-care person to take care of them.

• Arrange for a playtime at your own or another family's home. If the children need supervision, get it. Whatever you do, don't try to provide it yourself, unless you have unusually mature or self-sufficient children. You know your children, so do what makes the most sense.

• Get the children involved in homework or activities they enjoy. It's not enough to tell them to find something to do. Work with them to find a place, gather the materials, and arrange the circumstances that are likely to keep them involved.

• Have the children become involved in a parallel activity. If you love reading the Sunday *New York Times*, get your child snuggled up next to you with his or her favorite book and share the time quietly.

2. *Block out time for specific activities.* Another way of diminishing interruptions is to organize them. Develop specific times and days on which to handle predictable interruptive activities. For example, schedule special times for

- making and taking phone calls
- receiving visitors
- taking appointments
- having meetings with supervisors or supervisees
- going to luncheon appointments
- seeing salespeople
- socializing at work
- being alone with your children

Again, I urge you to put time limits on each activity, and stick to them.

III. **TIME ROBBER**: Invitations
   SOURCE: External
   FEELING: *"How can I say no to Uncle Jake's party? It would disappoint him so."*
   DESCRIPTION: If interruptions are Superwomen's number-one time robber, invitations are a close second. Actually, invitations often come first as interruptions in the form of phone calls, drop-in visitors, telegrams, and even flower deliveries. Some invitations are not formally extended—you are expected because you have appeared on schedule over a period of years, like going to your parents' home for Christmas.

Problems arise when you want to say no but feel you should say yes, and when you want to say yes but it makes sense to say no.

WHEN SHOULD YOU SAY YES? HOW DO YOU SAY NO?

SOLUTIONS

1. *After receiving an invitation, whether in person or over the phone, never respond immediately.* Give yourself some time. Acknowledge the invitation, thank the person or group

extending it, and tell them you need to consult your calendar (or your spouse or whomever) to see if the date is free. Give them a specific time by which you will respond, such as tomorrow before noon. Then think it over. See if you want to say yes.

2. How to determine when you should say yes. Ask yourself the following:

Do I want to accept this invitation? (Yes or no.)

Why yes; why no? After you have answered these questions, ask your spouse or children, or colleagues, the same if they too were invited.

Is it important to me? (Yes or no.)

Why yes; why no?

Is this something I can not *do?* (Yes or no.)

What is the worst thing that will happen if I don't accept it?

Let's apply these questions to a couple of real-life situations. In the first situation, let's say my family and I have been asked to attend a Christmas party with relatives who have made it known that they really don't like me. It's a party to which I am asked to bring some of the food, and there is to be an exchange of presents. In the past, it has not been a pleasant experience, but we have gone because I think that my uncle's feelings would be hurt if we didn't. Up to now, we have automatically accepted the invitation because it seemed like the "right thing to do."

If I apply the analytical questions to this situation, the answer is obvious.

Do I want to accept this invitation? (No.) Why? (Because I really hate to go to this affair.)

Does my husband want to go? (No.)

Do the children want to go? (Yes. They're ready for a Christmas party with presents anytime.)

Is this party important to me? (No, but my uncle is.)

Is this something I can *not* do? (Yes.)

What will happen if I don't accept the invitation? (I'm not

really sure, but I think my uncle would be disappointed, and my other relatives would be horrified if I broke the "tradition." Maybe I should talk with my uncle about it. I'll invite him to join us for our regular Christmas; and, frankly, I don't really care how the others feel. Well, I do. I hate it when people have a reason to put me down; but, considering the source, I guess I can tolerate it. My actions are not meant to hurt anyone. As a matter of fact, going to that party "hurts" me. So, by not going, I will save myself from a generally uncomfortable experience. I'm not going to go.)

Do you see how it works?

3. *How to say no when you think you should say yes.* Remember, you have a perfect right to say no. In saying yes when you really want to say no, you are being dishonest. To put it bluntly, you are lying.

Develop a "no" response that has the following ingredients:

A. *Acknowledge the invitation.* ("John, thanks very much for the dinner invitation.")

B. *Specifically state that you cannot accept it.* ("I'm afraid I'll have to say no at this time.") Don't give ambiguous or loophole answers, such as: "I don't *think* I will be able to come," or, "If things get cleared, I'll be there." First, those are lies; second, those are surefire ways of getting yourself to that dinner in spite of yourself.

C. *If it is appropriate and legitimate, tell why you cannot accept the invitation.* ("I'm going out of town for the weekend.") Don't make up excuses that you will have to cover later on. If the reason is simply that you don't want to go, then say that you cannot accept the invitation or, if it is true, that you have plans.

D. *If the person is someone whom you would like to see under other circumstances, make a counteroffer.* ("I can't go Saturday evening, but why don't we meet at my house for breakfast the following Saturday?") But do this only if you want to, not because you feel guilty.

Saying No Is a Big Deal

You are not alone if saying no is a big deal for you. Deciding to say no has much greater meaning for women than for most men. Harvard University psychologist Carol Gilligan says that concern for others is absolutely central in the way women make decisions. While men often make a decision based on principles, women are much more concerned about the impact a decision (such as saying no) makes on the people involved.[7]

Many women tell me that when they say no they feel they are pushing people away or deserting or rejecting them. They feel they are hurting others when they say no. Because these same women often report feeling pushed away, deserted, rejected, and/or hurt if someone says no to them, they may assume that others will feel the same way. Many of us don't want to say no to others because, in fact, we don't want people to say no to us. But people say no to us anyway, especially the men in our lives, who do not live under the same psychological constraints as we do.

Finally, some women are reluctant to say no for fear of arousing anger in others. Anger is a very uncomfortable emotion for women. They find it unacceptable in themselves, and they are terrified of it in others. Some women will do almost anything to prevent anger from developing in themselves and in others. They think that if they never deny others anything, if they never say no, they can prevent anger from emerging. Of course, such timidity often produces the opposite effect.

What Happens When You Deny Your Needs

If you deny your needs, if you do whatever other people want without regard to what you want, you stand a good chance of becoming a martyr.

In assuming a martyr role, you might feel powerless and

cheated, resentful and angry, without a sense of self, lacking in self-esteem. Need I say more?

Learning to say no is an acquired skill, like learning to ski. You get better at it with practice. Using this little two-letter word judiciously can have very positive time-management consequences, and it can help you to feel better about yourself and less resentful of others.

This doesn't mean that you will never do a favor for a friend, go to a boring party, or participate in a community event. It simply means that you will gain some control over how often you will do such things.

4. *How to say no when you want to say yes, but it makes sense to say no.* Some Superwomen not only *feel they should* do it all, they really *want* to do it all. They don't want to say no to anything, in spite of the fact that they are overcommitted, have too much to do, and are on the brink of physical collapse. This could be called the "I don't want to give up anything" syndrome.

Under these circumstances, you must ask yourself some very basic questions: Why do I want to accept this invitation? Is it important to me? (Yes or no.) Why yes; why no? How does this invitation relate to who is important to me? Is this something I can *not* do? (Yes or no.) What is the worst thing that will happen if I don't accept it? Am I being seduced by an unimportant possibility?

IV. **TIME ROBBER:** The "do it" approach to everything
    SOURCE: Internal
    FEELING: *"I must do it myself."*
    DESCRIPTION: Whether at home or at work, Superwomen tend to *do* a lot. They *do it themselves rather than ask for help or delegate or pay someone to "do it" for them.* Most of us "do it" without thinking. It's an automatic response we have to the demands around us. By always doing it, we set all kinds of precedents for the people around us *not* to do it (and unintentionally we teach our daughters to do the same).

If I have a report that must be photocopied, I usually just do it. Unless the circumstances were extreme, I can't imagine my husband ever just "doing it." His first impulse would be to find someone to photocopy the report for him. These sex-differentiated responses are repeated in hundreds of other situations.

HIS AND HER WAYS OF "DOING IT"

Superwomen bake cookies for school parties	Men tell someone else to order and deliver them
Superwomen clean houses	Men hire housecleaners
Superwomen respond personally to all their phone calls	Men have their secretaries respond, determine the nature of the business, and then delegate whatever must be done
Superwomen cook dinners	Men have them cooked by spouses, caterers, or restaurants
Superwomen personally buy gifts for all occasions for family, friends, or business colleagues	Men ask somebody else to do that for them
Superwomen write out or dictate all their correspondence	Men assign the task to their secretaries

And men never feel guilty about any of those decisions. Men would never even consider doing many of the things on which we expend enormous amounts of energy.

This "do it" orientation is very reflective of traditional socialization. In "doing it" you are demonstrating how

____ nice you are

____ supportive you are

____ hardworking you are

____ detail conscious you can be

____ response oriented you are

____ unselfish you are

SOLUTION

Start using the anti-doing-it formula. You really don't have to be the one-woman band for everything you're involved with. What you need is a formula by which to determine what it is *you* choose to do. Consider the following Anti-Doing-It Formula:

- *Does this really need to be done? Why?*
- *Can someone else do it? Who?*
- *Do I want to do it? Why?*
- *Is it important for me to do it? Why?*
- *Is this something that I can* not *do? Why?*
- *What is the worst thing that will happen if it doesn't get done?*
- *If I choose to do it, who can help?*
- *Can I pay someone else to do it? Who? How much?*
- *How much time will I save if I hire or ask someone else to do it?*

V. TIME ROBBER: Crises

SOURCE: Internal and external

FEELING: *"Help!"*

DESCRIPTION: Crises of any type are stressful and time-consuming. Unavoidable crises are those over which we have no control. They are "acts of God," such as freak accidents. We can't prevent them. We can only respond to them with our best judgment. We can also develop individual or family emergency procedures and prepare a list of emergency resources that include the best medical/legal/financial people available. In the next section I will outline a crisis-management procedure.

Avoidable crises are another thing. Superwomen often live from crisis to crisis, handling each as it arises; that is, they *react* to a wide range of problems rather than *prevent* them. Why? Alec MacKenzie lists six major causes of crises.[8] They include

- lack of good planning
- failure to monitor things as they go along in time to make corrective actions when needed
- failure to anticipate problems
- procrastination
- mechanical breakdowns
- human error

I add to this list two other factors:

- communication breakdown
- inadequate resources

SOLUTIONS

1. *To prevent crises you must use good planning skills, develop contingency plans and backup systems, be flexible, and allow time in your schedule for the unexpected.*

A. *Anticipate problems.* Think ahead a bit to feel out what might go wrong. You know and I know that something will go wrong; it's just a matter of what and when. Be prepared.

B. *Develop contingency plans and backup people or systems.*

Since something will go wrong—the child-care person will get sick; the clothes dryer will break down; the car won't start; one of your children will get chicken pox, and then the other one will too; your purse and your credit cards will be lost or stolen; you will forget some special person's birthday; your boss will ask for a thirty-page report in a week; or you will ruin the roast—you must develop contingency plans and backup systems. This means that you must get—in advance—the names of recommended resources from friends, colleagues, and professionals. Every time you hear of a good plumber, an excellent baby-sitter, a great place for take-out food, whatever—write the name and phone number in the address section of your calendar. Also, talk with neighbors, friends, or family about their potential availability for emergency situations. You will feel much more secure going about your everyday business knowing that there are some people out there on whom you can count.

A *contingency plan* is an orderly procedure you follow when normal events change, a plan designating who will do what in the event that such-and-such occurs. You need contingency plans for predictable crises, such as when the school calls you to say that your child is sick or when your car won't start.

C. *Be flexible. Allow time for the unexpected.* Very often, crises develop because we want things to go exactly as we had planned; then, when they don't, we drive ourselves crazy trying to make them conform to the original plan. Part of this comes from a kind of perfectionism, part from a kind of inflexibility. However, having contingency plans and established backup systems does help us to be flexible. The most important aspect of being flexible is developing a flexible state of mind. This is especially important with minor issues. We must be able to react to situations with a perspective something like: "Well, this is not working out the way I expected. . . . Now, what else can I do?"

Another aspect of being flexible is giving yourself a cushion of time around appointments and events. For example, Michael LeBoeuf suggests that one should estimate how much time a given activity or task will take and multiply it by 1.25. If a dental appointment should take an hour, give yourself an hour and fifteen minutes. He allows himself 1.50 of the given time if he is going to do something unfamiliar.[9] You don't want to plan your time so closely that you always find yourself just barely making appointments or being just a little (or a lot) late. That creates unnecessary high blood pressure, anxiety, guilt, and a reputation for undependability.

2. *To deal with crises, minor or major, one must follow an organized procedure, including the following:*

A. *Stop what you are doing.* As I have indicated before, Superwomen often try to carry on all regular activities and deal with a crisis at the same time. Minor crises may require that you stop what you are doing until you can gather the resources and develop plans to take care of the crisis. Major crises, however, predicate that you stop all but the survival activities of your life. Cancel all activities, appointments, and engagements until your life gets back to normal.

B. *Call on your spouse or the most important person in your life.* Crises are not times to go it alone. From the very outset, you must communicate with someone, getting his or her support and assistance. Ask people for help. Go to your best friends. How many times have you helped your friends and family in times of crisis? Plenty, I bet. Now it's your turn, even though it may not be a comfortable role for you.

C. *Diagnose the situation.* This may seem obvious, but very often crises are not just one event or one problem. They may develop as a result of a series of things. Obviously, before you can do anything to relieve a situation, you need to know what's wrong.

D. *If appropriate, seek expert advice on the situation.* The kinds of people you might consult range from repair persons to physicians, designers, caterers, travel agents, or teachers.

E. *When appropriate, buy or borrow the services you need.* Crises are not good times in which to be penny-wise and pound-foolish. If you need to spend some of your financial resources, do it. That is what "rainy day" funds are for. This is a time when the resources of friends, family, and others might also be needed.

F. *For major crises, alert key people, such as your employer, as to what is going on.* You don't have to go into great detail explaining your problems, but it is basic courtesy to let your employer or supervisor know that you may not be able to work or that you may be less available due to a crisis situation. Often, employers are very sympathetic if they know something of your problem. If they don't, they can get irritated about your absence or seeming lack of productivity.

G. *For minor or major crises, inform your children.* Again, you have to use your judgment about what to say and how much detail to give. Much of this will depend on the ages and maturity of your children and whether they are accustomed to receiving such information. At the very least, you can say something like, "Johnny, I am likely to be impatient today because the car broke down." Or, in the case of a major crisis that involves the children, give them an opportunity to talk with you about it, ask questions, and express feelings. This is very important.

Teachers, child-care persons, and parents of your children's best friends probably would appreciate being informed of major issues affecting your children. They can then deal appropriately with them. These people can be wonderful, supportive resources for you and your children.

H. *Take appropriate actions.*

I. *Take care of yourself.* Crises are times when you are most likely to ignore your most basic needs. Get plenty of sleep, eat properly, and, somehow, relax. It is imperative that you take care of yourself so that you can muster all your resources to deal with the crisis.

J. *When the crisis is over, evaluate what happened.* Look back over the crisis. Was there any way it could have been prevented? Is there any way you can now prevent it from occurring again? Were your resource people helpful? Who was and who wasn't? Did your actions work well for you? What would you do differently if this happened again?

I have left out one time robber, and it is the worst one of

all. Can you guess what it is? Like Pac-Man (or -Woman), it chomps away at our time every day, every week, every month. It robs time from women, calls them, commands their attention. One can never really finish dealing with it because the demands are infinite. It's "bigger than a breadbox," "more powerful than a locomotive"—it's a bird, it's a plane, . . . it's *housework!* And it is big enough to need a chapter of its own.

11

Housework:
How to Do Less
of It

TIME-ROBBER: Housework
SOURCE: External (complicated by internal socialization)
FEELING: *I'll never get all this done!*
DESCRIPTION: A few years ago, my husband, Mort, and I collaborated on a book about two-career couples. I told Mort then that I wanted to write the household chapter, thinking that I could "pick the brains" of some of the world's most famous housekeeping gurus (who shall remain anonymous). What I wanted was assistance in managing my home *and* some cogent advice about how to get my husband to do more (every woman's fantasy). Here is what I found:

____ "Ten Easy Steps to Having Sparkling Windows"
____ "How to Have Glorious Walls and Ceilings"
____ "Giving Your Clothes a Rest"
____ "Saving Money by Buying Whole Chickens, Sides of Beef, and Wheels of Cheese"
____ "Removing Waxy Buildup with Elbow Grease"

I couldn't believe it! I was outraged, furious, and disappointed. I wanted help in managing my home, not more busywork!

While I was looking for some good management ideas, I was also looking for a housekeeping list—something that organized all the tasks and responsibilities involved in keeping a house, so that I wouldn't have to keep track of them in my head. I couldn't find that, either. All I found were more tips on cleaning my wood, pewter, crystal, and velvet-curtain interlinings.

I was so frustrated by the lack of real, helpful information that I vowed someday to tackle this area myself. Therefore, what I will do in this chapter is (1) define housework and discuss why it is such a "problem"; (2) describe a management process to help you get the household organized; and (3) help you understand why *you* do it and *he* resists.

WHAT IS HOUSEWORK—A REAL DEFINITION

Dr. Joanne Kliejunas defines housework as:

> . . . the sum of unpaid labor performed by household members which serves one or more of the following purposes:
>
> **1.** Providing household members' physical and/or psychological subsistence (preparing food, teaching a child to read)
>
> **2.** Enabling household members to meet institutional commitments outside the household such as doing paid work or attending school (home repair, attending parent-teacher conferences)
>
> **3.** Producing a good or service used by household members (sewing clothes, nursing a child)
>
> **4.** Maintaining a quality of household life "reasonably" expected with the culture, class, and/or community in which the household is situated (washing dishes, laundering clothes)
>
> **5.** Acquiring the foods or services necessary to accomplish any of the above purposes from sources out-

side the household (shopping for groceries, taking a
household member to the dentist)

6. Organizing or facilitating any of the above purposes (menu planning, contacting and meeting home-
repair persons).[1]

I found Dr. Kliejunas's postdefinition remarks even more
interesting. She said that "existing theories of housework's
value do not specifically define housework; they seem to assume a common understanding of its components."[2] In other
words, although housework is a complicated set of tasks and
services involving the management of people, property, and
equipment, most people, even researchers, assume that everyone knows what is involved. Therefore, no one has bothered
to write a description of housework or its functions!

Housework Is Like Jell-O

Can you imagine what would happen if one ran a business
based on a "common understanding of its components"? That's
a little like saying that you're going to organize Jell-O.
Housework is the only major work area I know of whose
definition and description remain in the heads of one segment
of our population—women—and is, as a result, a product of
their special training, personal experience, and influence by
the media. As such, it remains amorphous, variable, and un-
organized, which explains, in part, why it has been so difficult
over the years to manage it, and so impossible to assess a
monetary value to. *It also explains, in part, why housework
has been so difficult to delegate to the men in our lives.*

With regard to the latter point, let me give you an example.
If I asked my husband to straighten up the house, based on a
"common understanding" of what is involved, how likely do
you think it is that he would do it according to the standards
and procedures I have in my head? Unless I have explained to

him in detail what I have in mind (unlikely), or written out for him what I have in mind (even more unlikely), the chances of his "doing it right" are one in a thousand (or ten thousand or more). Needless to say, my view of "common understandings" is that they lead quickly to misunderstandings, disappointments, and anger. Let me add to this anecdote the fact that my husband does not like to be told what to do, and that he is uncomfortable performing "a female job," and you can see that I have created a setup for me to be angry and disappointed.

Before we move on to the management of housework, I will summarize some of Joanne Kliejunas's observations about housework. I think this will give you a better idea of why it is a problem area and a time robber.

Some Research Findings About Housework

1. Women still do the major portion of housework whether or not they work outside the home.

2. Men and other household members are only slightly more likely to do housework if the woman is employed.

3. The number of children is the biggest factor in determining how much time is spent in housework.

4. Household technologies often make additional work for the houseworker, because they encourage higher standards of cleanliness and more frequent performance of tasks. Some new technologies have even created new tasks for houseworkers.

5. Housework has a poor image.

6. Housework is absolutely necessary but not valued by society in general.

7. The practice of sharing housework is tentative and rare. Women continue to do most of the housework to avoid the interpersonal "hassles" their insistence on sharing would create.

8. Men's lives would change dramatically if women refused to do housework.[3]

In *American Couples,* Philip Blumstein and Pepper Schwartz bring out some very revealing facts about housework.

1. Even if husbands are unemployed, they do much less housework than do their full-time-employed wives. This is the case even among couples who profess egalitarian social ideals, including equal sharing of all housework. While these men do more housework than those who are in favor of a traditional division of labor between the sexes, they are still far behind their wives. Shared responsibility turns out to be a myth.

2. Among middle- and upper-middle-class two-career couples, some husbands encourage their wives to invest themselves in their work and contribute to the family's standard of living. The wives still do more housework than the husbands, but some of the burden may be shifted to hired help.

3. Try as they might, Blumstein and Schwartz could not find a significant number of men who fit the description of "househusband."

4. Married men's aversion to housework is so intense that it can sour their relationships with their wives. The more housework they do, for whatever reason, the more they fight about it.

5. Couples who are not married but who live together expect their partners to work outside the home. Each partner pledges to provide for himself or herself, and both contribute to the financial support of the household. Women in such relationships do less housework than do working wives, but the men who live with them become no more involved with household duties than do husbands.

6. When women work it gives them "more power, respect, and self-fulfillment. They gain status in the household. When a woman earns money, she acquires more of a voice in the decisions she and her husband make. If she makes a success of herself, she is not expected to do as much housework—a sure sign that she is elevated in her own and her husband's eyes."[4]

Most of Us Are Still Using Horse-and-Buggy Methods

Housework is a never-ending job, accomplished mostly by women (even when they work full-time outside the home), for which few effective management techniques have been developed. Women, especially Superwomen, tend to utilize many of the horse-and-buggy methods used by their mothers or grandmothers to keep their homes. As a result, many women are overwhelmed by the enormity of the details. Even when Superwomen know about and practice good management techniques at the office, many don't utilize them in their own homes.

Ayako, a manager at a Minneapolis high-tech firm, explained it this way:

> In my company I am known as one of the best managers in the division. Thanks to a special executive-training program I went through, I learned all about things like planning, decision making, and resource allocation. I also learned about being a supervisor. Believe it or not, that was the most difficult part of the training, because I used to think I had outstanding people skills. In high school and college I had been president of everything, and everybody used to tell me how good I was at leading. So, before the course I couldn't believe I would learn very much about how to be a supervisor. Boy, was I wrong!
>
> In the beginning I couldn't "hear" my instructor when she told me I was a lousy communicator. I figured she was a lousy instructor. I almost dropped the course.
>
> After a while I began to see what she was talking about. I found that she was right about my not being able to communicate. I must say it's been difficult for me to change the way I handle people, but I'm really getting pretty good at it now. Unlike before, I'm ask-

ing people to do things, telling them directly what I want from them, and giving them feedback.

It's still a different story at home, though. While I would never dream of expecting my secretary to keep my office organized, I often find myself "hoping" that my husband will help me around the house. While I would never dream of giving a trainee a project to do without first giving her (or him) some instruction, at home I'm always asking the kids or my husband to do things without showing them how. While at the office I never yell or scream or carry on about something not getting done (or done right), at home I'm always losing my cool. To put it in a nutshell, at work I am a very effective, competent professional. At home, I feel like a real basket case. I hate it and I hate me at home. I wish I could do something about it!

Do You Feel Any of These Ways?

Before anything else, let me predict that if you are feeling any of the ways described above, there is a good chance that

_____ your household does not have a manager, in the true meaning of the word

_____ your home seems chaotic a lot of the time

_____ your housekeeping standards, at least in some areas, are too high

_____ you are doing too much yourself

_____ there are no limits to the time you devote to your housework

_____ you do not know how to delegate effectively

_____ you get little help from other household members or others

Am I right? Think about it. And before you run off to do something else, let me tell you some ways to change all this.

At first it might sound foreign and it may feel uncomfortable, but in the end, I think it will make sense to you.

YOUR HOME NEEDS A MANAGER

In his book *Management: Tasks, Responsibilities, and Practices,* Peter Drucker describes what managers do. He says that managers set objectives, organize, motivate and communicate, and measure performance.[5]

Who Is the Manager?

Who in your household is the manager? You? Your partner? Someone else? Even if you have (or want to have) an egalitarian household in which you share tasks, *someone* (and I emphasize *one*) must have ultimate responsibility for what goes on in your home.

If the manager in your household is someone other than you, please hand this book to him or her right now. If it is you, please read on. If you are saying to yourself, "No one else is going to be manager and I'm not going to do it either," you have a problem. If no one else is going to do it, then the job is yours, whether you want it or not. You have the choice of managing your household poorly or managing it well.

I don't want to make your life more complicated. The purpose of designating a manager is to make things easier. I don't want you to do more, I want you to do *less*. I want you to have more time to do things that are enjoyable, fun, and rewarding.

What a Manager Should Do

Let's say that a household manager is the person who has over-all responsibility for the "work" of a house. As such, the manager's job is to do the following:

1. Set goals
2. Organize household activities
3. Anticipate problems
4. Determine the use of resources
5. Delegate tasks (communicating with household members and staff, motivating them, and measuring their perfor-mance)

Setting Goals

In my work with other women, most have established that while they spend a lot of their time on it, housework is not an essential element in their lives; however, they do want to get housework under control and to do less of it. Many also add that they would like to see their partners or spouses do *more*. What kind of goal statements about housework might you make that would take into account dimensions of what, where, when, and how much?

Some Goal Examples

Here are a few examples:

1. *I do not want to spend more than two hours per weekday (Monday through Friday) and six hours per weekend on housework or on errands related to housework.*

2. *I want my husband to match the time I spend on housework and not resent that time.*

3. *I want my children to learn to pick up after themselves,*

to contribute to household chores as their ages permit, and increasingly to take care of their own household needs such as cooking, washing and drying their clothes, cleaning their rooms, and making their lunches.

4. *I want to hire out most routine housecleaning tasks to a person or service who comes to my house twice a week and who needs little supervision after the initial training period.*

5. *I want my house to be organized so that I have what I want when I need it and can easily find what I need. That means we need a lot of storage space and systems for dealing with mail, bills, and clutter.*

6. *I want our family to spend most of our at-home time relaxing, enjoying ourselves, and having a good time.*

7. *At all times, I want to remember that everything doesn't have to be done!*

THE BENEFITS OF MAKING SOME HOUSEHOLD CHANGES

Here are the benefits of making some changes in how your household works:

- The woman doesn't feel overwhelmed with housework.
- The woman doesn't feel angry at and resentful of household members.
- The family understands the nature and scope of housework.
- Tension around housework issues is reduced.
- The woman doesn't associate "care" by family members with their involvement in housework.
- The woman has some leisure time.
- The family has leisure time together.
- The family spends minimum time bickering about chores and errands.
- Children of both sexes and at all age levels know how to perform household activities.
- Male and female children learn nontraditional ways of handling the household.

• Family members don't feel guilty about their lack of participation.

• The household uses outside resources as finances permit.

• The woman allows family members to perform household tasks in their own ways.

• The woman and partner communicate about housework and other issues.

• The woman spends a limited amount of time on housework, which leaves her free to pursue essential issues and spend time with important people.

I am sure you can think of a dozen more items.

ORGANIZING HOUSEHOLD ACTIVITIES

The key to organizing your household activities is to have a written list of them.

In appendix B, I have organized a sample Household Activities List by function and frequency.

First, look over the list and add anything important I may have omitted. Second, remembering that "everything doesn't have to be done," ask the following questions of each activity on the amended list:

"Everything Doesn't Have to Be Done"

• *Is this really necessary?* If yes, keep it. If no, eliminate it.

• *Is this something that can not be done?* If yes, drop it. If no, keep it.

• *Am I being compulsive about this?* If yes, figure out how you can simplify or reduce the activity. If no, keep it.

• *Who else can do it?* (We'll cover this in the delegation section.)

My motto is, when in doubt, dump it. The time you take now to eliminate or simplify these activities will save you hours in the future. While it is your function as manager to make these decisions, and because others in your household will be affected, it might be politic for you to discuss the process with them. It wouldn't harm them to see what is really involved in keeping a house. Many men and children found reading this list "a revealing experience."

Anticipating Problems

Households are fraught with potential problems. Perhaps housework is where the saying, "If anything can go wrong, it will," got started. Anticipating and preventing household problems is the best way of dealing with them. The organizational techniques, the systems, and even the equipment and services recommended in this chapter are designed to help you control your housework instead of letting it control your life.

First, you must get housework "in perspective." Try reading Erma Bombeck or Fran Lebowitz. They have unusual ways of looking at the world, and especially at the home, that tickle my funny bone. When you can laugh at your problems, they are cut down to manageable size.

Determining the Use of Resources

When you're constantly in a *do-it* frame of mind, as many Superwomen are, it's difficult to think about what help is available to you, even though it might be right in front of you. Every household has some resources. Take a look at your property or home itself. (Perhaps you can make better use of the space.) Consider the equipment in the home. (Are you making adequate use of your work savers?) How about the people who live in the home? (Are you calling on their available time, knowledge, skills, and abilities?) Are you allocating money realistically to get help? Have you researched the potential outside resources (people, services, equipment, and information) that you might use?

The reality is that most of us have spent months, perhaps years, doing things in a half-baked way because we haven't had the appropriate equipment. I have gone for months without such things as a potato peeler, good knives, or a step stool. I still don't have a microwave oven or a good vacuum, but it's on my list *to do* sometime soon.

People Resources

Who are the people in your home? Is there a partner or spouse? Are there children or stepchildren? Are there in-laws, friends, roommates, or boarders? No matter who they are, each of these people represents to you, as manager of the household, a potential resource in time, energy, information, and skill.

It is my belief that no one (except infants or individuals who are ill or physically disabled) should have a free ride when it comes to the work of the house. This does not necessarily mean that everyone should share equally; circumstances may dictate otherwise. But neither does it mean that one person should become the sacrificial household lamb.

You may find it difficult to believe, but children have a need to contribute. Their contributions depend on how they are asked, what they are asked to do, what kind of feedback they receive, and at what age the asking begins. We'll go into greater detail about these questions in the section on delegating.

In a recent article in *The Moneypaper,* a financial publication for women, psychologist John Platt is quoted as saying that "one of the biggest mistakes a parent can make is always giving, without expecting anything in return."[6] To prevent you from making that mistake, you might want to refer to appendix C, where I list the housework children at varying ages can do.

Don't forget the "other people" in your household, even if they are guests. There are both "nice" and effective ways of eliciting help from these people.

"Home Rules"

Minimally, you can and should expect all members of your household to pick up after themselves. I rather like the following "Home Rules" as a standard of that expectation:

> If you sleep on it . . . make it up
> If you wear it . . . hang it up
> If you drop it . . . pick it up
> If you eat out of it . . . put it in the sink
>   (better yet, in the dishwasher)
> If you step on it . . . wipe it off
> If you open it . . . close it
> If you empty it . . . fill it up
> If it rings . . . answer it
> If it howls . . . feed it
> If it cries . . . love it[7]

But please do not limit your thinking about resources to the "in-house" people in your household. Many women do that.

Money to Pay for Outside Resources

If I asked you, right now, "Why don't you hire someone or some service to do the housework?" I bet your answer would be one of the following:

"No, I don't have the money."
"No, it's too expensive."
"No, I don't want to be exploitive."
"No, I don't want some stranger in my house."

"No, it's too much of a hassle."
"No, I don't have time to find anyone."
"No, my husband wouldn't approve of it."

These "excuses" are the standard responses of many women who are reluctant to spend financial resources on outside help.

Even among high-income women there is an incredible resistance to spending money on household services traditionally performed by women. Men, however, are not as reluctant. If they have a plumbing problem, they hire a plumber; if they have a gardening job, they hire a gardener; if they have a party, they hire a caterer. If a man is too busy, he doesn't think twice about assigning the job to an outside source. For a variety of emotional rather than logical reasons, most women would rather "do it" than "buy it." Even when women's husbands encourage them to "buy it," they often resist.

WHY WE DO IT RATHER THAN BUY IT

Why? I think part of it reflects the conflicts women feel about giving to themselves. After all, asking the butcher to deliver the meat involves an extra expense, an imposition, and an unnecessary "indulgence." Another explanation might be that women don't want their husbands or children to feel they have abandoned them as a result of their working outside the home; they feel that they must "pay for the sin of working." There are also women who choose not to work but who have to. Sometimes their resentment about working comes out in self-punishing, martyrlike ways. By denying themselves even the most minor of time-saving expenses, they are saying, "Look at how hard I am working to take care of you. You should really appreciate me and what I am doing." Of course, they don't actually say it, but that's what they are thinking and that's the message everyone gets.

Another explanation is that some women don't spend money on help because they want to avoid criticism for being lazy, a spendthrift, and self-indulgent. And, of course, some Superwomen do it because they pride themselves on being superb homemakers. They want *A*'s in this arena too.

HIRING OUTSIDE HELP

Women have rejected hiring outside help with a passion that outweighs any reasonable examination. As Letty Cottin Pogrebin says, "Why is it okay to hire someone to fix the toilet if the husband can't/won't, but not okay to hire someone to clean the toilet if the wife can't/won't."[8] As we begin to earn money for our work outside the home, we *must* begin to spend some of it on outside resources to relieve ourselves and our families of the overwhelming burden of housework. To find money in your budget for buying housework resources, I suggest first that you look at how you are spending your money now. Where could you cut a few corners to come up with extra money? Could what you are now spending on "lunches out," makeup, or clothes be cut? What about magazine subscriptions or gift purchases?

Dru Scott sums it all up when she asks you to "take a moment to consider the value of your time per hour (whether in dollars or in 'psychic pay') versus the cost of professional help for these tasks." She says that "there are an enormous number of skilled people available to serve you by the hour for a fair fee . . . so don't hold yourself back by believing your time is not that important."[9]

I can't tell you *how much* to spend—that depends on your circumstances. But I can tell you what kinds of services are available and what you can buy for specified amounts of money. In appendix D I have outlined what these resources are.

Remember that you can buy parts of a person's time or service. You can buy a half-day's worth of a cleaning person's time, three hours from a teenage helper, or an hour from an errand runner. Many women are inhibited about buying services because they think too big. They think they will have to hire a full-time housekeeper (and that's okay) or an every-week gardener (and that's okay) or cater the whole affair (and that's okay) or have a live-in nanny (and that's okay, too). Set aside some money, determine what you can buy with it, and then find someone to fill that need.

DELEGATING TASKS BY COMMUNICATING WITH HOUSEHOLD MEMBERS AND OUTSIDE STAFF:
Motivating Them and Measuring Their Performance

One of my clients speaks about how difficult it is to delegate:

> Every time I think about delegating I get a knot in my stomach. The "vibes" about having somebody do something for me are very negative. I think part of it comes from having watched my mother. She used to work herself to death and then lay a big guilt trip on me for not helping her, or she would nag, nag, nag about everything that needed to be done. God, she drove me crazy.
>
> My dad's way wasn't much better; in fact, I think he was worse. He used to come into the house and immediately give orders. "Do this, do that..." and then he'd do his own guilt trip: "When I was a kid I was up at six o'clock in the morning working for my dad. You kids don't know what work really is." Or, worse, "Your poor mother works so hard, and all you do..." I used to think to myself, but dared not say, "You turkey, why don't *you* do something to help her!"

I hated what went on, and frankly, that's why I have a hard time today. I don't want to nag or tell my kids how hard I worked or lay guilt trips ... so I usually end up doing almost everything myself (just like my mother). But I feel resentful about that too—I really don't know what to do.

As children we saw our mothers' nondelegative and ineffective style and our fathers' equally ineffective, authoritarian style. I believe that most women who grew up under traditional circumstances feel the same way.

However, just as you probably learned ineffective ways of delegating, you can also learn some very effective ways.

Before we move on to the five steps to effective delegation, I will summarize which behaviors definitely don't work. I want to show you how your behavior can elicit nonproductive feelings and responses in yourself and others.

Ineffective Delegation Technique	Others' Nonproductive Responses	Result
1. You continue to do it all.	They continue to let you.	You feel tired, angry, stressed, and resentful.
2. You hope (perhaps even hint) that someone will notice how hard you are working and will take it upon himself or herself to "pitch in."	They don't notice or choose not to notice.	You feel angry and upset.

3. You do almost everything and let your family's lack of helpfulness build inside.	They comment about how you haven't seemed very happy lately... is there anything wrong? Your children and husband tell you you are grumpy.	You feel unhappy and get sick and believe yourself to be inadequate or "wrong."
4. You decide to let things go.	They talk about how chaotic things are ...where are their clean clothes?	You feel guilty at the chaos, unappreciated for past efforts.
5. You get upset and cry. You tell them how you can't do it all anymore.	They feel sorry and guilty and promise to help out more.	They help for a few days, then go back to old ways. You feel hopeless.
6. You get upset and angry. You tell them they are a bunch of ungrateful slobs.	They tell you you are a demanding bitch.	You feel resentful and guilty.
7. You tell them what you want done.	They resist doing it openly or covertly.	You are furious.

| 8. You announce that because it's only fair, from now on this is going to be an egalitarian household where everyone shares the housework. | They ignore your announcement. The "more liberated" agree in principle but disagree in actions. | You want to run away from home. |

The major reason women don't get help with housework is that they don't ask for it.[10]

What Behavior Do You Want?

You have a better chance of getting what you want if you first think, "What behavior do I want? What can I do to increase the chances of getting it?" Remember, actions always beget reactions. For example, if you want loving, accusing someone of never giving it to you is unlikely to produce the results you want. Likewise, if you want your husband to take you out to dinner, you have very little chance of that occurring if all you do is hint at how tired you are.

How can you increase your chances for effectively delegating housework tasks to both in-house and outside people?

Delegating Steps

1. *Decide what task or tasks you want to delegate.* Don't just delegate the dirty work; interesting and rewarding tasks can be delegated, too.
2. *Determine who has the time, skill or potential skill, and possible interest to do the job.*
3. *Ask the child or adult to do the job.*
   A. *Describe the job.* ("Jenny, the kitchen garbage needs to be taken out to the trash cans.")
   B. *Give more information about it.* ("If the garbage isn't emptied it overflows, makes a mess, and the dogs get into it.")
   C. *Communicate your feelings.* ("I would really appreciate your doing it because I'm right in the middle of making dinner.")
   D. *Ask the delegatee specifically to do the job within certain time limits.* ("I'd like to have this done in the next five minutes.")
   E. *Listen to any replies.* ("Mom, I'm in the middle of my homework now. Can I do it later?")
   F. *If necessary, ask for clarification of the reply.* (MOM: "When do you think that will be?" JENNY: "In about fifteen minutes.")

It is very important that you carefully explain what you want done, including the standards you expect (How clean is clean?). Think of yourself as a teacher in this situation. The delegatee is a learner who needs to know what the assignment is and how to do it. I must warn you, effective delegation allows people to do things "their way." This isn't easy for most of us to allow. On one hand, you don't want to have to do a job over because it was done with no regard to your standards. On the other hand, to insist that someone do it perfectly according to your ways will probably result in their not being willing to do it again. It is sad but true that your way is not the only right way.

4. *Make sure the delegatee has the proper equipment to do the job.* For example, if you ask your daughter to mow the lawn, go with her to see that the lawnmower is where it's supposed to be and that it is in good condition; that, in addition, you have lawn clippers, a lawn rake, an outside broom, an empty garbage can, and anything else she will need to do the job correctly.

5. *After the job has been completed, check the work and thank the delegatee for doing the job. If appropriate, comment on how well the job was done. If appropriate, help the delegatee to understand how to do the job more easily, better, and faster next time. Always* thank someone for his or her efforts, even though you have done the same job thanklessly over the years. You are much more likely to have a repeat performance if you positively reinforce (to use psychologese) the behavior you want. You are rewarding behavior that is important to you. Be careful not to criticize, belittle, blame, accuse, name-call, or lecture about a job that is not done to your standards. This is easy to do because that's what many of us heard when we were growing up. Everybody makes mistakes or misjudges things. Mistakes sometimes are a way of learning. In fact, mistakes are inevitable, and therefore you can expect them, tolerate them, and even benefit from them.

Don't be concerned if this procedure doesn't work perfectly the first time. Often it takes practice to do it effectively. Please, don't give up after a couple of tries.

By the way, these steps should be used with adults and children alike. *Children have just as much right to be treated with respect and dignity as do older people.* As "right" as it may feel, it is equally *ineffective* to tell, demand, order, threaten, or ask a child to serve you as it is to do that with adults. I tell you this not because I am a mushy-headed permissive parent, but because treating children with respect and dignity is what works.

What if Someone Says No

What if someone says no or doesn't do what you requested?

There are *two* answers to any question that begins, "Will you . . . ?" One is yes (the expected and desired one); one is no (the unexpected and unwelcome one).

Many women I know are so shocked and upset when someone says no to them that it takes them three days to recover. Find out *why* he or she is saying no to you. Most of us never take time to do that—we're in such a hurry to get upset.

If someone says no to you and offers a logical explanation ("No, I can't pick up the cleaning after work; I have a meeting to go to"), accept it. Perhaps you can come up with an alternative ("Well, if you can't do it then, would you stop by the cleaners in the morning on the way to work?").

What if someone says no to you and doesn't explain why? In a nonattacking way, ask why. As a therapist, I find that both men and women often cut short conversations before they get complete messages. By not giving each other enough information about what we are thinking or feeling, we open the way to misinterpretation. Then one person or the other may feel taken advantage of, uncared for, maligned, or even attacked. *Talk!* Allow each person to find out what the other is thinking.

What If Someone Doesn't Follow Through

What do you do when people do not do what you ask them to? What you *shouldn't* do is assume that they haven't done it because of some ulterior motive. Often there is another good explanation. What you do first is to ask *why* such-and-such is not done, again without attacking. If the explanation is reasonable, follow through in the ways we have just described:

Come up with an alternate request or find another way of getting your need met.

When the answer is unreasonable, you have a number of choices. If it is infuriating or confusing, say so. It is important to express appropriate feelings about something that has not been done, provided you attack the behavior—*not* the person or his or her character. ("I'm furious that we don't have desserts for the party tonight. You promised you would pick them up!")

Another thing you can do is to suggest a way to correct the situation. ("I know you forgot to pick up the desserts, so how about going down to the ice-cream shop and getting some sherbets instead?")

Or you can toss the problem back and let the other person figure out what to do. ("I'm sorry, but I have my hands full right now. You need to come up with a dessert solution. The guests are arriving in half an hour.")

Delegating household tasks to others can double or triple your effectiveness in your home. You will be able to relax occasionally at home without being compelled to work constantly. By learning to delegate, you not only save yourself time, you save yourself from experiencing nonproductive and upsetting feelings about yourself and the people around you.

A SUMMARY OF HOUSEHOLD-MANAGEMENT TECHNIQUES

What follows is a summary of what you have accomplished in the household area up to this point. First, you have designated a manager for your household. Second, you have determined what needs to be done in the household by going through the Household Activities List, using the formula of eliminate-simplify-anticipate. (Remember, eliminate whatever activities you can. Simplify or reduce the activities themselves. Anticipate problems that will occur.) Third, you have determined what your resources are in people and money. You have also considered which outside resources you will use. Finally, you have learned something about how to delegate. The next step is to introduce and implement these steps in your household.

INTRODUCING MANAGEMENT TECHNIQUES TO THE "FAMILY"

A household "family" may be just a spouse or partner, and/or some children, and/or some other family members, and/or roommates, and/or boarders. Unless you live alone, the following step is appropriate for any kind of family group.

Call a Household Meeting

1. *Call a household meeting for a convenient, specific time, a specific duration, and in a comfortable setting.* Include children, depending on their maturity, over the age of four or five. If they are between the ages of four and eight, you might want to provide them with something to do for the "talking" part of the meeting. But do involve them, even in conversation, when it seems appropriate. The sooner you ask children to begin acting in adultlike ways, the sooner they will. After you have established the meeting time and place, post that information where everyone will be reminded of it. (For example, put a sign on the refrigerator that says: FAMILY MEETING: *Sunday evening, in the living room by the fireplace, 6–6:30. Hot chocolate will be served!*)

2. *Before the meeting, prepare an agenda, including the following items:*
A. *A statement about why you are calling the meeting.* This may be the most important part of the whole meeting, because

what you say in the beginning will probably set the mood and the direction for what follows. If you are nervous about doing this, write out what you are going to say. Even if you are not nervous, make some notes . . . you don't want to forget any important points.

Be honest, direct, and descriptive. For example, you might talk about how housework is a big job, and say that in order for everyone's life to be more relaxed and easier, you would like to introduce some management and organizational techniques. You could summarize some of the things you have read in this chapter so that everyone shares an understanding about the meaning and complexity of housework. Say whatever you think will be most effective and appropriate for you and your family's circumstances.

B. *A description of the current housework situation.* Without sounding like a martyr or an accuser, describe what is currently taking place in your household. Use the Household Activities List to show everyone the variety and scope of housework activities.

C. *An accounting of both the costs and the benefits in continuing with the status quo and in making some changes.*

Your "Plan"

D. *Your tentative plan for managing housework activities and getting the household organized includes*

• written ideas for redistributing housework (This initial plan calls for some small changes. I know you would love to hand it all over; but realistically you have a much better chance for changes if you start small.)

• your description of what you have eliminated and simplified, what *your* participation will be, what you are suggesting their participation be, what money will be set aside for "outside resources," what "outside resources" you are suggesting, and their costs

   • your suggestion of a weekly family meeting (if you don't already have one) to coordinate activities and housework assignments

3. *Chair the actual meeting*. As manager of the household, you are in charge. Be firm—stay in charge. Don't let someone else try to take over. Bring along your written agenda and follow it carefully.

4. *Ask household members to respond to your tentative plan by requesting feedback and alternate suggestions*. My bet is that you are going to get a wide range of responses, not all positive, but not all negative, either. Be prepared for that. Give people plenty of room to respond. Realize that you are asking your family members to change, and people usually resist change, especially when it comes from an external source. Try hard not to defend your plan, but listen first to what people have to say. Slowly move into a problem-solving mode. If objections are raised, ask for alternate solutions. Tell them that unless they come up with better solutions, yours will stand. If they don't like their job assignments, ask them to choose others, or go through the list asking for volunteers. If they say they don't want to do anything, tell them that that is unacceptable.

Be encouraging, positive, and appreciative of their involvement. Tell them how good you feel about their willingness to hear the plan.

5. *Negotiate differences between your plan and their suggestions into a trial plan of action*. First, acknowledge what you agree on. Second, pull from the discussion the specific things over which there is disagreement. Third, for each disagreement, discuss why each of you has a different position. Find out why the other person has his position and what his needs are. Be as specific as you can about feelings and thoughts. And, as difficult as it may be, try to understand each person's position. Fourth, for each disagreement, spend some time brainstorming options other than those you have proposed. Fifth, come to an agreement that meets some of the needs of each person.

6. *Assign a trial period in which to implement your plan.* Usually, it takes a couple of weeks to a month to get the feel of a new plan of action. This does not mean that if something really isn't working you have to wait a month to correct it. On the contrary, it is very important that you remain flexible and make small corrective actions as you go along. I strongly suggest that you continue short family meetings on a weekly basis to talk about how things are going and to give household members a chance to make suggestions for change. This is also a good time to talk about what is "right" about the plan.

If you have real difficulty with any of the aspects, consider getting assistance. You can take classes in assertiveness, consult with a mental-health professional about communicating more effectively with your family, or read any of the very helpful books listed in the bibliography.

The family member with whom you will have to do most of your communicating is your husband (or partner). Understanding his attitude about the division of household duties is absolutely vital.

WHY YOU DO IT AND HE DOESN'T

Before we talk about why "he" doesn't do the housework, let's go over the research statistics substantiating the fact that "he" doesn't. Many would argue that in fact men do as much housework as women do. The studies say the opposite.

What Studies Say About Men's Involvement

• When the wife is not employed outside the home, the average time spent on housework each day is eleven hours and six minutes (more or less, depending on the number of children).[11]

• When the wife is employed outside the home, the average time spent on housework is eight hours and forty-two minutes per day (again, depending on the number of children).[12]

• When men are asked, when their wives are asked, or when outside observers actually clock the amount of time men spend on housework, it has never been found to be more than one and a half hours per day, whether the husbands' wives were homemakers or were employed outside the home.[13]

In other words, women continue to perform 80 percent of all work in the home.

According to a national study on husbands and housework, there are four different groups:

"• Those who believe in the traditional division of labor and *do not help* around the house (39 percent)

• Those who believe the man should help but whose actions suggest that they *do not follow through* (33 percent)

• Those who have ambivalent attitudes but *say they do help* with the housework (15 percent)

• Those who *regularly perform* household chores and have little difficulty adjusting to the role (13 percent)"[14]

I think you might find one other piece of data very interesting. A University of California researcher recently found, in studying a large number of families where the woman worked outside the home, that "husbands did more housework and child care when their wives were employed, but the amount of time spent on these chores did not approach equality; nevertheless, these husbands and wives frequently *had the perception that they shared the work equally.*"[15]

Housework Is a Major Source of Arguments and Anger

This is just one dimension of the problem. Studies show that housework is the major source of family arguments and violence.[16]

Many women whose husbands don't contribute to housework are furious with their husbands. Some express their anger directly. Many others express it as depression, by withholding sex, or in irritability with children. Sometimes it erupts into a tirade after a long period of withholding feelings.

Frankly, I know of no area in our lives—including sex, children, money, or in-laws—concerning which there is more polarization between the sexes. I don't know of another area in which male and female ways of thinking, feeling, and action could be more different.

Nevertheless, this area of seemingly irreconcilable differences is one we can do something about. The solution is not simplistic: "Well, if *he* would just do it, then there wouldn't be any problem." It is far more complicated than that.

In other parts of this book I have tried to give you an understanding of how and why many women hold on to housework. I will now address male resistance. I am not pretending expertise in the area of male psychology; I can't get "into the skin of a man" and know what it's like to be one, because I haven't experienced the world as he has. But I can relate what I've learned through research, interviews, and counseling.

Perhaps the best way to explain why men don't do housework is to report what some of them have said to me in answer to that question. I'll give you their initial "short" replies, then describe some of the feelings and thoughts behind the answers. You probably hear your husband's replies and then add your own interpretation of what he really means. I note some of these female interpretations as well.

"WHY DON'T YOU DO HOUSEWORK?"

1. HE: *I help my wife all the time.*
   SHE: *He helps me once in a while.*
   HE: *If she asks me to take out the garbage, I do. I take care of the trash and the cars and the yard. I sometimes barbecue and always serve the wine and the after-dinner drinks.*

   Comment: Men do complete traditional male chores around the house—those things associated with the outdoors and certain other tasks they saw their fathers do.

2. HE: *I would do more housework if she would ask me.*
   SHE: *I don't want to have to ask him all the time. Does he have to ask me to do the laundry or make supper? Of course not!*
   HE: *Truly, if she would just ask me, I'd do more. I just don't think about doing things. How do I know what she wants if she doesn't ask me? I'm not a mind reader.*

   Comment: One of the major barriers to getting help with housework is that women do not ask for it. Men don't feel responsible for housework, so they don't think about it unless someone brings it to their attention.

3. HE: *It's not my job.*
   SHE: *That really burns me up. It's his house, too; why doesn't he do anything?*
   HE: *I have to be honest with you—I'd rather have*

her do it. Besides, it's her job. My mother did it and her mother did it before her. Housework is woman's work.

Comment: Apparently it is in men's self-interest not to do housework. There are obvious benefits that they don't think about very much, if at all. They especially don't think of the consequences their attitudes and behaviors have on women. For some men, this traditional attitude affirms masculinity: They are "real men" when their women do what they are "supposed" to do.

---

4. HE: *I don't want her telling me what to do.*
   SHE: *My God, anytime I ask him to do anything, he has a temper tantrum.*
   HE: *Every time my wife asks me to do something, I feel like a little boy. I hate that! I will not be ordered around by some woman.*

   Comment: Our society has taught men that their traditional role is to control and dominate women. Some men think this is a reaction to being dominated by their mothers. Others think this is part of an inherent male makeup.

---

5. HE: *I don't want to do it.*
   SHE: *He's lazy, mean, and uncaring.*
   HE: *When I come home from work, I'm exhausted. I don't want to do all that crap. Have I gone to college, gotten an M.B.A., and worked my way up in the firm to come home and do housework? No way! Besides, my wife can do all those things better than I can. I'm good at computers, not dishwashers.*

Comment: For generations, women have been providing men with care and services, and many men want no part of that traditional servantlike role.

---

6. HE: *I've got better things to do with my time.*
   SHE: *So do I, you chauvinist.*
   HE: *Listen, I'm taking care of this family pretty damn well. What do you want from me?*

   Comment: Many men put everything they have into their work because they feel so financially responsible. Even when their wives work, men feel that ultimately it is up to them to provide. As a consequence, they spend all their time working or preparing (mentally and physically) for work. Almost everything else seems irrelevant.

---

7. HE: *I just feel that too much is expected of me now.*
   SHE: *Too much of him! I'm the one who has to be a Superwoman!*
   HE: *This is really a difficult time to be a man. My wife is always asking me to change. I understand that she needs help with the house and the kids, but I don't think it's possible for me to meet all her expectations. When I don't, she gets angry and I get defensive.*

   Comment: While women are struggling with the issues of being Superwomen, many men are feeling the need to become Supermen in response. They too are feeling confused, angry, and helpless; but, having been trained by our society to suppress feelings and refuse to analyze them, men have more difficulty expressing these feelings.

8. HE: *That's not what I bargained for.*
   SHE: *You're just spoiled, that's all.*
   HE: *When my wife and I got married twenty years ago we had a set way of doing things. I went to work and brought home the money, and she stayed home and took care of the house and the kids. Now she wants to change things. I can't understand why she wants to go back to work—we certainly don't need the money. I certainly don't understand how in the world she could expect me to start doing housework.*

   Comment: The men who find it most difficult to start doing housework are probably those who are middle-aged, who have had their services and care provided without question for many years, and who have conservative ideas of what is appropriate for men and women to do. They are often surrounded by male friends and colleagues who see the world in the same way they do. They often express bewilderment and chagrin over the way things are now.

---

9. HE: *I don't care if it gets done. It's not important to me.*
   SHE: *He doesn't care about it and he doesn't care about me. He is the most self-centered, insensitive man I know.*
   HE: *Really, housework has no meaning for me. So what if the dishes don't get done today? So what if the furniture isn't vacuumed or the clothes aren't washed? They'll get done somehow—they always do. If my wife doesn't do it, we'll hire somebody who will.*

   Comment: Some men have no idea of what is involved in keeping a household running smoothly and how that relates to their quality of life. They are totally unaware of the organization, activities, and enormity of the work and the skills it requires. They protect themselves from doing the work if they don't know what it is; but some have been protected from it by never having been asked to participate.

---

10. **HE:** *I'd rather be sailing [or golfing or playing tennis].*
   SHE: *I can't believe him. In the middle of a thousand things to do he runs off to go sailing. Talk about irresponsible...*
   HE: *Look, I have to take care of myself. If I don't sail, I really get uptight and tense. If I stay that way I know I'm in for a collapse. My wife doesn't understand this at all. How can she? She doesn't take care of herself at all. She always thinks that when I'm playing or exercising I'm loafing. I don't even talk to her about it anymore.*

   Comment: Men do seem able to take better care of themselves physically than most women do. While sailing could be a way out of doing housework, it also represents, as the man above indicates, an important way for him to relax. When their health depends on it, men will go sailing rather than do housework, and that is often upsetting to women.

We're Asking for More than Just Housework

What does all this mean? We are not just asking men to do housework. Basically, we are asking them to change their sex-role behaviors and themselves. I think we are asking the men in our lives to do something that is frequently uncomfortable and disconcerting, sometimes threatening, and occasionally upsetting and even painful. This is not an easy task we have set for ourselves, nor is it one without consequences.

I don't want this information to dishearten you in your efforts to effect changes. On the contrary, my purpose is to let you know why—up to now—it may have seemed so difficult, and to help you formulate some ideas about how to do it more effectively in the future.

Whether your spouse is involved in housework probably will be determined by a number of factors:

- What kind of and how old a man he is
- What kind of and how old a woman you are
- The nature of your respective upbringings
- The types and stages of each of your careers
- Most important, what kind of relationship you have together

The older, the more conservative, the more traditional, the more insecure he is—the less likely he is to do housework. The more traditional, the more conservative, the less career oriented you are—the less likely he is to do housework. The more traditional his family was—his mother acting as housewife and his father acting as breadwinner and doing no housework—the less likely he is to do housework. The more involved he is in his career, the less likely he is to do housework. Finally, the more distant, noncommunicative, noninteractive, and tense the relationship is, the less likely he is to do housework. And the more these things are true, the less likely it is that he will change at all.

How to Get Him to Do More

Assess realistically what kind of man—and what kind of woman—you're dealing with. What is reasonable to expect? Remember all we have talked about previously with regard to change: that it's difficult, often resisted, best implemented in small, sequential steps, and needs to be rewarded. Remember too that change is most resisted when it is forced, expected, demanded, claimed, pushed, or threatened. Finally, remember that the circumstances under which it is *least likely* to occur are those involving anger, hostility, resentment, indignation, and antagonism, whether silent or spoken.

Rather than forcing men to change, which we can't do anyway, we need to elicit the changes; and that probably will involve our having to make some changes ourselves.

Here is my final advice about getting your spouse involved in housework:

First, I urge that *for you and for him,* buy as much outside help as you can afford. There is nothing inherently moral or good about either of you doing it.

Second, without getting angry, talk with him about housework, explain to him what is involved, show him the Household Activities List, ask him for help with solutions, and listen to what he has to say. You need to talk, negotiate, and then talk more. For many couples this is very difficult, but if you cannot talk with each other about housework, you really have no chance of solving the problems concerning it. If you cannot have differences about issues without painful stalemates, and if you cannot feel good about each other because of unresolved issues, perhaps housework is not *the* problem; perhaps having a less than open, communicative relationship is. You have to have a "real" relationship in order to deal with housework.

12

Playing the
Work Game and
Changing It Too

SHOE SALESMAN: *And what do you want to be when you grow up, little girl?*

LITTLE GIRL: *A mommy.*

MANY OF US grew up thinking that way. Our concept of what it would be like in the adult world was built around a fantasy of one day meeting Prince Charming, marrying him in a beautiful wedding ceremony, becoming a mommy to his darling children, letting him take care of us, and living happily ever after. Even those of us who didn't end up living exactly according to that scenario somehow still expect it to happen.

We didn't think much then about jobs and careers outside the home. The work-force statistics of the 1950s reflected those attitudes. In 1950, our population was 151 million. At that time there were 64 million people in the work force, of which 18.4 million (or 29 percent) were women.

Now, however—just over thirty years later—jobs and careers are very much on our minds. And the statistics reflect these concerns. Our population is 226.5 million; the total labor force is 105 million, and women hold 44.6 million (or 43 percent) of those positions. Well over half of the 86 million women age sixteen and over—52 percent—are employed.[1]

Further, the Urban Institute predicts that by 1990, 70 percent of all women between the ages of sixteen and fifty-four will work outside the home.[2] An article on working women in the *Los Angeles Herald Examiner* predicted: Today's young women are likely to spend thirty or more years in the paid work force. A married woman with no children will work an estimated thirty-five years. A mother of two will work twenty-two years. Even women with four or more children will spend seventeen years in paid jobs. *Only one out of ten women will never work outside the home.*[3]

Most women work outside the home because of economic need, yet our earning power is unimpressive. To illustrate this point, here are some recent statistics on women's annual salaries: 60 percent of all working women earn less than $10,000 a year; 33 percent of full-time working women earn less than $7,000 a year; only 1 percent of all working women earn over $25,000 a year.[4] In contrast, 50 percent of all working men earn at least $15,000 a year, and 11 percent of all working men earn $25,000 or more a year.[5] Women earn only 62 cents to a man's dollar.[6]

Even more significant are the facts and figures about women and poverty. Fifty percent of widows and single women live in poverty. Seventy-five percent of poor people in the United States are women and children. Five percent of families headed by men are at the poverty level, but in families headed by women, a staggering 25 percent live in poverty. Along those lines, you may be interested to know that 50 percent of all children can expect to live in one-parent homes at some time during their childhood.[7]

WHY DO WOMEN EARN LESS?

Why are the earning capacities of women so bleak? Part of it has to do with the Prince Charming fantasy. Many of us never expected to have to work. Therefore, unlike men, we didn't think about it, plan for it, or prepare for it, especially as a lifelong endeavor.

Then, once we did go into the work force, the vast majority of us—80 percent—moved into the female ghettos of clerical, services, retail sales, factory, or plant work. These positions represent only 20 of the 420 listed occupational categories, and their wages are significantly lower than those of the categories dominated by male workers. In short, most women work in underpaid, dead-end jobs.[8]

Another factor is that we are "foreigners" in the male work world. This was first pointed out by economist James March when he observed that women enter the male work world as immigrants with all the respective accoutrements of low status, low pay, and low power.[9]

Jessie Bernard has also noted that, like the European immigrants to the United States, women bring their "old-country ways" from the female world to the male work world. They stand out from the normal male employee in looks, actions, and attitudes. Like immigrants, women often remain segregated with their "own kind" not only in female-dominated occupations but in stereotypical female jobs. Many who move into male-dominated occupations or typical male jobs feel uncomfortable and vulnerable. Further, they have to learn to speak and read a new business language and figure out the meaning of all the gestures, nuances, and understandings that the male "natives" take for granted.[10]

Natasha Josefowitz points out that women in the male work world also have to deal with the double bind of playing the game according to the rules, while being punished for trying to do just that.[11] In her poem "Good Management Potential," Josefowitz very aptly describes the frustration of dealing with this double bind:

GOOD MANAGEMENT POTENTIAL

If I'm assertive,
I'm seen as aggressive.
If I'm aggressive,
I'm a bitch.
I won't be promoted.
Let's try it again.
If I'm nonassertive,
I'm seen as a patsy.
If I'm a patsy,
I won't be promoted.
Let's try it once more.
If I'm very careful,
I can go unnoticed.
If I'm unnoticed,
No one will know
I want to be promoted.
Any suggestions?[12]

Nastasha Josefowitz,
Is This Where I Was Going?

Thus, most of us didn't anticipate spending much time working outside the home, particularly while we were raising young children. We didn't plan or train for long-term participation in the work force; nor did we expect to support or help support ourselves and our families. We never thought much about functioning or competing in the work culture, except in limited ways. But today's economic and cultural realities bespeak a different kind of orientation. As a contemporary woman of this age, it is likely that

• we will spend a good part of our adult lives in the work force
• we will need to support ourselves and/or help to support our families
• we will work in environments created by men, operated

on policies and procedures developed by and for them, reflecting their ways of seeing and doing things

What we can do is to learn to play the work game, and, having accomplished that, we can then begin changing it to better meet our needs.

PLAYING THE WORK GAME

The first thing we can do to play the work game is to stop thinking about our work as "jobs." Jobs involve merely "being hired for a given service or period."[13] All the evidence points to women being in the work world for the majority of their adult lives. Like men, we need to think about our work in career terms. A career involves "a profession for which one trains and which is undertaken as a permanent calling ... with consecutive progressive achievements."[14] Even if you are a volunteer, you can think about the career implications of what you are doing in terms of gaining knowledge, skills, access, or experience. More than anything else, a career orientation involves a way of thinking about what you can do now to help you prepare for your future work.

The second thing we can do to play the work game is to know who we are, where we want to go, and what we must have and do to get there.

So, you say to me, how do I find out these things? Essentially, those are career-planning questions that are answered by going through a career-planning process. Career planning is simply a process of *articulating who you are as a person*— your background, your abilities, your interests, your personal characteristics, and your needs and preferences—*matching that with an occupation,* and *developing strategies for advancing in that occupation.* At the beginning of a career, it will help you to know what to do and how to choose a career that matches your needs and abilities. At the middle, it will help you to know if you are keeping on track and accomplishing what you set out to do. At the end of the career, you should be able to reap the benefits from all the years of careful planning. You can also use the techniques to phase out of work and phase into retirement activities.

For those of you who need assistance with your career-planning process, here are some places where you are likely to receive it: the Catalyst National Network of Career Resource Centers;* Government Employee Development offices; your employer's personnel office; your college or university's career-planning office; adult education/university extension courses and workshops; women's centers; private counseling services; women's organizations such as the YWCA. It is important that you take a good look at a program or service before involving yourself, particularly if you are paying for it. Find out before you enroll (1) what is involved; (2) who is offering it and what their credentials are; and (3) what past participants or clients think about the program or service.

The third thing we must do in playing the work game is to become aware of how certain Superwoman characteristics cause us problems in the workplace. Throughout this book we have seen how these characteristics affect us in the personal arena; now let us see how they affect us at work.

SUPERWOMAN CHARACTERISTICS CAUSE US PROBLEMS AT WORK

I. **SUPERWOMAN CHARACTERISTIC:** You are a very nice woman. You are people oriented, supportive, and nurturing.
   SOURCE: Internal

---

*The Catalyst Network is a group of 175 independent resource centers located in thirty-one states and three foreign countries that provide career and educational counseling and programs for individuals who wish to advance in their careers, change fields, or reenter the job market. A list of these centers can be obtained by writing to Catalyst, 14 East 60th Street, New York, NY 10022.

FEELINGS:

"Above all, I must be nice."

"I can't stand it when people don't like me."

"No matter what, in my office I want an atmosphere of caring and warmth."

"I want people to feel that I am accessible to them, available for support."

BEHAVIORS:

You have an open-door policy. Anyone can come in "to talk" at any time.

You allow a salesperson to use up a whole morning.

You are always available to "pitch in."

You allow other people's needs and problems to get in the way of your work.

In *Paths to Power*, Natasha Josefowitz says that "women are twice as accessible as men in similar positions." Further, the women in her study not only made themselves available to employees, colleagues, and clients, they even "left their offices more often to go and see if they could be helpful."[15]

As I have said many times there is nothing wrong with being nice, caring, supportive, or nurturing. The world needs more of these behaviors. However, problems arise when you allow such behaviors to control what you really want and need to do; problems develop when these behaviors inhibit your ability to work effectively. You end up feeling resentful when your work suffers because you take care of someone else's needs instead of your own. Chapter 10, "Better Manage Your Time— It's All You Have," is filled with suggestions about how to deal with people interruptions. If "nice behavior" is a problem for you at work, refer to that chapter.

II. **SUPERWOMAN CHARACTERISTIC:** You are very hardworking, yet you never have enough time to do what you would like to do.

   SOURCE: Internal

FEELINGS:

"I am being 'good' when I work."

"I'll relax later."

"I feel anxious unless I am working hard all the time."

"I must keep busy."

BEHAVIORS:

You work while you eat lunch (or eat lunch while you work).

Your calendar is cluttered with unending appointments and things to do.

You don't exercise or take time to relax.

Everything must fill a "work" purpose.

You work in the evenings, on weekends, and on holidays, and you expect others to do the same.

You find it difficult to enjoy vacations.

While it is true that some women have to work harder than their male colleagues in order to be taken seriously, others are nothing less than workaholics. In her book on the subject, Marilyn Machlowitz says that a workaholic is someone who is "a slave to a set schedule, merciless in [her] demands upon [herself] for peak performance . . . compulsively overcommitted."[16] Workaholics tend to work harder, not smarter.

Michael LeBoeuf says that workaholism often develops as a result of myths: "The more you sweat, the more you get" and "Activity means productivity." Regarding these myths, he says that much is made of hard work and success, but "hard work and failure occur just as often." Further, "many of us habitually confuse activity with results . . . it's not enough to be busy; rather, the question is what are we busy about." LeBoeuf suggests that one can beat the activity trap by setting goals and staying focused on them.[17]

Productivity expert Charles Garfield agrees: "Workaholics are addicted to work, not results . . . they work for work's sake and tend not to make a major impact. The workaholic never makes the discovery, writes the position paper, or becomes the chief executive officer." The real achiever, according to Garfield, "has a passionate commitment to work, but also knows how to relax, how to delegate activity, and how to surround himself with competent people."[18]

III. **SUPERWOMAN CHARACTERISTIC:** You are very detail conscious.
SOURCE: Internal
FEELINGS:
"I must be thorough and complete."
"I must keep things perfectly in order."
"I must have all the information before I go on."
BEHAVIORS:
You read every word in every report.
You spend a lot of time keeping files and reports orderly and neat.
You complete perfectly projects that are of little importance.
You spend hours writing addresses in your new address book.

As indicated in the Superwoman Quiz, sometimes a focus on finishing details makes a very positive difference. But very often this same mania for details will deter you from working on what is important. It will keep you busy but not effective.

If you have a predilection for working on details, you may have to retrain yourself. The higher you rise in an organization, the more general your skills will have to be. Secretaries deal with minutae; executives deal with long-range plans. Sometimes we fail to notice an opportunity to move up because we are so bogged down by the little things.

IV. **SUPERWOMAN CHARACTERISTIC:** You are short-term-response oriented.
SOURCE: Internal
FEELINGS:
"I get so distracted."
"I don't really know where I'm going."

"My life feels chaotic."

"I'm always running into people and things that need to be taken care of."

BEHAVIORS:

You move from one emergency to another.

You let whatever and whomever control your life.

You solve problems as they occur rather than anticipate them.

As young girls many of us were not taught how to set goals, how to plan for the future, how to determine our priorities, or how to commit to a course of action without being distracted. These skills are essential in the work world.

Margaret Hennig and Anne Jardim say that men set priorities; women try to do everything equally well. Men also plan ahead; women tend to concentrate on the present. They say that men decide on a goal and go after it; women wait to be chosen.[19] In an article in *New West* magazine, these highly respected management professors said that "contrary to the old cliché that women are more sensitive to others . . . in business it is the men who are aware of others and who adjust their behavior accordingly. Women are so concerned about their own work they often fail to notice what's going on around them. They miss warning signals, stop signs, and—worst of all—green lights."[20]

In predicting America's business future, the author of *Megatrends*, John Naisbitt, says that long-term planning is one of the ten most important orientations we can have in order to have a healthy future.[21]

Chapter 9, "Who Is Important, What Is Essential in Your Life?" shows how one sets goals and determines priorities. If you need help in planning ahead, refer to that chapter.

V. **SUPERWOMAN CHARACTERISTIC:** You are a perfectionist.

    SOURCE: Internal

    FEELINGS:

"I must be perfect in everything I do."

"I am never satisfied with what I do."
"I can't make a mistake."
"If I don't keep at it, I'll lose everything I've gained."
BEHAVIORS:
You keep close watch on everything you do; you play it safe rather than take risks.
You do it because others won't do it as well.
You have extraordinarily high standards for yourself.

Meyer Friedman and Ray Rosenthal, the men who made Type A personalities so famous, suggest that achievement-oriented males pay for their personality type with increased susceptibility to psychosomatic diseases, such as high blood pressure and heart disease.[22] Perfectionism—a predisposition to accept in yourself nothing less than excellence—is a major characteristic of Type A behavior and is legend among Superwomen.

When things go wrong, Superwomen tend to blame themselves. Theirs is an internal response—it's as if "they are what went wrong." They loathe themselves and their deficiencies. However, when things go wrong for men, they are less likely to personalize their dilemma. Often men place the blame on external sources—the situation, another person, or their bosses.

If we look first to ourselves for what is wrong in any situation, no wonder we have such high standards. No wonder we try to maintain control of projects and tasks. No wonder we don't take risks. We are so quick to feel responsible, to take the blame for whatever goes wrong around us, that we tend to play it safe.

Charles Garfield says that this is exactly the opposite of what peak performers do. "The peak performer is not a perfectionist. Perfection is an illusion and the top performer knows this. He or she tends to see the perfectionist as paralyzed by unrealistically high standards. The people [he talked] to were not so much interested in perfection as in doing the best job they could."[23]

Garfield also says that "peak performers have learned to take risks confidently by rationally considering and assessing all significant outcomes," and that they "continually attempt and often succeed at surpassing their own previous levels of accomplishment [not those of others]."[24]

What can you do to curb your desire to be perfect? First, stop being your own worst critic. Although it may be uncomfortable, begin saying good things about yourself. Reward and reinforce those things that you do well. Look to yourself, not to others, for approval. Second, begin to think about constructive criticism in a different light. Rather than seeing it as an indictment of you as a person, see it for what it is—feedback about an action or a part of your work. Finally, focus more on what helps you to feel good or confident. As we have seen throughout the book, Superwomen tend to neglect themselves. Don't do that anymore! At the very least, take some preliminary steps to be good to yourself. It's in your employer's best interest too.

VI. **SUPERWOMAN CHARACTERISTIC:** You have difficulty saying no to anyone.
   SOURCE: Internal
   FEELINGS:
   "If I say no, he won't like me."
   "If I say no, I may not get promoted."
   "If I say no, I'll be seen as a slouch."
   "If I say no, I'll make waves."
   BEHAVIORS:
   You say yes to all requests for your time and energy.
   You accept all invitations.

Girls were told that "it's not nice to say no." They were also taught not to express negative feelings, not to reject, refuse, criticize, challenge, or dismiss. On the other hand, boys were taught to do all those things so they could promote themselves in the work world.

In order to be effective, we must learn some new ways, the most important of which is to say no. In chapter 10 we outline in detail how to say no and when to say yes. Saying no is one of a number of skills involved in being an assertive person. If you find this area difficult, refer to one of the books on assertiveness listed in the bibliography, or take a class. It's not easy to change behavior, but any attempt you make to feel better about yourself will result in increased self-respect and respect from those around you.

VII. **SUPERWOMAN CHARACTERISTIC:** You find it difficult to delegate tasks.
   SOURCE: Internal
   FEELINGS:
   "I'd rather do it myself."
   "I don't want to impose on anyone."
   "I don't like to be told what to do—why should I tell someone else what to do?"
   BEHAVIORS:
   You do it, rather than delegate it.
   You redo it when someone else does it incorrectly.
   You finish it when someone else doesn't.

Superwomen have great difficulty in delegating tasks or responsibilities. Either they feel they should do it themselves or they are afraid to let someone else do it because it might not be done well enough to meet their standards. They worry before they delegate, and they feel guilty.

Many Superwomen end up doing a lot of extra work as they begin to supervise others. They pick up the pieces left by subordinates; they scrupulously check everything that leaves their department. Unknowingly, the Superwoman conveys a message to those who work for her: "I know best; I don't trust you." Obviously, this is not a particularly effective way of leading staff. It breeds dependence and resentment.

Garfield says that peak performers are "masters of delegation."[25] This is consistent with the requirements for upward mobility. Entry-level jobs often require one to be very good at some specific skills. But as you move into higher positions, you need to depend increasingly on others to get things done for you.

In chapter 11 we discussed delegating tasks within the home. These same techniques apply in the work situation. What do you have to lose by trying to delegate?

VIII. **SUPERWOMAN CHARACTERISTIC:** You don't feel very good about yourself.

    SOURCE: Internal

    FEELINGS:

    "I wish I were smarter."

    "They are better than I am."

    "I'm not as strong as I could be."

    "I can't do that."

    BEHAVIORS:

    You hold yourself back.

    You act shy.

    You apologize to others for your deficiencies.

    You act on others' needs, not your own.

In a recent issue of *Marriage and Divorce Today,* Dr. Christina Banks of the University of Texas identified self-confidence as the single most important personality trait a woman must have to be a successful leader in a profession, business, or community.[26]

Charles Garfield says that after commitment, self-confidence is the most important trait of a high performer.[27]

How does a woman gain self-confidence? It's not easy. Consider that we live in a world that calls women "the weaker sex" and where little boys grow up thinking girls are inferior and second-class. Add to this the fact that many of us had traditional parents who thought their job was to point out all our deficiencies. Also, many of us learned that to be a "good" person we should feel guilty and worry about everything all the time. Given all this, it's a wonder women have any self-confidence.

Building your self-confidence is the key to increased effectiveness in your work world. How do you do that? Here are some beginning steps.

1. *Know who you are as a person.* It is much easier to like yourself when you know what there is to like. Because we spent so many years focusing on what other people like and want, many of us have forgotten about our own preferences. Write down something about your abilities, your interests, your personal characteristics, your needs, and your preferences. Pay attention to that complex, interesting, dynamic person who lives inside you.

2. *Focus on your strengths.* Every woman's image of herself is a mixture of positive and negative aspects. Most of us dwell on the negative, which serves only to bring down our confidence. So, draw up a list of your positive traits. Read them aloud to yourself every day. Despite the popular belief that thoughts come from feelings, just the opposite is true. Feelings follow thoughts. Therefore, if you want to feel confident, it is important that you begin thinking more positively about yourself.

3. *Surround yourself with people who build your confidence.* Most of us have relatives, friends, or colleagues who like us and make us feel good. Spend time with these people rather than with those who put you down. You have control over whom you spend time with. Use the techniques offered in chapter 10 to make sure you have time to do this.

4. *Look around you at the women who appear self-confident and act like them.* Notice that self-confident people stand tall; they walk, talk, and look in confident ways. Women who are not confident often say to me, "If I could just feel confident, I would be able to do all that." But I say to them, "Feelings often follow effective actions." For now, concentrate on self-confident actions; the feelings will come later.

No one controls your thoughts, your feelings, or your actions, except you. Only you can begin to control the circumstances that will lead to your having more self-confidence. It's in your hands.

IX. **SUPERWOMAN CHARACTERISTIC:** You don't take very good care of yourself.

SOURCE: Internal

FEELINGS:

"I'll exercise when this project is over."

"I'll begin eating better when things get under control at the office."

"I'll stop smoking when my calendar is less hectic."

"I'll relax when I finish school."

BEHAVIORS:

You eat on the run.

You don't exercise regularly.

You work rather than relax on the weekends.

You never stop pushing yourself.

You have difficulty sleeping.

Successful women are healthy women. They take care of themselves. In Garfield's research on peak performers, he found they were healthier than the average person—and for good reasons. They know that when they are tired or under mental stress they are less efficient. Peak performers are never "too busy" for relaxation and exercise. Garfield says that by investing time in fitness, high performers actually save time.

You also must eat well. A diet that is low in fat, salt, and sugar; high in complex carbohydrates (fruits, vegetables, grains); and moderate in animal protein (fish and chicken) will not only help you keep trim, but will help you feel more energetic.

X. **SUPERWOMAN CHARACTERISTIC:** You don't feel that you have any control over your life.

SOURCE: Internal and external

FEELINGS:

"I feel hopeless about my work situation."

"I'm in a rut."

"There's no relief in sight."

"I deserve a promotion—why doesn't it happen?"

BEHAVIORS:
You live your life the same every day.
You don't try anything new.
You complain a lot about the state of things.
You wait to be chosen or appreciated.

There are both internal and external barriers to women's succeeding in the workplace. Researchers Anne Harlan and Carol Weiss of the Wellesley College Center for Research on Women have noted that the issue seems no longer to be "getting in." Most corporations have made great strides in identifying and breaking down barriers to entry into management. Rather, they suggest that the challenge today is in identifying and eliminating barriers that prevent women's advancement.

In their three-year study comparing women's and men's advancement in management they found the following:

> The extent of similarities between men and women managers was far greater than predicted. Both sexes revealed profiles of high power and achievement drives, good self-esteem, and strong motivation to manage. However, equal proportions of men and women also experienced problems and barriers usually considered to limit only women's advancement such as unfocused career plans, dead-end or blocked career paths, and limited access to mentors.
>
> Women managers experienced sex bias in a number of both subtle and overt forms including stereotypic attitudes, greater pressure on women to perform exceptionally well, some exclusion from particular managerial positions, overprotection from supervisors and peers, and inappropriate sexual remarks.[28]

Let us talk about the former—unfocused career plans, dead-end or blocked career paths, and limited access to mentors—and what to do about them.

WORK GOALS

Many women feel that if they do a good job, that is enough. They think that someone above them will not only notice their work but appreciate and reward them for it with praise and promotions. Unfortunately, that is not the way it "works" in the work world. In order to get praise and promotions you have to plan for them. You have to develop strategies to get them. You have to make success happen for you.

In order to advance and be successful in your occupation you must know where you want to be. Above all, you must have work goals.

In chapter 8 I defined goals and listed step-by-step procedures for following through on them. If you recall, we followed the social worker Myra in the pursuit of her career goals. I won't repeat here what those procedures are. The major questions you want to answer in setting your career goals are: What do I want to be doing in five or ten years? What do I want to be earning in that time? How will the answers to these questions affect my lifestyle? What must I do to get to that place?

DEVELOPING A CAREER PATH AND FINDING MODELS TO FOLLOW

A career path includes all the intermediary positions and experiences leading to work goals or a particular position. All of us have career paths, whether or not we are aware of it. Some are sedentary, providing little advancement; others are fast-moving, providing both career advancement and success.

If you want your career path to be of the latter type, perhaps the best thing to do is to take a look at the women and men ahead of you to see what paths they have taken. Look for some models of success. Pay particular attention to the women ahead of you, because their paths may be closer to yours than those of men in the company. If your job area or company does not have women in positions higher than yours, go outside your area. Seek role models through colleagues, women's-network groups, anywhere and anyplace where you think they might be found.

Once you have found a good role model, make a point of meeting her. Ask her for information; find out what choices she has made, what skills and abilities she has, the process for promotion she has used. Notice everything about her—how she acts, how she talks, whom she knows, how she spends her time, what organizations she joins. If you want to develop a successful career path, study her success.

Another way of examining successful career paths is to read about them. Magazines and newspapers are filled with information about high-achieving professionals. Read these articles and extract what seems relevant to you and your situation. Recently, many books have come out on women and success. Some of the better ones are listed in the bibliography.

Once you have determined what is involved in creating a career path that will lead you to your goals, begin acting on that information immediately. Decide which activities and people will lead you to those goals. Use all the planning and time-management techniques discussed in this book. Focus on what is most important and relevant to getting you where you want to go.

In order to play the work game, you must become the most credentialed, knowledgeable, skilled employee you can be. That means:

1. *Finding out what the top educational requirements are in your occupation and making specific plans to attain them.* Do you need an M.B.A.? An M.A.? A Ph.D.? A certain level of competency or certification? A license? What do you need to reach the top of your profession?

2. *Learning about the professional organizations in your occupation and how one affiliates with them; when and where local, regional, and national meetings are held; what publications or newsletters are available.* For example, if you are

a new manager in the personnel department of your company, you will probably want to know about the American Management Association, the American Association of Training and Development, the Organizational Development Network, and the Employment Management Association. Are there local chapters in your area? If so, find out which are the strongest. If not, at least subscribe to a publication or newsletter. If you want to become more professional, become a part of your chosen field's professional group. Keeping up with the people and information that are the "state of the art" in your profession can only help you to do a better job.

3. *Absorbing as much as you can about your company or organization.* It is easy to lose sight of what is happening in your company when you are involved in your own productivity. In order to advance, however, you must know about things beyond your job and even beyond your department. You need to know about your company. Does it have an annual report? Have you read it? If you have difficulty understanding what it says, have someone explain it to you. Find out how your company is organized. Who are the principal people and what do they do? What is your department and how does it relate to other departments? What do other departments and the people in them do? How does your company compare to others in the field? Who are the competitors? Which companies are considered the best in the field? Why? Where are they located? Let your natural curiosity be your guide in this information search. The knowledge you gain should be not only interesting but useful in representing yourself as a knowledgeable, promotable employee.

4. *Gaining job skills through in-service training programs, working with a supportive boss or colleague, and attending "outside" educational courses or workshops.* You must have the knowledge and skills necessary to do the job you have been hired to do. But you also must learn general management skills if you want to progress.

The Catalyst organization suggests that you learn how to

communicate, plan, organize, negotiate, and delegate.[29] Natasha Josefowitz says that effective managers must, above all, be able to "read, write, count, and speak in public."[30] John Naisbitt agrees. He says that more than ever we must have basic reading and writing skills.[31] He also urges workers to become computer literate, since 75 percent of all jobs by 1985 will involve computers in some way.[32]

Finally, Peter Drucker gives the following as the five practices one can learn to be an effective executive:

- Know where your time goes.
- Gear your efforts to results rather than to work.
- Build your effectiveness and the effectiveness of those around you on strengths, not weaknesses.
- Set your priorities and stay with these priority decisions.
- Know the right steps in the right sequence to make effective decisions.[33]

5. *Becoming an expert on the male work world by observing, identifying, and learning appropriate behaviors for the work world.*

6. *Developing a system of female contacts within and outside your organization to provide you support, information, advice, contacts, and access.*

7. *Establishing a personal attitude that there isn't any problem, situation, or task you can't handle, because if you can't solve it, handle it, or deal with it now, you have the personal resources to find out how to do it later.*

Once you begin to play the work game effectively, while gaining power and authority, you can begin to change some of the rules of the game to make your life and the lives of other women less difficult. I know this can happen.

Some years ago my husband and I gave a talk on two-career couples at Stanford University. About six months after the talk I received a call from a young woman who had just graduated from Stanford. She said, "You don't know me, but I heard your talk on two-career couples last May. I was a student then. I am now a computer programmer at [a large midwestern organization], and I just want you to know that when I get to a position where I can have a say in what goes on here, I'd love to invite you and your husband to come and speak about two-career couples. Would you?"

Two years later I received a call from the same young woman. "Hi, remember me?" she said. "I'm in a position to invite you now." Mort and I were invited to speak—and we did so. We were then invited back to train managers on issues relating to two-career couples. That company now has a two-career-couple club; a child-care-resource person; changes in policy and procedures regarding sick leave for parents of ill children; and a few other changes—all because of one woman's efforts.

You *can* make a difference. You can make changes in an organization that will help not only you but other women and men employees who are concerned about their roles as family members. The following are possible changes you can make.

CHANGING THE WORK GAME

Most policies and procedures operating in the work world today are designed to meet male needs, the male life calendar, and male time schedules. In many cases, the *employee* is viewed as being male, a sole wage earner who has a wife to support him emotionally at home. Females are regarded as exceptions to the rule.

Antinepotism

Antinepotism policies prevent members of the same family from being hired by the same company. Further, conflict-of-interest policies prohibit their hiring someone whose spouse works for a rival firm. According to a Catalyst survey of the top thirteen hundred corporations, 82 percent of the responding companies do not forbid husband and wife to work at the same company, but 72 percent exclude the possibility of a couple's working in the same department![34] The danger in an antinepotism policy is that the hiring, firing, promotion, and position of employees can be made on the basis of sex. More and more couples are procuring educations together, choosing similar careers, and meeting each other at places of employment. They will encounter problems if the antinepotism policy is not eliminated.

Child Care

The 1981 Economic Recovery Tax Act allows an employer who provides child care to declare these expenses as ordinary and necessary business expenses. Employees who receive this benefit are not required to report the amount received as taxable income. Employers are free to provide child care in any one of three ways:

- An on-site daycare center
- Payment to an off-site center
- Reimbursement for dependent care services (baby-sitters or housekeepers)

Since women comprise nearly half the work force, we are in a position to demand and expect an employee package that includes child care. Tremendous stress can result from trying to work and parent at the same time. In addition, when a mother takes a job, a primary consideration is always child care. How competent is it? How close? How dependable? How expensive? This consideration is just as important as salary.

Mothers who work and whose employers assist with child care are absent fewer times, change jobs less often, enjoy their jobs more, and are more productive.

Transfer Policies

Companies should provide ample time for consideration and planning of a transfer. The careers of both spouses must be taken into account. If a transfer is requested, the company should assist in the transfer of the other employed spouse.

Whether your career mandates a move or your spouse's does, you have a right to request and receive time to decide and assistance for both of you; you also have the right to refuse the move if relocation disadvantages outweigh advantages. It is no longer a matter of Mary packing up the kids and the house to follow John across the country.

Now it is Mary and John examining both careers, both possibilities for advancement, both incomes. Unless companies go out of their way to assist, transfers will be rejected, talent lost, and productivity decreased. Additionally, travel expectations must include awareness of family responsibilities. No one is going to last long in a job that requires airport shuttling every other week.

Flexible Hours

Nearly six thousand European companies are on flextime, as compared with about ninety thousand federal employees and a few hundred private companies in the United States. Flextime means that within limits set by management an employee can choose starting and quitting times. Thus, "morning" people who produce most from seven till noon are free to do just that; "evening" people are encouraged to do their work at their peak-energy hours. Flexible hours provide wider options for child care and for two-career couples, reduced stress, fewer parking and traffic problems, less absenteeism, decreased turnover, improved morale, more time for family and recreational activities, less wasted time at work, and more time for continuing-education programs. There have been so many studies, reports, and trials over the past several years that most analysts, planners, and corporations predict flextime as both inevitable and essential for today's family. Consolidated Edison, Digital Equipment Corporation, Massachusetts Mutual Life, and Equitable Life Assurance Society are among the companies that provide successful flextime options.

Part-Time Employment*

Many companies and many employees report that part-time employment is more productive and more satisfying than full-time employment.[35] Options include

- one or more people working part-time at one job ("job sharing")
- work performed partly at home, partly in an office (obvious advantages for child care)
- consulting work on special projects as required (paid by the hour)
- a position with one person doing the "heavy" professional tasks, and one doing the "light" clerical work

Companies willing to incorporate such options will find increasing numbers of talented and qualified men and women seeking employment, staying longer, and working more effectively.

*The National Network for Work Time Options is a consortium of 20 groups around the country promoting permanent part-time employment, job sharing and other alternative work schedules. For futher information contact New Ways to Work, 149 North Street, San Francisco, CA 94103.

In-Service Training

Companies should offer counseling and information referral services for two-career couples, and for transfer complications, stress reduction, time management, parenting and working conflicts, and financial and legal problems. If companies take more responsibility for the well-being of their employees, far fewer problems will arise at the job and at home. When employees are offered lunchtime seminars or on-the-job classes addressing familiar complaints and problems, the employees feel more valued and not so overwhelmed.

Cafeteria Benefits

Cafeteria-compensation plans allow employees a selection of benefit packages that most closely meet personal needs. Options are available in the areas of life insurance, maternity benefits, medical coverage, educational subsidies, vacations, investments, and retirement annuities. Employees must have the ability to make meaningful choices about their careers and, within those careers, the benefits and services that contribute to lives and jobs that work.

Leave Options

There are various kinds of leave options: maternity leave, paternity leave, sick leave, and leave to attend to sick children.

While sick leave is taken for granted and maternity leaves are common, paternity leave and leave to attend to sick children are not. Some of the changes we must work for in this are (1) maternity and paternity leaves that allow employee parents to spend six months to a year with their newborns without fear for their jobs or loss of upward mobility in the organization; (2) sick leaves for parents and/or stepparents to respond to children's physical and emotional needs; (3) sick leave to care for elderly parents.

The time has arrived for employers, who are often parents themselves, to recognize the need for these organizational changes. Workers—male and female alike—can no longer afford to choose companies that neglect family concerns, employee well-being, and flexible options. The upwardly mobile, educated, competent employee will seek those corporations that provide the perquisites that distinguish one job from another.

Epilogue

Where Do We Go from Here?

IT'S IMPORTANT for us, individually and collectively, to get the Superwoman Syndrome under control, because we are, in a sense, pioneers on the frontier of a changing world. We must anticipate what the future will be for women, for men, for relationships and families, and for society in general so that we can plan for the future without fear and be ready to adapt.

WHAT DO THE FUTURISTS SAY?

First, they predict that only one out of ten women will *never* work outside the home. That means you and your daughters should prepare for careers even if you plan to be wives and mothers. In fact, by 1990, 40 percent of family income will be contributed by wives. The "traditional family" will be eclipsed by such arrangements as families with a female head or those with a male head with children from a previous marriage or marriages. Not only is divorce becoming more acceptable, but staying single, postponing marriage, and "living together" will increasingly become alternatives to early marriage.

Divorce is changing the way men relate to their children. With mothers no longer present when divorced fathers have to cope with their children, men are faced with new dilemmas.

Sometimes they back out of their children's lives because they can't handle the new responsibilities. Others are becoming more sensitive and spontaneous as they learn how to communicate with their children. This is a problem that will grow, because it is expected that by 1990, 27 percent of all children will live with a single parent—3 percent with their fathers and 24 percent with their mothers. More women are going to wait to become mothers until after the age of thirty-five, especially since postponing motherhood appears not to be harmful for babies or mothers.

As the children of the baby boom move into successful work positions, the changes that have been taking place will intensify. There will be fewer children per family, and the mothers will be more career oriented. They will be better educated and more aware politically, and they'll pressure both congress and employers to provide for child care. And—more good news— the number of American households with incomes of $50,000 or more (1980 dollars) will triple by the mid-1990s.

WHAT ABOUT THE CULTURAL TRENDS?

Provided that we don't blow ourselves up or go into a worldwide depression, we face a better future. Our society will place less emphasis on material things and equate success more with personal fulfillment. There will be more equality of work roles between the sexes. "The good life" will be a goal for more people who will be concerned with ecological issues and health and who have a conviction that there is more to life than working. At work, a new breed of employee will be demanding options in working time, in retirement plans, and in job tasks, and choices about when to work, when to learn, when to take leisure time, and when to retire, rather than following a set schedule.

So, it seems that the changes we have been dealing with in our lives are only the beginning, and, as we all know now, we women cannot handle everything ourselves. Striving to be

Superwomen is not the answer. Throughout this book, I've urged you to talk with your husband or partner, sharing your expectations and his, because the changes to come must be faced together. That is what my husband, Mort, and I decided to do with this last chapter: discuss the future. Because we counsel couples and families, what we say reflects the problems and solutions being worked out by them. Because we are man and woman, husband and wife, father and mother, our personal attitudes are bound to surface. Of course, what follows is edited conversation, but we have not deleted the emotional reactions that are part of relationships. Here are our feelings as well as our thoughts.

WHAT WE SEE FOR THE FUTURE

MARJORIE: During the writing of this book, I've felt as though I had to focus on negative aspects of the changes in our lives, but as I reached the concluding chapters, I began to feel that good things were going to come out of this rough, transitional time—for both men and women.

MORT: What do you mean?

MARJORIE: I think we're moving toward healthier ways of living, both for men and women. It's no secret that women feel more confident and better about themselves as people when they have the recognition that goes with succeeding in a job outside the home. And men should be freer to enjoy life outside work if they don't have to bear that "forever and ever" financial responsibility they've been carrying.

MORT: It's true that men don't want to work as hard, and they do look positively toward their partners' contributions; but even with working wives, they still feel that the financial responsibility is one that they own. They'd like to reduce the pressure of the load; they don't want to be sick or dead by the time they're forty-five. They want to get more out of life from friends, wives, and children, but what they don't want is to trade one set of stresses for another. They don't want to come home from work and begin working again at all the chores their working wives used to do. Especially, they don't want to do what women tell them to do.

MARJORIE: Then how do you think women should handle the problem?

MORT: First, I think men are tired of being labeled "the problem." They're tired of hearing that they aren't changing. They have changed and they are changing. They see the results of stress in their lives; even the companies they work for see it. Companies find that when men lead more-balanced lives, they are more productive. The men I talk to just don't want women to tell them what the problem is, what the solution is, and what they're supposed to do about it.

MARJORIE: That male power-dominance thing is coming through, isn't it? Hearing constantly that you are a problem destroys a man's self-confidence and makes him angry. I guess one of the things we women need to work on is how to get messages across without making men angry with us. That probably means we're going to have to be more direct, more honest, less complaining, and less manipulative.

MORT: You said complaining and manipulative; I didn't. I think you're going to get into trouble with women if you label them that way.

MARJORIE: I'm not calling them that, but because of our unique training, we've learned to get our needs met indirectly, because somehow the message has been that it's not nice or ladylike to get them met any other way.

MORT: As it happens, the workplace may be the place where women learn how to do that. Part of what management training is all about is effective communication. Like the woman you described who wouldn't think of waiting for her secretary to become aware on her own that she needs to type a letter, but who waits for her family to decide to help her at home—perhaps if she brought some of her management skills home, things would be different. Women are learning how to solve problems, how to say what they want, how to get their needs met at the workplace. Interestingly, learning how to develop good relationships at work might help them to have better relationships at home. This is true for men, too. Another thing I think is likely to occur is that as men and women meet in the workplace and become friends and colleagues, there may be more real friendship developing between men and women at home. A woman who works is more likely to understand what her partner's work pressure is all about. The more each partner in a relationship can understand and empathize with the other, the better the relationship is likely to be.

MARJORIE: I think you're right about that, but right now I think we're in for some rough times between men and women, unless men begin participating a little more (you notice I say a *little* more) in the household and with their children. I don't think bright, competent, educated women are going to put up with men who are unwilling to participate in a sharing kind of relationship. You notice I say "sharing," not "equal sharing." Many women tell me they want to have a man in their life, but they are no longer willing to be the only person giving in the relationship. They don't want to be with a man who needs to be taken care of. In that case, it's easier and more pleasant to be without a man.

MORT: Marjorie, that's really infuriating to most men. It's quite clear that men are doing more and that this trend is likely to increase. What men find difficult to accept is that they get little credit for what they do, and an incredible list of complaints about what they don't do. Men and women may give in different ways. Women continue to set ground rules for what they expect, what they want, and how they want it delivered. I can tell you that most highly competent, successful men—the kind of men most women look for—simply will not respond to a behavioral checklist.

MARJORIE: I know it. But we're living in the eighties, the era of two-career couples. If a woman is helping to provide for her family, it only makes sense—from a behavioral point of view—that she have some help with the home parts of her life. You know as well as I do that there are consequences to all behaviors. The consequence of letting your wife do it all is that she is likely to get angry, resentful, and maybe even sick. Does that make sense?

MORT: No, but I do think couples need to take a look at what the situation is beyond the wife's pointing a finger at the husband. You know, that doesn't work either. I think many men will probably be happy to "let her go"—they'll find someone else to take care of them.

MARJORIE: There are consequences for that, too. I don't think men think much about what it means to have a more traditional woman be dependent on them financially and in almost every other respect. Most men with whom I have talked say it drives them crazy. If a woman has to look to others for a vicarious sense of achievement, for a sense of who she is, she's likely to have low self-esteem and be depressed. What's it like to live with a depressed, unconfident person? I think that it's too easy to say, "Well, I'll just go find someone else who will adore me." Being adored may occur in the early part of a relationship, but unless it's reciprocated, feelings of resentment and anger are likely to build. So what does the guy do—go on to the next adoring woman, and the next? You and I both know that a life of that kind is pretty empty and superficial.

MORT: Of course the solution isn't simply to abandon one woman and then go on to the next. Clearly, the fifty-percent divorce rate says that for both men and women, in traditional and dual-career households, couples have a tendency to give up on a relationship that isn't working and move on to another one. What really has to occur is that the needs of both men and women must be met, even if the ways for meeting them are to change. Women do need help in balancing roles—and men can demonstrate their caring by offering help. Men do want to feel loved and cared for, however, and women cannot place that need in the "whenever I have time after everything else is done" file.

MARJORIE: It seems to come down to a matter of recognizing priorities, doesn't it? Women want to be able to develop their full potential outside their homes, and they think the men who love them should help them by taking over some of the home responsibilities—not just grudgingly doing chores. And men still want women to regard them as the most important part of their lives, even if women are assuming a share of the financial responsibility. Both the man and the woman have to recognize that the loving and caring come first, then the willingness to cooperate so that each can have the wider horizons each wants.

MORT: And if there are children? I think we agree that children need and deserve parents who are deeply involved with them. It's hard enough to be a parent full-time, let alone when you're juggling that role in addition to your career.

MARJORIE: You're right. We jump into parenthood without any preparation, we practice at being a parent on the kids we love, and, when we work away from home, we do this most important job on a part-time basis.

MORT: Perhaps what we need is to provide high school and college students with some basic information about relationships and family systems. Given that the teenage years are so difficult anyway, two things can be accomplished: They'll learn something about how to communicate better with their own parents; and they'll learn about how to be better parents themselves.

MARJORIE: This is one area where one's own parents may not be the best teachers. I think it would be extremely useful to teach our young people the latest we know about the tenets of good parenting. We as a society could stand to be knowledgeable about such things as conflict resolution, problem solving, leadership, and building self-esteem. Perhaps if young couples face parenthood with the kind of insight that education in family life could give them, they might approach the problems of parenting more intelligently. It certainly makes sense that they should know something about it, considering the new kinds of challenges the "traditional family" will be meeting in the future.

MORT: I like the idea of participating children. I think in this new broad-horizon family, children should feel they are also a working part of the unit. That was accomplished easily in rural families, where what needed to be done was obvious and children were given more responsibilities as they matured. Children in a working family should have a sense of being worthy of the love and care they get from their parents by having the opportunity to participate.

MARJORIE: You mean the way our kids helped in getting this book together?

MORT: You bet. They feel they contributed, and they did in more ways than just letting Mommy alone when she was writing.

MARJORIE: I think our government and industry need to help parents out, too. There should be a child-care industry that is available, affordable, and has high standards *for every child who needs it*. With the growing number of one-parent households, there will be more children who need good care when their parents are away at work.

MORT: I think state and local groups can be helpful, too. For example, I think we need to bring back regular schooldays beginning at eight or nine and ending at three-thirty. Many children are out almost by noon. I also think we should eliminate the so-called short schooldays and provide optional vacation programs and/or activities, as well as pre- and postschool programs and activities.

MARJORIE: If we're going to do that, then I think we need to offer teachers and administrators overtime pay to develop and attend these programs, which brings up one of my favorite subjects. I think we need to increase salaries and benefits to teachers so that we can attract more of the best and the brightest in our country.

MORT: Let's talk about what the colleges and universities might do. They can provide the training and certification for a new child-care industry.

MARJORIE: Yes, and I also see a place for them to study and disseminate information to the public about all the changes we're going through. As I said earlier in the book, we're quick to pick up on technological changes in this country, but not so quick to deal with sociological change.

MORT: I also think colleges and universities can inform and

train educators and health and mental-health professionals about these things. They need to be told about contemporary families and their issues: two-career families; raising competent, healthy children; and the differences between men and women.

MARJORIE: What else?

MORT: Well, I see some very smart group developing a housekeeping industry to meet the needs of working families. I could also see the government getting involved by providing training as a part of a program such as the job corps. Even further, I can see businesses making available housekeeping services as one of the cafeteria-benefit options. Whenever business sees a need, things get done.

MARJORIE: In addition to the housekeeping industry, I see service industries (including utility companies and maintenance-and-repair people) becoming more consumer oriented. More and more I think we working couples are going to patronize, and even pay more for, people we can count on to do a good job and be available before and after regular work hours.

MORT: You know, it doesn't have to stop there. I think there is tremendous power in consumer hands. We should also look to the professions to be more responsive to our needs. We need physicians, attorneys, psychologists, and accountants who will meet us before and after regular working hours and who are sensitive to working families' needs. I think service utilizers will respond to those who are on time for appointments, provide short-term child care, and understand the complicated nature of families today.

MARJORIE: I think it's time to wake up to the fact that we are really in the 1980s, not the 1940s. I think it's time we begin acting responsibly in the workplace, in the home, as consumers, and as parents.

MORT: One of the things the social psychologists tell us is that change has two dimensions—the first is anxiety (because we don't know what's happening), and the second is excitement (because anything is possible). It's obvious that we're in the middle of a variety of changes. The trick is to keep the excitement and anxiety in balance.

MARJORIE: We're getting all excited, aren't we, about the way things *should* be. We're pointing out how big a job it is and will be to keep our lives full of human goodness regardless of how much time all of us spend outside our homes. It's so big a job that we want to round up all the resources of our society to help. What does that say about the importance of the matter?

MORT: Obviously, it's too important to be handled in a make-shift way. Today's Superwoman needs all the help she can get from everyone; her husband, her children, and society need to assume their share of the responsibility.

MARJORIE: That's what I've had in mind all along. I hope *The Superwoman Syndrome* helps women *and* men to understand better what is going on in their lives. My wish is that women who read this book won't have to act like Superwomen anymore in order to feel wonderful about themselves and the people around them. It's not the more you do, but the quality and care of what you do, that makes for a real super woman.

THE EIGHT SUPERWOMAN COMMANDMENTS

And Everyday Responsive Readings

---

1. THY TIME HAST VALUE . . . THOU SHALT NOT SURRENDER ALL THE HOURS OF THY DAYS AND NIGHTS TO OTHERS

(My time is valuable . . . I am not on twenty-four-hour call)

2. THOU NEEDST NOT ACHIEVE PERFECTION IN ALL THINGS

(I don't have to be perfect at everything)

3. ALL THINGS ASKED OF THEE NEED NOT BE DONE

(Everything doesn't have to be done)

4. THOU SHALT LEARN TO SAY NO

(I must learn to say no)

5. THOU SHALT ATTEND TO THINE OWN NEEDS AS THOU WOULDST TEND TO THE NEEDS OF OTHERS

(I must take care of myself as I take care of others)

6. THOU SHALT LAY A PORTION OF THY BURDENS UPON OTHERS, NOT KEEP UNTO THYSELF THE DOING OF IT ALL

(I can delegate it, buy it, ask for help, or not do it all)

7. THOU SHALT GIVE TIME FIRST UNTO THOSE THOU LOVEST AND THAT WHICH MATTERS MOST IN THY LIFE

(I must give my time first to the people and things most important in my life)

8. FIX THINE EYES UPON WHAT IS RIGHT, NOT UPON WHAT IS WRONG OR WHAT PASSETH WITH THE MOMENT

(I must focus on what is positive in my life, not on what is negative or trivial)

WHOSOEVER FOLLOWETH THESE PRINCIPLES WILL NOT SACRIFICE ALL ON THE ALTAR OF SUPERWOMANHOOD, BUT WILL SECURE UNTO HERSELF AND HER LOVED ONES JOY AND FULFILLMENT

Notes

Chapter 1. Are You a Superwoman?

1. Ellen Goodman in Jeanette Branin, "She Outlines the Realities for a Change," *San Diego Union*, June 29, 1977.

Chapter 2. What Is the Superwoman Syndrome?

1. Hans Selye, *The Stress of Life* (New York: McGraw-Hill, 1978), 174.
2. *Stress Management Primer*, Scripps Clinics and Research Center, 1981, 1.
3. Thomas H. Holmes and Richard H. Rahe, "The Social Readjustment Rating Scale," *Journal of Psychosomatic Research* 11(1967), pp. 213–218.

Chapter 3. "From Ver Did You Came?"

1. John P. and Georgene H. Seward, *Sex Differences* (Lexington, Mass.: Lexington Books, 1980).
2. Horace B. and Eva Champney English, *A Comprehensive Dictionary of Psychological and Psychoanalytical Terms* (New York: David McKay, 1958), 508.
3. Jessie Bernard, *The Female World* (New York: Free Press, 1981).

4. Ibid.

5. Ibid.

6. Ibid.

7. Betty Friedan, *The Feminine Mystique* (New York: W.W. Norton, 1974).

8. Margaret Hennig and Anne Jardim, *The Managerial Woman* (New York: Pocket Books, 1976).

Chapter 4. How Men Really Feel

1. Mary Braylove, "Husband's Hazards for Middle-Aged Men, A Wife's New Career Upsets Old Balances," *The Wall Street Journal,* Monday, November 9, 1981.

Chapter 5. Why Today's Relationships Are So Difficult for Us

1. Donald H. Bell, *Being a Man* (Lexington, Mass.: Lewis, 1982).

2. Harvey Fields, "On the Job Training," *The New York Times Magazine,* January 1, 1984, 29.

3. *Marriage and Divorce Today,* January 24, 1983.

4. Georgia Witkin-Lanoil, *The Female Stress Syndrome* (New York: Newmarket Press, 1984), 81.

5. Bell, *Being a Man,* 151.

6. Lois Leiderman Davitz, "The Big Secrets of Adoring Couples," *McCall's,* November 1983, 169.

7. Natasha Josefowitz, *Is This Where I Was Going?* (New York: Warner Books, 1983), 61.

8. Luise Eichenbaum and Susie Orbach, *Understanding Women* (New York: Basic Books, 1983), 52.

9. Bell, *Being a Man,* 56.

10. Constantina Safilios-Rothschild and Marcellinus Dijkers, "Handling Unconventional Asymmetries," in *Working Couples,* eds. Rhona and Robert N. Rapoport and Janice M. Bumstead (New York: Harper and Row, 1978).

11. Marjorie Hansen Shaevitz and Morton H. Shaevitz, *Making It Together as a Two-Career Couple* (Boston: Houghton Mifflin, 1980).

Chapter 6. The Key To Having a Good Relationship

1. Virginia Satir, *Making Contact* (Millbrae, Calif.: Celestial Arts, 1976).
2. Virginia Satir, *Peoplemaking* (Palo Alto, Calif.: Science and Behavior Books, 1972), 30.
3. Ibid., 12.
4. Ibid., 13.
5. Virginia Satir, *Conjoint Family Therapy* (Palo Alto, Calif.: Science and Behavior Books, 1967), 73.
6. Satir, *Peoplemaking,* 76.
7. Ibid.
8. *Marriage and Divorce Today,* June 13, 1983.
9. Dorothy Corkille Briggs, *Your Child's Self-Esteem* (Garden City, N.Y.: Doubleday, 1975), 179.
10. *Marriage and Divorce Today,* March 14, 1983.
11. "A Happy Marriage—the Main Ingredient," *Vogue,* November 1981.
12. Lois Leiderman Davitz, "The Big Secrets of Adoring Couples," *McCall's,* November 1983, 95.
13. Donald H. Bell, *Being a Man* (Lexington, Mass.: Lewis, 1982), 101–102.
14. Susan Polis Schutz, "I Do Not Want To Change You," *Yours If You Ask* (Boulder, Colo.: Blue Mountain Press, 1978), 83.

Chapter 7. Motherhood: What Has Changed and What Has Not

1. Jessie Bernard, *The Future of Motherhood* (New York: Dial Press, 1974), vii.
2. California Commission on the Status of Women, October 1983.
3. Jan Norman, "Married Working Mothers Feel Most Stress," *The Register* (Santa Ana, California), July 2, 1982.
4. California Commission on the Status of Women, October 1983.
5. *Marriage and Divorce Today,* August 29, 1983, 3.

6. Grace Baruch, Rosalind Barnett, and Caryl Rivers, *Lifeprints* (New York: McGraw-Hill, 1983), 22.
7. Ibid., 141.
8. Ibid., 143.
9. Ibid., 143.
10. Ibid., 144.
11. Ibid., 16.
12. Ibid., 87.
13. Ibid., 93.
14. Ibid., 94.
15. Claire Etaugh, "Research Evidence and Popular Views," *American Psychologist* 35, no. 4 (April 1980), 309–319.
16. Mary C. Howell, "Effects of Maternal Employment on the Child," *Pediatrics*, September 1973, 327–343.
17. Claire Etaugh, "Effects of Maternal Employment on Children," *Merrill Palmer Quarterly*, April 1974, 71–97.
18. Ibid.
19. Ibid.
20. Baruch, Barnett, and Rivers, *Lifeprints*, 78.
21. Ibid., 80.
22. Marjorie Hansen Shaevitz and Morton H. Shaevitz, *Making It Together as a Two-Career Couple* (Boston: Houghton Mifflin, 1980), 67–75.
23. Margaret Hennig and Anne Jardim, *The Managerial Woman* (New York: Pocket Books, 1976), 151.
24. Baruch, Barnett, and Rivers, *Lifeprints*, 149.
25. Jessie Bernard, *The Female World* (New York: Free Press, 1981), 165–166.
26. Ursula Vils, "Testing Aptitude for Parenthood," *The Los Angeles Times*, May 1, 1978.
27. Shaevitz and Shaevitz, *Making It Together*, 77–78.
28. Sir Edwin Arnold, "Mothers," Stanza 6, *The Future of Motherhood* by Jessie Bernard.

Chapter 8. Raising Happy, Productive Kids

1. Fitzhugh Dodson, *How to Parent* (New York: Signet Books, 1971), 21.

2. Dorothy Corkille Briggs, *Your Child's Self-Esteem* (Garden City, N.Y.: Doubleday, 1975), 2–3.

3. Ibid.

4. Gene Hawes and Helen and Martin Weiss, *How to Raise Your Child to Be a Winner* (New York: Rawson Wade, 1980).

5. Ibid, 3–4.

6. Briggs, *Your Child's Self-Esteem,* 41.

7. Haim G. Ginott, *Between Parent and Child* (New York: Avon Books, 1965).

8. Spencer Johnson, *The One Minute Mother* (New York: William Morrow, 1983), 47.

9. Ibid.

10. Rebecca Sager Ashery and Michele Margolin Basen, *The Parents with Careers Workbook* (Washington, D.C.: Acropolis Books, 1983).

Chapter 9.   Who Is Important, What Is Essential in Your Life?

1. Horace B. and Eva Champney English, *A Comprehensive Dictionary of Psychological and Psychoanalytical Terms* (New York: David McKay, 1958), 235.

2. Luise Eichenbaum and Susie Orbach, *Understanding Women* (New York: Basic Books, 1983), 9.

3. Ibid., 97.

4. Ibid., 153.

5. Abraham H. Maslow, *Toward a Psychology of Being,* 2nd ed. (New York: D. Van Nostrand, 1968), 3.

6. Ibid., 4.

7. Ibid.

8. Grace Baruch, Rosalind Barnett, and Caryl Rivers, *Lifeprints* (New York: McGraw-Hill, 1983), 30.

9. *Webster's Ninth New Collegiate Dictionary* (Springfield: Merriam-Webster, 1983), 524.

10. Michael LeBoeuf, *Working Smart* (New York: McGraw-Hill, 1979), 35.

Chapter 10. Better Manage Your Time—It's All You Have

1. Dru Scott, *How to Put More Time in Your Life* (New York: New American Library, 1980).
2. Michael LeBoeuf, *Working Smart* (New York: McGraw-Hill, 1979).
3. Charles A. Garfield, "Achieving Peak Performance," Performance Sciences (Berkeley, Calif.).
4. Ruth Schwartz Cowan, *More Work for Mother* (New York: Basic Books, 1983).
5. Garfield, "Achieving Peak Performance."
6. Alec MacKenzie and Kay Cronkite Waldo, *About Time!* (New York: McGraw-Hill, 1981), 26.
7. Carol Gilligan, *In a Different Voice* (Cambridge: Harvard University Press, 1982).
8. MacKenzie and Waldo, *About Time!*, 26.
9. LeBoeuf, *Working Smart*.

Chapter 11. Housework: How to Do Less of It

1. Joanne C. May Kliejunas, "Being of Use: The Value of Housework in the Household and in the Economy," Ph.D. diss., Stanford University, 1982, 7.
2. Ibid.
3. Ibid.
4. Philip Blumstein and Pepper Schwartz, *American Couples* (New York: William Morrow, 1983), 153.
5. Peter F. Drucker, *Management* (New York: Harper and Row, 1973).
6. John Platt in Sharon Schneider, "Kids and Money," *The Moneypaper,* December 1983.
7. *The Locomotivator* 37, September/October 1982.
8. Letty Cottin Pogrebin, *Family Politics* (New York: McGraw-Hill, 1983), 163.
9. Dru Scott, *How to Put More Time in Your Life* (New York: Signet Books, 1980), 157.

10. Diana Silcox with Mary Ellen Moore, *Woman Time* (New York: Wyden Books, 1980).
11. Pogrebin, *Family Politics*.
12. Ibid.
13. Ruth Schwartz Cowan, *More Work for Mother* (New York: Basic Books, 1983).
14. Pogrebin, *Family Politics,* 146.
15. *UCI Update* (University of California, Irvine), August 1982.
16. Pogrebin, *Family Politics*.

Chapter 12.   Playing the Work Game and Changing It Too

1. Linda J. Waite, "U.S. Women at Work," Rand, December 1981.
2. Ralph E. Smith, ed., *The Subtle Revolution* (Washington, D.C.: The Urban Institute, 1979).
3. "Working Woman: The Myths and Facts," *Los Angeles Herald-Examiner,* November 1, 1983.
4. "The Feminization of Poverty," California Commission on the Status of Women, May 1983.
5. Ibid.
6. Weal Washington Report, no. 3, June/July 1983.
7. "The Feminization of Poverty," California Commission.
8. Ibid.
9. Jessie Bernard, *The Female World* (New York: Free Press, 1981).
10. Ibid.
11. Natasha Josefowitz, *Paths to Power* (Reading, Mass.: Addison-Wesley, 1980).
12. ———— *Is This Where I Was Going?* (New York: Warner Books, 1983), 5.
13. *Webster's Ninth New Collegiate Dictionary* (Springfield: Merriam-Webster, 1983), 659.
14. Ibid., 208.
15. Josefowitz, *Paths to Power,* 17.

16. Charlotte Curtis in Marilyn Machlowitz, *Workaholics* (Reading, Mass.: Addison-Wesley, 1980), 7.

17. Michael LeBoeuf, *Working Smart* (New York: McGraw-Hill, 1979), 14–16.

18. Charles A. Garfield in "Why Workaholics Work," *Newsweek,* April 17, 1981.

19. Margaret Hennig and Anne Jardim in Ruth Mehrtens Galvin, "Goal Consciousness: You Have to Have a Strategy," *New West,* April 11, 1977.

20. Ibid., 42.

21. John Naisbitt, *Megatrends* (New York: Warner Books, 1982).

22. Meyer Friedman and Ray Rosenthal in Georgia Witkin-Lanoil, *The Female Stress Syndrome* (New York: Newmarket Press, 1984).

23. Charles A. Garfield in "Better Than Good," *Mgr.,* no. 2, 1982, 8.

24. Ibid., 7.

25. Charles A. Garfield in Erik Larsen, "Why Do Some People Outperform Others?" *The Wall Street Journal,* January 13, 1982.

26. *Marriage and Divorce Today,* December 5, 1983.

27. Garfield, "Better Than Good."

28. Anne Harlan and Carol Weiss, "Moving Up: Women in Managerial Careers," Wellesley College Center for Research on Women, Working Paper no. 80, September 1981, i.

29. Catalyst staff, *Upward Mobility* (New York: Holt, Rinehart and Winston, 1981).

30. Josefowitz, *Paths to Power.*

31. Naisbitt, *Megatrends.*

32. Ibid.

33. Peter F. Drucker, *The Effective Executive* (New York: Harper and Row, 1966).

34. Catalyst staff, "Career and Family Bulletin," winter 1981.

35. Marjorie Hansen Shaevitz and Morton H. Shaevitz, *Making It Together as a Two-Career Couple* (Boston: Houghton Mifflin, 1980).

Bibliography

CHILDREN

Ames, Louise Bates, et al. *The Gesell Institute's Child from One to Six*. New York: Harper and Row, 1979.

Ashery, Rebecca Sager, and Michele Margolin Basen. *The Parents with Careers Workbook*. Washington, D.C.: Acropolis Books, 1983.

Auerbach, Stevanne, and Linda Freedman. *Choosing Child Care*. San Francisco: Parents and Child Care Resources, 1976.

Azerrad, J. *Anyone Can Have a Happy Child*. New York: M. Evans, 1980.

Bartz, Wayne R., and Richard A. Rasor. *Surviving with Kids*. San Luis Obispo, Calif.: Impact, 1978.

Bayard, Robert T., and Jean Bayard. *Your Acting-Up Teenager*. San Jose, Calif.: Accord Press, 1981.

Briggs, Dorothy Corkille. *Your Child's Self-Esteem*. New York: Doubleday, 1970.

Dunn, Rita, and Kenneth Dunn. *How to Raise Independent and Professionally Successful Daughters*. Englewood Cliffs, N.J.: Prentice-Hall, 1977.

Faber, Adele, and Elaine Mazlish. *How to Talk So Kids Will Listen and How to Listen So Kids Will Talk*. New Jersey: Stratford Press, 1980.

Farson, Richard. *Birthrights*. New York: Penguin Books, 1974.

Ginott, Haim G. *Between Parent and Child*. New York: Avon Books, 1965.

Glickman, Beatrice Marden, and Nesha Bass Springer. *Who Cares for the Baby? Choices in Child Care*. New York: Schocken Books, 1978.

Hawes, Gene R., Helen G. Weiss, and Martin S. Weiss. *How to Raise Your Child to Be a Winner*. New York: Rawson Wade, 1980.

Ilg, Frances L., and Louise Bates Ames. *The Gesell Institute's Child Behavior from Birth to Ten*. New York: Harper and Row, 1955.

Levine, James A. *Who Will Raise the Children? New Options for Fathers (and Mothers)*. Philadelphia: J.B. Lippincott, 1976.

Peck, Ellen, and William Granzig. *The Parent Test*. New York: Putnam's, 1978.

Pincus, Cynthia Sterling. *Double Duties*. New York: Chatham Square Press, 1978.

Pogrebin, Letty Cottin. *Growing Up Free*. New York: McGraw-Hill, 1980.

Price, Jane. *You're Not Too Old to Have a Baby*. New York: Penguin Books, 1978.

Schowalter, John E., and Walter R. Anyan. *The Family Handbook of Adolescence*. New York: Alfred A. Knopf, 1979.

Wallerstein, Judith S., and Joan Berlin Kelly. *Surviving the Breakup— How Children and Parents Cope with Divorce*. New York: Basic Books, 1980.

Whelan, Elizabeth M. *A Baby? . . . Maybe: A Guide to Making the Most Fateful Decision of Your Life*. New York: Bobbs-Merrill, 1975.

COMMUNICATION SKILLS

Baer, Jean. *How to Be an Assertive (Not Aggressive) Woman in Life, in Love, and on the Job*. New York: Rawson Wade, 1976.

Bower, Sharon Anthony, and Gordon H. Bower. *Asserting Yourself*. Reading, Mass.: Addison-Wesley, 1976.

Comfort, Alex, ed. *The Joy of Sex*. New York: Crown, 1972.

Crenshaw, Theresa Larsten. *Bedside Manners*. New York: McGraw-Hill, 1983.

Firestone, Robert, and Joyce Catlett. *The Truth. A Psychological Cure*. New York: Macmillan, 1981.

Fisher, Roger, and William Ury. *Getting to Yes. Negotiating Agreement Without Giving In*. Boston: Houghton Mifflin, 1981.

Masters, William H., et al. *Pleasure Bond*. Boston: Little, Brown and Co., 1976.

Satir, Virginia. *Peoplemaking*. Palo Alto, Calif.: Science and Behavior Books, 1972.

Tavris, Carol. *Anger*. New York: Simon and Schuster, 1982.

COUPLES

Bernard, Jessie. *The Future of Marriage*. New York: Bantam Books, 1973.

Blumstein, Philip, and Pepper Schwartz. *American Couples*. New York: William Morrow, 1983.

Friday, Nancy. *Men in Love*. New York: Dell Publishing Co., 1981.

Marcus, Genevieve Grafe, and Robert Lee Smith. *Equal Time*. New York: Frederick Fell, 1982.

Mornel, Pierre. *Passive Men, Wild Women*. New York: Ballantine Books, 1979.

Pogrebin, Letty Cottin. *Family Politics*. New York: McGraw-Hill, 1983.

Shaevitz, Marjorie Hansen, and Morton H. Shaevitz. *Making It Together as a Two-Career Couple*. Boston: Houghton Mifflin, 1980.

FOR YOUR ENJOYMENT

Bombeck, Erma. *Motherhood*. New York: McGraw-Hill, 1983.
——— *Aunt Erma's Cope Book*. New York: McGraw-Hill, 1979.

Bloomfield, Harold, with Leonard Felder. *Making Peace with Your Parents*. New York: Random House, 1983.

Goodman, Ellen. *Close to Home*. New York: Simon and Schuster, 1979.
——— *Turning Points*. New York: Doubleday, 1979.

Hansson, Carola, and Karin Liden. *Moscow Women*. New York: Pantheon Books, 1983.

Josefowitz, Natasha. *Is This Where I Was Going?* New York: Warner Books, 1983.

Lebowitz, Fran. *Social Studies*. New York: Random House, 1981.
——— *Metropolitan Life*. New York: Fawcett, 1981.

Schutz, Susan Polis. *Love, Live, and Share*. Boulder, Colo.: Blue Mountain Press, 1980.

———— *Yours If You Ask*. Boulder, Colo.: Blue Mountain Press, 1979.

HOUSEWORK

Brace, Pam, and Peggy Jones. *Sidetracked Home Executives*. New York: Warner Books, 1981.

Cowan, Ruth S. *More Work for Mother*. New York: Basic Books, 1983.

MALE AND FEMALE DEVELOPMENT

Bardwick, Judith M. *In Transition*. New York: Holt, Rinehart and Winston, 1979.

Baruch, Grace, Rosalind Barnett, and Caryl Rivers. *Lifeprints*. New York: McGraw-Hill, 1983.

Bell, Donald H. *Being a Man*. Lexington, Mass.: Lewis, 1982.

Bernard, Jessie. *The Female World*. New York: Free Press, 1981.

———— *The Future of Motherhood*. New York: Dial Press, 1974.

Brownmiller, Susan. *Femininity*. New York: Linden Press/Simon and Schuster, 1984.

Dowling, Colette. *The Cinderella Complex*. New York: Summit Books, 1981.

Durden-Smith, Jo, and Diane Desimone. *Sex and the Brain*. New York: Warner Books, 1984.

Eichenbaum, Luise, and Susie Orbach. *Understanding Women*. New York: Basic Books, 1983.

Farrell, Warren. *The Liberated Man*. New York: Bantam Books, 1974.

Friedan, Betty. *The Second Stage*. New York: Summit Books, 1981.

Gerzon, Mark. *A Choice of Heroes*. Boston: Houghton Mifflin, 1982.

Gilligan, Carol. *In a Different Voice*. Cambridge: Harvard University Press, 1983.

Levinson, Daniel J., et al. *The Seasons of a Man's Life*. New York: Alfred A. Knopf, 1978.

Pleck, Elizabeth H., and Joseph H. Pleck. *The American Man*. Englewood Cliffs, N.J.: Prentice-Hall, 1980.

Pleck, Joseph H. *The Myth of Masculinity*. Cambridge: Massachusetts Institute of Technology Press, 1982.

Sargent, Alice G. *Beyond Sex Roles*. St. Paul, Minn.: West, 1977.

Schutz, Susan Polis, and Katherine F. Carson, M.D. *Take Charge of Your Body*. Boulder, Colo.: Blue Mountain Press, 1983.

Seward, John P. and Georgene H. Seward. *Sex Differences: Mental and Temperamental*. Lexington, Mass.: Lexington Books, 1980.

Tavris, Carol, and Carole Offir. *The Longest War*. New York: Harcourt Brace Jovanovich, 1977.

Witkin-Lanoil, Georgia. *The Female Stress Syndrome*. New York: Newmarket Press, 1984.

PSYCHOLOGY

Fromm, Erich. *The Art of Loving*. New York: Bantam Books, 1956.

Maslow, Abraham H. *Toward a Psychology of Being*. 2nd ed. New York: D. Van Nostrand, 1968.

Rubenstein, Carin, and Phillip Shaver. *In Search of Intimacy*. New York: Delacorte Press, 1982.

Veroff, Joseph, Elizabeth Douvan, and Richard A. Kulka. *The Inner American*. New York: Basic Books, 1981.

STRESS MANAGEMENT

Farquhar, John W. *The American Way of Life Need Not Be Hazardous to Your Health*. New York: W.W. Norton, 1978.

Pelletier, Kenneth. *Mind As Healer, Mind As Slayer*. New York: Dell, 1977.

Selye, Hans. *The Stress of Life*. New York: McGraw-Hill, 1976.

————— *Stress Without Distress*. Philadelphia: J.B. Lippincott, 1974.

TIME MANAGEMENT

Best, Fred. *Flexible Life Scheduling*. New York: Praeger, 1980.

Gault, Jan. *Free Time*. New York: John Wiley, 1983.

Goldfein, Donna. *Everywoman's Guide to Time Management*. Millbrae, Calif.: Les Femmes, 1977.

Lakein, Alan. *How to Get Control of Your Time and Your Life*. New York: Signet Books, 1974.

LeBoeuf, Michael. *Working Smart*. New York: Warner Books, 1983.

MacKenzie, Alec, and Kay Cronkite Waldo. *About Time!* New York: McGraw-Hill, 1981.

Scott, Dru. *How to Put More Time in Your Life*. New York: New American Library, 1980.

Winston, Stephanie. *Getting Organized*. New York: Warner Books, 1979.

WORK

Blanchard, Kenneth, and Spencer Johnson. *The One Minute Manager*. New York: William Morrow, 1982.

Cohen, Allan R., and Herman Gadon. *Alternative Work Schedules*. Menlo Park, Calif.: Addison-Wesley, 1978.

Drucker, Peter F. *Management: Tasks, Responsibilities, and Practices*. New York: Harper and Row, 1974.

———— *The Effective Executive*. New York: Harper and Row, 1967.

Kanter, Rosabeth Moss. *Men and Women of the Corporation*. New York: Basic Books, 1977.

Kerr, Clark, and Jerome M. Rosow, eds. *Work in America*. San Francisco: Van Nostrand Reinhold, 1979.

Machlowitz, Marilyn. *Workaholics*. Reading, Mass.: Addison-Wesley, 1980.

Naisbitt, John. *Megatrends*. New York: Warner Books, 1982.

Olmsted, Barney, and Suzanne Smith. *The Job Sharing Handbook*. New York: Penquin Books, 1983.

Pleck, Joseph H., and Graham L. Staines. *The Impact of Work Schedules on the Family*. Ann Arbor, Mich.: Institute for Social Research, 1983.

Sargent, Alice G. *The Androgynous Manager*. New York: Amacom, 1981.

Yankelovich, Daniel. *New Rules*. New York: Random House, 1981.

WORKING WOMEN

Bernard, Jessie. *Women, Wives, Mothers*. Chicago: Aldine, 1975.

Bolles, Richard N. *What Color Is Your Parachute?* Berkeley, Calif.: Ten Speed Press, 1977.

Catalyst staff. *Marketing Yourself*. New York: Putnam's, 1980.

———— *Upward Mobility*. New York: Holt, Rinehart and Winston, 1981.

———— *What to Do with the Rest of Your Life*. New York: Simon and Schuster, 1981.

Harragan, Betty Lehan. *Games Mother Never Taught You*. New York: Warner Books, 1977.

Hennig, Margaret, and Anne Jardim. *The Managerial Woman*. New York: Pocket Books, 1978.

Josefowitz, Natasha. *Paths to Power*. Reading, Mass.: Addison-Wesley, 1980.

Josefowitz, Natasha. *You're The Boss*. New York: Warner Books, 1985.

Lenz, Elinor, and Marjorie Hansen Shaevitz. *So You Want to Go Back to School*. New York: McGraw-Hill, 1977.

Appendix A

Whether or Not to Have a Baby Resources

BOOKS

Bernard, Jessie. *The Future of Motherhood*. New York: Dial Press, 1974.

Boston Women's Health Book Collective. *Our Bodies, Ourselves*. New York: Simon and Schuster, 1976.

——— *Ourselves and Our Children*. New York: Random House, 1978.

Peck, Ellen. *The Baby Trap*. Los Angeles: Pinnacle Books, 1976.

Peck, Ellen, and William Granzig. *The Parent Test*. New York: Putnam's, 1978.

Price, Jane. *You're Not Too Old to Have a Baby*. New York: Penguin Books, 1978.

Rapoport, Rhona and Robert N., and Ziona Strelitz. *Fathers, Mothers and Society*. New York: Basic Books, 1977.

Whelan, Elizabeth. *A Baby? . . . Maybe*. New York: Bobbs-Merrill, 1975.

ORGANIZATIONS

A Baby? . . . Maybe Services, 165 West End Ave., New York, NY 10023

National Organization for Non-Parents, 806 Reistertown Road, Baltimore, MD 21208

Parenting by Choice, 110 West 86 St., New York, NY 10024

Planned Parenthood Federation of America, 810 Seventh Ave., New York, NY 10019

Pondering Parenthood, 405 West 118 St., New York, NY 10027

Zero Population Growth, 1346 Connecticut Ave., N.W., Washington, D.C. 20036

Appendix B

Household Activities

Automobiles
Babies and children
Family and social relationships and events
Finances
Food shopping and meal preparation
Household maintenance
• Bathrooms
• Bedrooms
• Dining room, family room, hallways, library, living room
• Gardens and yard
• Kitchen
• Laundry and clothing maintenance
• Miscellaneous
• Patios and porches
Pet care
Other:

AUTOMOBILES

TASKS AND HOW OFTEN TO BE PERFORMED	WHO DOES IT

Once a week
Check car
   " gas
   " oil
   " water
   " tires
   " battery water

Twice a month
Wash car

Every two months
Take car in for tune-up, oil change
Wax car

Once a year
Pay yearly registration/license fee

As needed
Take car in for regular and emergency repairs

OTHER:

BABIES AND CHILDREN

TASKS AND HOW OFTEN TO BE PERFORMED	WHO DOES IT

BABY

Once a day
Bathe baby, wash hair
Change bedclothes
Wash clothes
Wash diapers
Wash bottles and nipples
Make formula

Every two weeks
Clip nails

As needed
Change diapers
Feed baby (probably every 4 hours at first)
Make appointments for 6-week, 3-month, 6-month, 9-month checkups

OTHER:

SMALL CHILDREN

Twice a day or more
Feed child at meals
Transport child to and from nursery school or child-care center

Once a day
Dress child
Bathe child
Make school lunch

TASKS AND HOW OFTEN TO BE PERFORMED   WHO DOES IT

Prepare child for bed
Prepare child for school

Once a week
Arrange visits with friends
Organize child's chores
Wash hair
Clip nails

Once a month
Organize haircuts

Every six months
Make well-child visits to doctor and dentist

As needed
Buy clothes and shoes

OTHER:

OLDER CHILDREN

Once a day
Help child study
Make school lunch
Organize bath

Once a week
Arrange after-school activities, lessons,
   transportation
Arrange visits with friends
Organize chores

Once a month
Organize haircuts

TASKS AND HOW OFTEN TO BE PERFORMED	WHO DOES IT

Every six months
Make well-child visits to doctor and dentist

As needed
Arrange birthday parties
Arrange vacations, holidays, weekends
Attend school functions
Buy clothes and shoes
Buy school supplies

OTHER:

FAMILY AND SOCIAL RELATIONSHIPS AND EVENTS

TASKS AND HOW OFTEN TO BE PERFORMED	WHO DOES IT

Once a week
Correspondence: write and answer letters
Plan birthdays, anniversaries

As needed
Arrange visits with family
Arrange visits with friends
Organize attendance at religious services
Plan and execute social occasions at home
Plan for and organize special events
Plan and organize family vacations
Prepare for special religious observations
   (Christmas, Passover)

OTHER:

FINANCES

TASKS AND HOW OFTEN TO BE PERFORMED	WHO DOES IT

Once a day
Sort mail

Once a month
Balance checkbook
Do monthly bookkeeping chores
Pay bills

Every three months
Prepare quarterly income-tax forms

Once a year
Gather all information for income tax
Make insurance payments

As needed
Prepare medical insurance forms
Deposit checks to bank account

OTHER:

MEAL PREPARATION

TASKS AND HOW OFTEN TO BE PERFORMED	WHO DOES IT

DAILY MEAL PREPARATION	MON	TUES	WED	THURS	FRI	SAT	SUN
Breakfast							
Plan menu							
Set table							

Prepare food
Clean up dining area, put
  away food
Wash, dry, put away
  dishes

Lunch
Plan menu
Set table
Prepare food
Clean up dining area, put
  away food
Wash, dry, put away
  dishes

Dinner
Plan menu
Set table
Prepare food
Clean up dining area, put
  away food
Wash, dry, put away
  dishes

FOOD AND SHOPPING

TASKS AND HOW OFTEN TO BE PERFORMED   WHO DOES IT

Once a day
Check to see if any food items are needed

Every few days
Go to grocery store to pick up needed food items

TASKS AND HOW OFTEN TO BE PERFORMED   WHO DOES IT

Once a week
Plan menus for week
Check with family members to see if any special
  foods are wanted

Once a month
Go through pantry to see what food staples are
  needed
Buy food in bulk from discount stores

As needed
Plan and prepare for guests
Plan and prepare for special occasions

OTHER:

MEALTIME PLANNING

BREAKFAST MENU: *DAY:*   *TIME:*

Juice/fruit _____   Special considerations for
Eggs _____   infants, children, sick family
Cereals: cold _____   members, allergic family
         hot _____   members:
Pancakes/waffles _____   _____
Meat items _____   _____
Bread items _____   _____
Pastry items _____   _____
Beverages _____   _____
Other _____   _____

WHAT NEEDS TO BE DONE	WHO DOES IT	WHEN
Determine number of people	_____	_____
Plan menu	_____	_____
Defrost food, if required	_____	_____
Make coffee, tea, juice	_____	_____
Set table	_____	_____
Bake any required items	_____	_____
Prepare food	_____	_____
Clean up dining area, put away food	_____	_____
Wash, dry, put away dishes	_____	_____
Clean up kitchen area	_____	_____
Other	_____	_____

LUNCH/DINNER MENU:

Cocktails _____

Hors d'oeuvres _____

Soup _____

Salad _____

Entree _____

Vegetables _____

Fruits _____

Breads _____

Dessert _____

Beverages _____

Wine _____

Other _____

Special considerations for infants, children, sick or allergic family members:

_____

_____

_____

_____

_____

_____

_____

_____

_____

_____

WHAT NEEDS TO BE DONE	WHO DOES IT	WHEN
Determine number of people	_____	_____
Plan menu	_____	_____
Develop grocery list	_____	_____
Shop for groceries	_____	_____
Defrost food	_____	_____
Set table	_____	_____
Make coffee, tea	_____	_____

WHAT NEEDS TO BE DONE	WHO DOES IT	WHEN
Make initial preparations	_____	_____
Bake any required items	_____	_____
Prepare food	_____	_____
Serve food	_____	_____
Clean up dining area, put away food	_____	_____
Wash, dry, put away dishes	_____	_____
Clean up kitchen area	_____	_____
Other	_____	_____

GUEST LUNCH/DINNER MENU

DATE: **TIME:**

Cocktails _____

Seating arrangement:

Hors d'oeuvres _____

Soup _____

Salad _____

Entree _____

Vegetables _____

Fruits _____

Breads _____

Special considerations of guests (e.g., John O. doesn't eat seafood):

Dessert _____

Beverages _____

_____

Wine _____

_____

Other _____

_____

WHAT NEEDS TO BE DONE	WHO DOES IT	WHEN
Set date, determine guest list, type of lunch/dinner	_____	2–4 weeks before
Call guests or send invitations	_____	2–4 weeks before
Plan menu, develop grocery and supply list	_____	3 weeks before
Order any special foods, flowers	_____	2 weeks before
Bake any foods that can be put into freezer	_____	1 week before

WHAT NEEDS TO BE DONE	WHO DOES IT	WHEN
Prepare foods that can be refrigerated	_____	1 day before
Shop for grocery list	_____	1 day before
Pick or buy flowers for table	_____	Day of party
Defrost food	_____	Day of party
Set table, put out placecards, write out timetable for party	_____	Day of party
Make initial preparations	_____	Day of party
Prepare food, coffee, tea	_____	Day of party
Serve food	_____	Day of party
Clean up dining area, put away food	_____	_____
Wash, dry, put away dishes	_____	_____
Clean up kitchen area	_____	_____
Serve after-dinner drinks	_____	_____
Other	_____	_____

HOUSEHOLD MAINTENANCE

TASKS AND HOW OFTEN TO BE PERFORMED	WHO DOES IT

BATHROOMS

Once a day
Put out clean towels
Straighten up clutter

Once a week
Wash floor
Check bathroom supplies and purchase items needed
Clean combs and brushes
Clean mirror
Clean/polish tile on countertop and shower area

Clean shower stall
Clean sink
Clean toilet
Clean tub
Empty wastebaskets
Sweep floor
Vacuum carpet
Wash countertops

BEDROOMS

Once a day
Make bed
Hang up clothes
Straighten up clutter
Put away toys and games

Once a week
Change sheets
Clean fireplace
Clean mirrors
Clean telephone
Clean under bed
Dust blinds and shutters
Dust furniture
Dust lampshades
Dust pictures and frames
Empty wastebasket
Vacuum carpet, floors, furniture
Clean windowsills
Wash sheets and pillowcases

Once a month
Remove cobwebs
Polish furniture

TASKS AND HOW OFTEN TO BE PERFORMED	WHO DOES IT

Test smoke detector
Go through magazines and discard

Every six months
Clean walls, woodwork, light-switch plates
Turn mattress
Wash windows
Wash mattress pad
Clean light bowls

Once a year
Shampoo carpets
Clean walls and ceilings
Clean out bookcases, closets, cupboards, drawers,
   shelves

As needed
Replace light bulbs

OTHER:

DINING ROOM, FAMILY ROOM, HALLWAYS, LIBRARY, LIVING ROOM

Once a day
Straighten up clutter
Put things away

Once a week
Clean fireplace
Clean mirrors
Clean telephone
Dust blinds and shutters
Dust furniture
Dust lampshades

TASKS AND HOW OFTEN TO BE PERFORMED   WHO DOES IT

Dust pictures and frames
Empty wastebaskets
Vacuum carpet, floors, furniture
Clean windowsills

Once a month
Go through magazines and discard
Move and vacuum furniture, under furniture
Polish furniture
Remove cobwebs

Every six months
Wash woodwork, light-switch plates
Wash windows
Clean light bowls

Once a year
Clean walls and ceilings
Clean out bookcases, closets, cupboards, drawers,
    shelves
Shampoo carpet

OTHER:

GARDENS AND YARD

Once a week
Mow lawn
Sweep sidewalks or wash with hose
Water plants, trees

Twice a week
Water lawn

TASKS AND HOW OFTEN TO BE PERFORMED	WHO DOES IT

Every two weeks
Weed yard

Once a month
Spray plants for diseases

Every six months
Fertilize lawn and plants

Once a year
Prune bushes, trees

OTHER:

KITCHEN

Twice a day or more
Wash dishes or fill dishwasher

Once a day
Clean sink
Empty dishwasher
Empty garbage
Put away toys and games
Straighten up clutter
Wash pots and pans

Once a week
Clean telephone
Clean toaster, can opener, blender
Dust blinds, shutters
Dust furniture
Dust pictures and frames
Move furniture, sweep or vacuum
Polish faucets

Remove cobwebs
Sweep, damp-mop floor
Vacuum floor and moldings
Wash countertops
Empty wastebasket

Once a month
Clean inside and top of refrigerator
Clean microwave oven
Clean oven inside and out
Go through magazines and discard
Polish furniture
Shake out or wash scatter rugs
Wash canisters, knickknacks, jars
Clean hood of cooktop or range
Clean knobs and clock on stove

Every three months
Clean cupboard doors
Clean dishwasher and refrigerator doors
Clean drip pan of refrigerator
Clean stove fan
Clean fireplace/grill/barbecue
Clean inside of windows
Defrost freezer
Wax floor
Clean under sink

Every six months
Clean light fixtures
Clean out and organize closets, cupboards, drawers,
    shelves
Clean out and organize pantry
Clean walls, woodwork, light-switch plates
Polish silver and silverware

TASKS AND HOW OFTEN TO BE PERFORMED	WHO DOES IT

Wash windows
Wash or dry-clean curtains

Once a year
Strip old wax from floor and rewax
Shampoo carpet
Wash or change shelf paper

As needed
Empty trash compactor
Replace broken china, glass, cutlery
Replace light bulbs
Replace caulking on sink
Replace trash-compactor bag
Replace washers on faucet
Replace vacuum bags
Sharpen knives
Scrape and bleach cutting board

OTHER:

LAUNDRY AND CLOTHING MAINTENANCE

Once a day
Put away clothes

Once a week
Check clothes for stains
Clean floor
Clean laundry sink
Clean out dryer, wash top
Clean out purse and wallet
Empty wastebasket

TASKS AND HOW OFTEN TO BE PERFORMED   WHO DOES IT

Starch shirts
Mend/iron clothes
Polish shoes
Remove cobwebs
Spot-clean stained clothes
Sweep, damp-mop floor
Take clothing to cleaners, pick up
Vacuum floors and moldings
Hand wash delicate clothes
Wash countertops

Once a month
Clean or polish purse and handbags
Polish faucets
Wash out washer

Every three months
Clean under sink

Every six months
Clean closets, cupboards, drawers, shelves
Clean light fixtures
Clean walls, woodwork, light-switch plate
Sort seasonal clothing
Wash windows
Wash or dry-clean curtains

Once a year
Wash or change shelf paper
Strip old wax, rewax floor

As needed
Sort, wash, dry, fold, put away laundry
Purchase clothing
Remove lint from dryer

TASKS AND HOW OFTEN TO BE PERFORMED	WHO DOES IT

Replace light bulbs
Replace caulking on sink

OTHER:

MISCELLANEOUS

Once a week
Water plants
Put trash out for garbage collection

Once a month
Throw out old newspapers and magazines
Wash out garbage/trash cans, plastic wastebaskets
Fertilize plants
Clean walls, woodwork, light-switch plates
Remove cobwebs
Wash scatter rugs
Wax floors

Every three months
Replace batteries in smoke detector

Every six months
Turn mattresses
Wash mattress pads
Clean light bowls
Clean and organize cupboards
Clean out medicine cabinet
Wash shower curtain
Wash windows

Once a year
Clean air-conditioning filter
Clean heating-unit filter

TASKS AND HOW OFTEN TO BE PERFORMED   WHO DOES IT

Have chimney swept
Strip wax from floors, rewax
Shampoo carpets
Clean ceilings
Clean out bookcases, closets, cupboards, drawers,
  shelves

As needed
Handle immediate household repairs or service (leaky
  toilet, broken washer, etc.)
Have septic tank cleaned
Organize long-term household improvements
  (painting, fence building, etc.)
Replace diseased or dead plants
Change washers on faucets
Repair caulking on sinks, tub, shower
Replace light bulbs
Wash or dry-clean curtains

OTHER:

PATIOS AND PORCHES

Once a week
Clean or sweep patio/porch
Water plants

Once a month
Fertilize plants
Remove cobwebs
Wash patio furniture

Every two months
Clean out gutters

TASKS AND HOW OFTEN TO BE PERFORMED   WHO DOES IT

Every six months
Buy new plants
Repot old plants
Sweep and wash patio/porch walls

As needed
Replace broken, worn furniture
Replace diseased or dead plants
Replace light bulbs

OTHER:

PET CARE

TASKS AND HOW OFTEN TO BE PERFORMED   WHO DOES IT

Twice or more a day
Walk dog

Once a day
Feed animals

Every few days
Change kitty litter
Clean animal/bird cage

Every year
Get license for animal
Take animal to veterinarian for shots

TASKS AND HOW OFTEN TO BE PERFORMED   WHO DOES IT

As needed
Buy special food
Take animal to groomer
Bathe animal
Take sick animal to veterinarian

OTHER:

Appendix C

Examples of Work Your Children Can Do

3–4 YEARS OF AGE

(Children of this age need lots of reminders and lots of guidance)

Dress self (put on pants, socks, shoes, sweater, dress)

Pick up and put away toys

Empty wastebasket

Help set table, clear dishes

Put dirty clothes in hamper

Close drawers in room

5–6 YEARS OF AGE

(This age group also needs reminders and guidance)

Set and clear table

Feed pet

Help put away groceries

Dust

Pick up own games, toys, clothes

Take out trash

Water plants with direction

Assist with meal preparation

Make bed

Clean out pet box, cage

7–8 YEARS OF AGE

(The years 7–10 are very industrious ones. Children of this age group like to feel adultlike. Tasks should reflect this.)

Sweep floor, walks
Make own school lunch
Help with grocery shopping
Rake leaves
Walk dog
Polish own shoes

Vacuum
Wash, dry, put away dishes
Fill and empty dishwasher
Help with parties
Help with meals

9–10 YEARS OF AGE

Wash car
Prepare simple meals
Bathe dog
Use washer/dryer with directions
Put out trash for garbage collector

Water yard or plants
Polish silver
Straighten up rooms
Fold and put away clean clothes
Paint
Clean and organize drawers, closets

12 AND OVER

•

(Children over 12 need and want to feel independent. Tasks should reflect this.)

Shovel snow
Mow lawn
Iron
Do laundry
Wash floors, mirrors, windows
Purchase own clothing
Run errands

Wash clothes by hand
Clean refrigerator
Clean own room thoroughly
Plan menus
Prepare meals
Replace light bulbs
Baby-sit younger siblings

Appendix D

Household Services

In hiring outside services, make sure they are geared to *your* needs, not theirs; *your* hours, not theirs. Remember, you are hiring them to make your life easier, not more difficult. You want to hire a service whose people are competent, pleasant, and prompt, and who require little or no supervision. A good rule of thumb is to interview three references before you use a new service. The following are among those you might choose and their approximate charges:

Answering service ($45 per month)
Secretarial service ($5.70–$12 per hour)
Gardening service ($60 and up per month)
Pool service ($60 per month)
Bookkeeping and/or tax preparation service (depends on the job)
Milk-delivery service (variable)
Laundry and cleaning service that picks up and delivers (variable)
Chauffeur or driving service ($30 per hour)
Catering service (costs too variable to note)
Catalog service (handling and mailing costs variable)
In-home personal grooming services: hairdresser, masseuse ($30 per hour), manicurist ($10), exercise coach ($12 per hour)
Errand service ($5–$10 per hour)
Diaper service ($35 per month)
Shopping service (usually no charge)

Drugstore delivery service (usually no charge)
Housekeeping or cleaning service ($7.50 per hour)
Wardrobe-consultant service ($95 for 2½ hours)
Travel service (no charge)
Home-repair service (depends on the job)
Messenger service ($15–$20 per hour)
General pick-up-and-delivery service (depends on the job)
Window-cleaning service ($17.50 per hour per worker)
Rug- and furniture-cleaning service (depends on the job)
Painting service (depends on the job)
Cooking service (too variable to list)
Companionship service (for disabled) (variable)
House-sitting service ($15 per day)
Baby-sitting service ($3.50–$4 per hour)
Tutoring service ($17 per hour)
Bartending service (depends on the job)
Dog-walking service ($8–$15 per day)
Typing service ($3.50 per typed page)
Party service (depends on the job)
Children's-party service (depends on the job)
Package-wrapping service (too variable to list)

FORM A: SERVICE/REPAIR PERSON MESSAGE

Date _____

To _____

From _____ (your name)

As you know, I cannot be at my house when you are here to

service the _____ (broken appliance, plugged drain, etc.).

This is what needs to be serviced

Item(s) _____

Location(s) _____

Symptom(s) _____

_____

_____

Description of work needed

_____

_____

_____

_____

_____

Other:

Appendix E

Sources of Workers Outside the Household

In addition to the "normal, working" population (adults between the ages of twenty-one and sixty-five), both younger and older people often end up being the best resources. They have the time, some amount of flexibility to their lives, and the desire to work less than full-time. Among the groups you might consider are high-school students, college students, college dropouts, young people "in transition," retirees, senior citizens, and displaced homemakers.

The places you might find these resources are

- Classified ads in local newspapers
- *Pennysavers* and neighborhood newspapers
- Word-of-mouth requests to neighbors, friends, colleagues
- Notices on bulletin boards in supermarkets and churches (your own and others)
- Yellow Pages of telephone directories
- Salvation Army and other such organizations
- Employment agencies (public and private)
- Displaced-homemaker agencies
- Church and synagogue groups (or on their bulletin boards or in their newsletters)
- Senior-citizen groups
- High-school and university student-employment offices

- Announcements in newspapers of new kinds of businesses, such as errand services, "nanny" employment agencies, etc.
- Temporary-office-worker services

INDEX

A

I